Women and Work through a Comparative Lens
Gender and the Urban Labor Markets of Premodern Brabant and Biscay

MEDIAEVALIA LOVANIENSIA
Studies in Medieval History, Society, and Culture

ML

Editorial Board
Geert Claassens (KU Leuven)
Jelle Haemers (KU Leuven)
Jeroen Deploige (Ghent University)
Brigitte Meijns (KU Leuven)
Chanelle Delameillieure (KU Leuven – KULAK)
Baudouin Van den Abeele (UCLouvain)

KU LEUVEN, BELGIUM

Women and Work through a Comparative Lens

Gender and the Urban Labor Markets
of Premodern Brabant and Biscay

Nena Vandeweerdt

LEUVEN UNIVERSITY PRESS

This book is part of the activities of the research projects: *BARMER. From the ship to the market. Economic Activity, Social Relations and Armed Conflicts in the Port Cities of Atlantic Europe at the End of the Middle Ages* (ref. PID2020-118105GBI00); and *Violencia y transformaciones sociales en el nordeste de la Corona de Castilla (1200-1525)*, Research Project funded by MICIU (ref. PID2021-124356NB-I00); Research Group *Sociedades, Procesos, Culturas (siglos VIII a XVIII)*, funded by the Basque Government (ref. IT1465-22)

Financial support by PhD Fellowship FWO – Research Foundation Flanders (ref. 1173418N and 1173420N); Juan de la Cierva grant funded by MICIU/AEI/10.13039/501100011033, the European Union NextGenerationEU/PRTR (ref. JDC2022-050194-I); Fonds Lamberts-Van Assche; Universitaire Stichting van België; KU Leuven Fund for Fair Open Access; and the Open Book Collective.

Published in 2025 by Leuven University Press / Presses Universitaires de Louvain / Universitaire Pers Leuven. Minderbroedersstraat 4, B-3000 Leuven (Belgium).
© 2025, Nena Vandeweerdt
All TDM (Text and Data Mining) rights reserved.

This book is published under a Creative Commons Attribution Non-Commercial Non Derivative 4.0 License. For more information, please visit https://creativecommons.org/share-your-work/cclicenses/

Attribution should include the following information:
Nena Vandeweerdt, *Women and Work through a Comparative Lens: Gender and the Urban Labor Markets of Premodern Brabant and Biscay*. Leuven: Leuven University Press, 2025. (CC BY-NC-ND 4.0)

Unless otherwise indicated all images are reproduced with the permission of the rightsholders acknowledged in the illustration credits. All images are expressly excluded from the CC BY-NC-ND 4.0 license covering the rest of this publication. Permission for reuse should be sought from the rightsholders.

ISBN 978 94 6270 494 7 (Paperback)
ISBN 978 94 6166 696 3 (ePDF)
ISBN 978 94 6166 697 0 (ePUB)
https://doi.org/10.11116/9789461666970
D/2025/1869/48
NUR: 684

Layout: Crius Group
Cover design: Andre Klijsen
Cover illustration: Fresco depicting a market scene. Located at the Issogne Castle, Valle d'Aosta, Italy. Source: Archivi dell'Assessorato Beni e attività culturali, Sistema educativo e Politiche per le relazioni intergenerazionali della Regione autonoma Valle d'Aosta – fondo Catalogo beni cultural. Picture by Giorgio Olivero. By concession of Regione Autonoma Valle d'Aosta.

Table of Contents

List of Figures	7
List of Tables	8
Acknowledgements	9
Abbreviations	11
A Note on Numbers	11
Introduction. Comparing Women's Work	**13**
1. Institutions and Their Impact: The Guild Debate	16
2. "How Society Worked"	21
3. A North-South Comparison	28
4. Mapping the Terrain: Biscay and Brabant	31
Bilbao	31
Antwerp	34
Mechelen	35
5. Sources	37
6. Chapter Organization	42
Chapter 1. Tracing Women's Work	**45**
1. Female Labor Sectors, Women's Work, and Town Ordinances	46
Bread Trade	47
Fish Trade	52
Itinerant Informal Traders	58
Merchants	63
Artisan Workers	66
The Hidden Workforce	69
2. Women's Financial Status	70
3. Conclusion	82
Chapter 2. Shaping the Framework	**85**
1. The Household Economy in Brabant and Biscay	86
Widows	88
Spousal Cooperation	90
Never-Married Household Members	98
Shifting Away from the Household Paradigm	101

2.	Craft Guilds: The Stronghold of the Brabantine Urban Economy	106
3.	Operating Informally: Main Street or Margins?	116
4.	Conclusion	126

Chapter 3. Limiting Women's Work — 129
1. Bilbao's Council and the "Protection of the Consumer" — 131
2. Brabantine Guilds and Town Councils — 138
   Economic Motivations, Gendered Outcomes — 140
   The 'Guild Effect' — 145
3. Growing Restrictions? — 158
4. Conclusion — 168

Chapter 4. Wielding the Framework — 171
1. Influencing Regulation — 172
   Wielding Authority — 174
   Direct Influence — 178
   Consent, Bargaining, and Leverage — 181
2. Going to Court — 185
   Biscayan Tradeswomen in Court — 186
   Risk-Taking and Forum Shopping — 194
   The 'Poverty Argument' — 201
   Group Recognition — 205
3. Conclusion — 210

Understanding Women's Work — 213

Bibliography — 225
1. Archival sources — 225
   Biscay — 225
   Brabant — 225
2. Printed sources — 226
   Brabant — 226
   Biscay — 226
3. Secondary sources — 227
4. Digital sources — 240

Index — 241

List of Figures

Figure 1. The duchy of Brabant in the fifteenth century   15

Figure 2. The lordship of Biscay in the fifteenth and sixteenth centuries.   15

Figure 3. Map of Bilbao at the end of the fifteenth century.   32

Figure 4. Map of the existing occupational brotherhoods in premodern Biscayan towns.   68

Figure 5. Deciles of taxpayers by amount of tax paid in the registers of Bilbao (1470), Antwerp (1537), and Mechelen (1544), showing the percentage of women and men in each decile. Tax amounts are given in *maravedís* (Bilbao) and *stuivers* (Antwerp and Mechelen).   80

Figure 6. View of the sixteenth-century Mechelen Meat Hall with its adjacent informal market stalls. Drawing by JB. De Noter, eighteenth century.   118

Figure 7. Drawing of the formal section of the medieval fish market on IJzerenleen Street in Mechelen.   119

Figure 8. Five-year moving averages showing (a) the total number of new members per sex and (b) the proportion of new female members in the mercers' guild of Antwerp (1516–1555).   159

Figure 9. Statue by Joaquín Lucarini in homage to the Bizkaian *sardineras*, Santurtzi (1963).   167

Figure 10. Fifteenth-century fresco depicting women traders in a market scene. Located at the Issogne Castle, Valle d'Aosta, Italy.   223

List of Tables

Table 1. Overview of the available entrance lists and membership lists for Antwerp and Mechelen ca. 1400–1600.   42

Table 2. Total number and percentage of taxpayers by demographic category and marital status (for both men and women) in the house rent levies of Mechelen (1544) and Antwerp (1537), along with median tax amounts in *stuivers* (st) for each group.   72

Table 3. Total number and percentage of taxpayers by demographic category and marital status (for both men and women) in the tax register of Bilbao (1470), along with median tax amounts in *maravedís* (mrs) for each group.   73

Table 4. Women's occupations in the taxation survey of Bilbao (1470), ordered by median tax amount in *maravedís* (mrs).   76

Table 5. Women's occupations in the house rent levies of Mechelen (1544) and Antwerp (1537), organized by median tax amount in *stuivers* (st).   78

Table 6. Number and percentage of men and women in the available entrance lists and membership lists from Mechelen and Antwerp.   108

Table 7. Number and percentage of new members, by fee category, in the entrance register of the Antwerp mercers' guild (1516–1555). The categories include full entrance fee, half entrance fee, and unknown.   112

Table 8. Number and percentage of new female and male members, by occupation and fee category, in the Antwerp mercers' guild (1516–1555).   114

Table 9. Overview of registered sentences by type of offense and gender of the accused, based on the Mechelen fishmongers' guild's sentence books (1492–1561).   152

Acknowledgements

This book is based on my doctoral research, carried out between 2017 and 2022 at KU Leuven and the Universidad de Cantabria, with the support of a PhD Fellowship from the Research Foundation – Flanders. I owe special thanks to my supervisors, Jelle Haemers and Jesús Ángel Solórzano Telechea, whose guidance, trust, and expertise were invaluable throughout this project. Their encouragement beyond the dissertation has meant a great deal to me.

In the final two years of the project, I had the privilege of further developing this work under the funding and the framework of a Juan de la Cierva Postdoctoral Fellowship at the Universidad del País Vasco/Euskal Herriko Unibertsitatea. I am particularly grateful to Iñaki Bazán Díaz for his support.

The research environments in Leuven, Santander, and Vitoria-Gasteiz provided a welcoming and supportive setting. The feedback from colleagues during seminars and conversations helped shape this book. I owe much to the insights of Heleen Wyffels, Minne De Boodt, Laura Calvo García, and Maïka de Keyzer, whose comments and encouragement were especially valuable at key stages of the research.

Shennan Hutton, Anne Montenach, Danielle van den Heuvel, María Montserrat Cabré Pairet, Paul Trio, Peter Stabel, and María Isabel del Val Valdivieso generously shared their expertise and feedback at different stages of the research process. I am also grateful to the anonymous reviewer of this book, as well as to the colleagues I encountered at conferences and workshops, whose questions and suggestions enriched this work. I also extend my sincere gratitude to the editorial team at Leuven University Press for their support in bringing this book to publication.

This research would not have been possible without access to the archival sources that underpin it, and I wish to thank the staff of the various institutions that facilitated this access. I am especially appreciative of the City Archives of Mechelen, where both staff and volunteers offered invaluable assistance.

My deepest thanks go to my family and friends, whose love and encouragement helped carry me through this process. A special shout-out goes to Esther De Reys, who, as a fellow writer, was always ready to provide thoughtful feedback. Curiosity and enthusiasm—the two qualities that sustained me throughout this writing process—are ones I can always count on my siblings to reinforce, and for which I am ultimately grateful to my parents. It is to them that I warmly dedicate this book. Above all, I am thankful to my husband, Diego, with whom I have shared this journey—across continents and chapters alike.

Abbreviations

AFB: Statutory Archives of Biscay (*Archivo Foral de Bizkaia*)
ARChV: Archives of the Royal Court and Chancellery of Valladolid (*Archivo de la Real Audiencia y Chancillería de Valladolid*)
SAA: City Archives of Antwerp (*Stadsarchief Antwerpen, FelixArchief*)
SAL: City Archives of Leuven (*Stadarchief Leuven*)
SAM: City Archives of Mechelen (*Stadsarchief Mechelen*)

A Note on Numbers

This book uses a dot (.) as the decimal separator and omits thousands separators in its tables and figures.

INTRODUCTION

Comparing Women's Work

Wandering through the streets of many European towns, one can still trace the outlines of their medieval past. What remains hidden behind these familiar façades, though, are the daily lives and interactions of the townspeople—activities that profoundly shaped the urban landscapes we know today. These interactions were not uniform but varied significantly depending on place and context. For instance, on the IJzerenleen—one of the main arteries of Mechelen in present-day Belgium—no trace is left of Gheertruyde van den Broeke, a fishmonger's wife who, in the beginning of the sixteenth century, traded vigorously, disputed with town and guild officials, and collaborated with her husband to keep the household's business afloat. Similarly, Antwerp's Kraaiwijk, once a lively center of small businesses, now shows no signs of the daily trade taking place there, in addition to the frictions caused by it, such as the 1442 case where a married couple was ordered to cease selling fish oil because of the stench it caused.

In the northern Spanish town of Bilbao, a comparable bustle animated the fifteenth- and sixteenth-century docks and adjacent market square. Boats and smaller dinghies brought goods into this harbor town, where men and women unloaded and sold merchandise. Women fishmongers could be found in Bilbao as well as in Mechelen and Antwerp. Women like Mayora de Iturribalzaga, Catalina Nafarra, and María Pérez de Bermeo—whose stories we will encounter in the chapters to come—played central roles as vendors, shaping the daily rhythms of the marketplaces. The interactions between these tradeswomen and town authorities, among traders themselves, between husband and wife, and with the institutions organizing trade are the subject of this book.

Yet the gendered structure of economic life differed markedly between northern Spain and the Low Countries. In Bilbao, women held primary roles in certain trades, negotiating their positions informally within a system dominated by a powerful town council. In Mechelen and Antwerp, by contrast, the economic activities of many men and women, often operating within household economic units, were more formally organized through the strong network of craft guilds. For decades, historians have sought to explain these contrasts through the lens of a North-South divide: a narrative that depicted northern European women as enjoying greater freedoms, while their southern counterparts faced tighter constraints. Yet this narrative, built largely on separate case studies, tells us little about the diverse ways gender dynamics were constructed in urban economies.

This book begins where that debate leaves off. It compares the position of women active in small-scale trade in Antwerp and Mechelen in Brabant (present-day Belgium and the Netherlands, see figure 1) with that of their counterparts in Bilbao in Biscay (in the northern Spanish Basque Country, see figure 2) during the second half of the fifteenth and the first half of the sixteenth century. By placing distinct urban contexts side by side, it examines how institutional frameworks, interacting with individual circumstances, shaped women's economic opportunities. The central question guiding this study is: What was the impact of distinct institutional frameworks on women's labor opportunities? In providing an answer, two further questions are addressed: How did women actively navigate and wield institutions to shape their individual labor opportunities? And what other factors influenced the ways in which institutions affected women's work?

Through a comparative analysis of Brabant and Biscay, this book reveals that the presence or absence of strong socioeconomic institutions produced distinct labor markets and, consequently, different kinds of economic opportunities for women. However, the impact of institutions was neither uniform nor solely restrictive. Distinct local contexts created a complex interplay of factors—including cultural values, social and financial status, legal structures, sectoral differences, and marital status—that influenced each woman's individual experience on the urban labor markets. These interwoven factors not only shaped differences between regions but also produced variation within towns themselves. Ultimately, this study argues that meaningful insights into women's economic roles emerge through comparison—not to rank societies, but to reveal the complex interplay of institutions, collective frameworks, and individual circumstances that shaped women's lives.

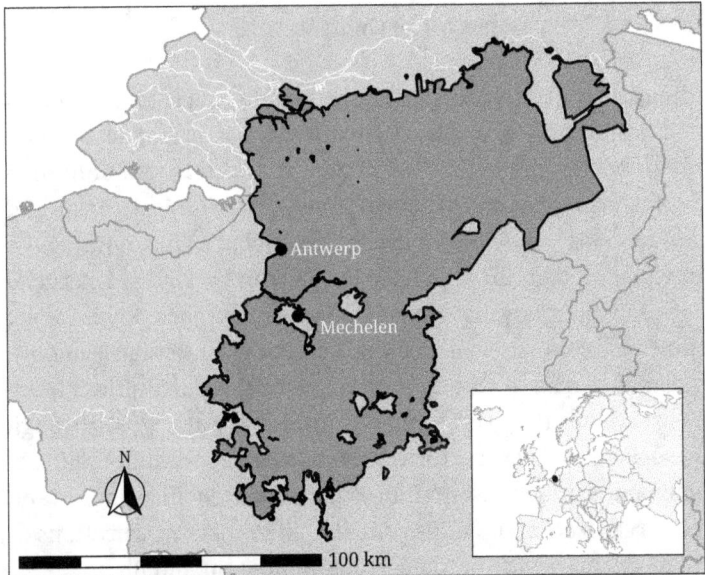

Figure 1. The duchy of Brabant in the fifteenth century.[1]

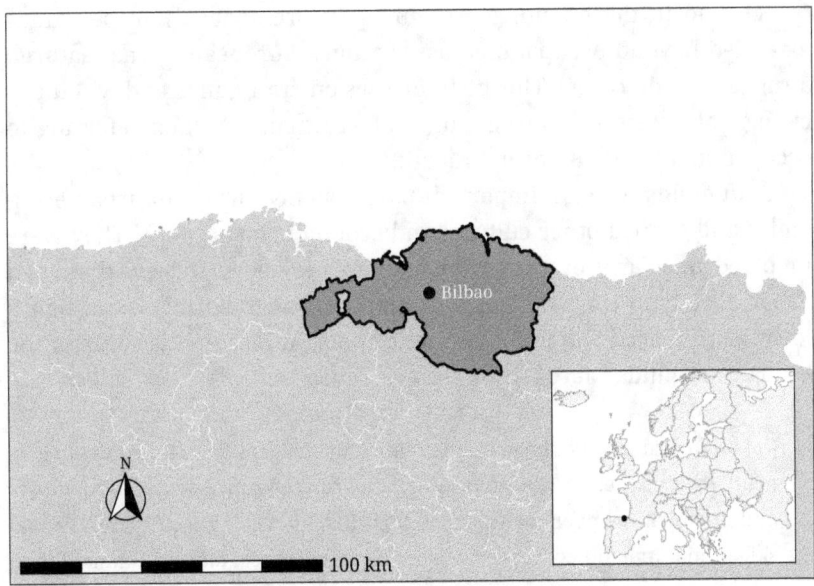

Figure 2. The lordship of Biscay in the fifteenth and sixteenth centuries.

[1] The data of the borders of the Duchy of Brabant can be found at: Stapel, Rombert, 2020, 'Duchy of Brabant GIS Collection', https://hdl.handle.net/10622/UOKBYL.

1. Institutions and Their Impact: The Guild Debate

Understanding the impact of institutions on women's economic opportunities is crucial to the study of women and work in premodern times. Institutions can be broadly defined as networks of actors that adhere to formal and informal norms and practices to structure political, social, and economic interactions.[2] They have proven essential to understanding the dynamics of women's labor in premodern urban Europe and are a crucial building block for this study. Using a comparative approach, I will reflect on how institutional contexts—particularly guilds, the household economy, and the informal market—shaped women's work opportunities. Town governments served as the overarching institutional framework through which these socioeconomic structures gained, or failed to gain, organizational capacity and legitimacy. Differences in the household economy and in the formal organization of guilds contributed to marked variations in women's roles within specific market sectors in Brabant and Biscay.

Gender historians broadly agree that institutions had a significant impact on women's economic opportunities. The institutions taking the foreground in these studies are guilds. In premodern Europe, guilds extended beyond occupational associations; European towns featured a range of guild types.[3] This book focuses on craft guilds and will interchangeably use the terms 'guilds' and 'craft guilds' when referring to occupational corporations in Brabant.

Craft guilds were an important part of many European urban economies and shaped other cultural and economic institutions. They were involved in nearly every aspect of their members' lives and shaped urban society in ways that, as we will see throughout this book, significantly influenced women's economic opportunities. In his study of the Brabantine guilds, Marc Jacobs defines a guild as:

> [...] an institution that has obtained official privileges from a higher government, making them a 'collective entity' that can recognise people as members and in which members are granted jurisdiction over a specific professional skill or manipulation of material products (as resource, tool, or commodity).[4]

---

[2] This definition is derived from: Ogilvie, "Whatever Is, Is Right'?', 650; Hunt & Shepard, 'Introduction. Producing Change', 8.

[3] Ogilvie, *Institutions and European Trade*, 19.

[4] Jacobs, 'De ambachten in Brabant en Mechelen', 588–9.

As legal entities, guilds could renegotiate their privileges and exert influence over economic regulation. Nico Slokker, for example, emphasizes their jurisdictional authority and economic power.[5] Yet guilds were not merely economic regulators. They often began as occupational communities that also provided religious, social, and cultural functions—roles they continued to perform until their abolition in the late eighteenth century.[6] In many parts of Europe, their political functions were equally significant.[7] In the Southern Low Countries after 1300, guilds were "both instruments of popular politics and mobilisation, and deputised branches of the urban government which carried out military and legal functions."[8]

This political power enabled guilds to push for *Zunftzwang*—the requirement that anyone working in a guild-regulated trade be a guild member or hold a guild license.[9] The guilds in these towns often made strenuous efforts to gain monopolies and become the exclusive providers of commodities, even if, in practice, they could never attain complete monopolies.[10] Jan Dumolyn has shown how guilds in the urban Low Countries sought to represent the entire urban commune, claiming a central place in civic identity and governance.[11]

Given the patriarchal character of premodern towns, it is no surprise that guilds framed themselves as masculine institutions. As Bert De Munck has noted, the dominant craft guilds drew their legitimacy from the idea that "fathers, men and masters [...] formed the link between the city as an aggregation of economic households and the city as a body politic—or the larger household."[12] Guilds were, in many ways, flagships of patriarchy. Membership was tightly controlled and seldom extended to women in their own right. Moreover, as this study also shows, guilds frequently sought to protect their economic privileges from informal competition,

---

[5] Slokker, *Ruggengraat van de stad: de betekenis van gilden in Utrecht*, 11–2.
[6] Eisenbichler, 'Introduction: A World of Confraternities', 2.
[7] Ogilvie, *The European Guilds*, 36–82.
[8] Dumolyn, 'Guild Politics and Political Guilds', 31.
[9] Ogilvie, *The European Guilds*, 11; Howell, *Women, Production, and Patriarchy*, 106.
[10] De Munck, *Guilds, Labour and the Urban Body Politic*, 185. As Peter Stabel has argued, only a few corporations actually tried to win a full monopoly in their market sectors. Most of those sectors were in food trades or sales of basic essential products. As I will show in this study, in the absence of masculine guilds, these sectors were dominated by women workers. See: Stabel, 'Guilds in Late Medieval Flanders', 193–4.
[11] Dumolyn, 'Guild Politics and Political Guilds', 30–1.
[12] De Munck, *Guilds, Labour and the Urban Body Politic*, 205.

often at the expense of women and other outsiders. While some women were able to participate in guild life—the significance of the household and the existence of certain more open or even feminine guilds allowed for women's participation in the guild context—it is precisely the masculine and exclusionary character of craft guilds that lies at the heart of the so-called Guild Debate.

The visibility and importance of guilds have sparked significant debate about their impact on premodern urban economies. The corporations have often been depicted either as drivers of innovation and efficiency or as backward, reclusive entities stifling progress. While this book does not aim to address the overall impact on urban economies, the two sides of the debate provide valuable insights for studying women and work.

One of the most forceful critiques of guilds comes from Sheilagh Ogilvie, who argues that their exclusivity and pervasive influence over urban life not only constrained women's participation in the economy but also hampered overall economic efficiency. Guilds, she contends, institutionalized male privilege and reinforced patriarchal cultural values.[13] As Claire Crowston summarizes in her influential overview of the Guild Debate, Ogilvie "draws a stark boundary between privileged insiders and dishonored and impoverished outsiders [...]. She also denies the possibility of alternate, possibly 'feminine' forms of social capital outside the guilds."[14] Ogilvie's concept of institutional enforcement recurs throughout this book, particularly in chapters 3 and 4, where its effects and limitations become especially visible through the comparative method. The Biscayan case study, where no guilds organized small-scale trade, offers a unique opportunity to examine what happens when such institutions are absent. This setting challenges the rigid dichotomy between 'feminine' social capital and exclusion, showing that women's work and agency cannot be fully understood within the binary framework of guild inclusion versus outsider status. By temporarily removing guilds from the equation, we gain a clearer view of the broader institutional and cultural dynamics shaping women's economic opportunities.

Already before Ogilvie, scholars such as Maryanne Kowaleski and Judith Bennett drew attention to the restrictive effects of guilds on women's work. While guilds typically excluded women from the core economic

---

[13] Ogilvie, 'How Does Social Capital Affect Women?'; Ogilvie, *The European Guilds*; Ogilvie, *A Bitter Living*.

[14] Crowston, 'Women, Gender, and Guilds', 24.

activities they organized, even those women permitted to work within guild structures were not treated as workers. Rather, they appeared in guild records as dependents—wives, daughters, widows, or servants of male masters. Furthermore, guild inclusion, when granted, came with many restrictions, leaving mostly the low-status, low-paid trades in the hands of women, as guilds were not interested in formally organizing them according to their own male structures.[15] These mechanisms of marginalization will be explored in detail in the Brabantine case studies, where guilds played a central role in structuring economic life.

The exclusionary pattern of guilds is particularly visible in studies of historical change. Judith Bennett, in her analysis of English brewsters, showed how women were gradually forced out of brewing between 1300 and 1600 as the craft became professionalized and increasingly subject to guild control.[16] A similar pattern appears in Martha Howell's *Women, Production, and Patriarchy in Late Medieval Cities*, which provides a clear view of the guilds' role in women's declining positions in high-status work. While the guild system was rooted in household-based production, it was precisely this overlap between domestic collaboration and market work that enabled the corporations to justify the exclusion of women as independent workers. As we will see, these dynamics are reflected in the Brabantine towns, where guilds actively sought to protect their privileges from informal competitors, many of whom were women. I further argue that even the household economy, which formed the backbone of many women's labor strategies in Brabant, came under guild scrutiny and hostility when it threatened to undermine their control over the organization of work.

Comparing Brabant and Biscay reveals a more nuanced view of what has been called the guild effect. In the Brabantine towns, we will see the exclusionary dynamics commonly associated with guilds: the restriction of women's access to lucrative trades and their confinement to peripheral roles. Yet this pattern was not universal. Many scholars have long noted the spaces within corporative structures where women did gain access—particularly as family members of guild members or as participants in all-female guilds. These women often benefited from having their work recognized and protected within corporative frameworks. Steven Epstein and Maarten Prak, who present strong opposition to Ogilvie's hypothesis,

---

[15] Kowaleski & Bennett, 'Crafts, Gilds, and Women in the Middle Ages'.
[16] Bennett, *Ale, Beer, and Brewsters in England*.

rightly highlight the constructive impacts of guilds on the economic opportunities of insiders. They underscore the advantages guilds offered to insiders: formal training systems, structured professional networks, and collective investment in developing skills. From this perspective, guilds fostered stability and innovation, particularly for those admitted to their ranks.[17]

Although most gender historians acknowledge the restrictive nature of guilds for women overall, many have also nuanced this view—or sidestepped the question of the 'guild effect' altogether. Recent scholarship on women's labor in the urban Low Countries often centers on those women who were integrated into guild life.[18] Ariadne Schmidt's study of early modern Dutch guilds, for instance, emphasizes the positions that women could hold, rather than the numerous barriers others encountered.[19] This emphasis may reflect the dominant role that guilds played in the economic organization of towns in the Low Countries, which makes it difficult to look beyond the corporations—to detect the women who were excluded, or to consider economic activity outside guild control.[20] In many cases, the archival record itself reinforces this view. In Antwerp and Mechelen as well, surviving documents predominantly frame women's work within a guild context, making it challenging to access evidence of informal or non-corporate labor. This archival bias has, in part, obscured the relevance of Ogilvie's critique in studies of the Low Countries, even though the underlying issue—guilds limiting women's access to economic opportunities—remains difficult to deny.

By placing Biscay alongside Brabant, this book adopts a broader comparative perspective on the role of institutions in shaping women's

---

[17] Epstein & Prak, Guilds, *Innovation and the European Economy*, 5–24.

[18] My initial engagement with gender studies also stemmed from this perspective, as reflected in my earlier work: Vandeweerdt, 'Van den vleeschouweren oft pensvrouwen'; Vandeweerdt & Haemers, 'Working Women: Women's Professional Activities in and outside the Craft Guilds', 121–46 (English translation of the original 2019 Dutch text). Other studies that align with this school of research include, among others: Coomans, 'Policing Female Food Vendors'; Deceulaer and Panhuysen, 'Dressed to Work'; Hutton, 'Women, Men, and Markets'; Stabel, 'Women at the Market'; Van Dekken, *Brouwen, branden & bedienen*.

[19] Schmidt, 'Contested Authority', 217–8.

[20] Of course, the studies cited above acknowledge the limitations imposed by guilds and their impact on the wider urban female workforce. However, research that focuses on alternative segments of that workforce remains more limited and includes, among others: Schmidt & van Nederveen Meerkerk, 'Reconsidering the 'Firstmale-Breadwinner Economy'; van Nederveen Meerkerk, 'Segmentation in the Pre-Industrial Labour Market'; Lambert, 'Merchants on the Margins'.

work opportunities. In Biscay, most commodity trades remained informally organized; in Bilbao, the region's main commercial hub, guilds did not organize small-scale trade, unlike in Brabantine towns such as Antwerp and Mechelen. This institutional contrast offers a unique opportunity to assess women's labor both in the absence of guilds and within guild-dominated contexts—highlighting how such corporations could simultaneously restrict and support women's economic activities. In this sense, my approach parallels that of Daryl Hafter, who, rather than comparing regions, focuses on institutional change over time. In her study of eighteenth-century France, Hafter highlights how guild dissolution and the rise of wage labor destabilized women's positions. For many women, guilds had offered relative security; their disappearance led to greater precarity in a male-dominated labor market.[21] Similarly, the Biscayan case shows that the absence of guilds made certain trades more accessible to women and fostered a sense of occupational identity among them, yet it also left their work more precarious and less institutionally protected.

2. "How Society Worked"

While most scholars agree that powerful institutions shaped women's labor positions, they never exclusively determined women's roles in premodern urban economies. Institutional dynamics intersected with a range of other factors—including social and financial status, marital status, legal structures, cultural norms, and sectoral differences—that collectively shaped women's economic opportunities. These intersecting factors, taken together, offer "valuable clues as to how societies in the past worked."[22] This book does not aim to reconstruct those building blocks from scratch. Many scholars before me have taken on the Herculean task of mapping out the frameworks within which women operated. Rather than revisiting those efforts, this study builds on them by offering a comparative perspective that highlights how institutional structures and individual circumstances coexisted and interacted in two very distinct contexts.

First, the concept 'work' needs clarification. Recent studies have criticized the definition of 'work' as remunerated activities with economic

---

[21] Hafter, *Women at Work in Preindustrial France*.
[22] Ågren, *Making a Living*, 6.

value, which had sufficed for earlier scholars.[23] Critics point out that men and women's work in premodern society extended beyond this account. Much of their work was focused on their own households rather than on the market.[24] Work for premodern people requires a broader interpretation than our current questionable definition. The comparative objective of this study has made the selection of work fields one of the most important criteria for demarcation. This approach has allowed me to apply microstudy methodology to different case studies, ensuring the compatibility of source material and results, despite the absence of a systematic 'big data' study. Consequently, this study does not cover all work fields but rather centers on women's positions in market-oriented activities in small-scale trade and production. It focuses on a group of urban residents who, through these occupations, made a living.[25]

This perspective does not mean, however, that women's activities always corresponded to our contemporary definitions of work, nor that the various source types we will encounter all painted a uniform picture of work. Market-oriented activities were not necessarily remunerated, nor were they always considered work. For example, the women we will encounter in the Spanish courts in chapter 4 spent their time not only selling wares but also defending their activities, making the defense part of their market-oriented endeavors. Similarly, the fishmongers' wives in the Mechelen case study, discussed in chapters 3 and 4, did not necessarily receive a direct income from their market-oriented work. When Gheertruyde van den Broeke, the fishmonger's wife, was sentenced to a pilgrimage for allowing her niece to sell fish informally, she did not gain directly from these actions. Instead, they were part of managing her household economic unit. While the comparison of a narrow range of market sectors facilitates the inclusion of broad geographic areas, the multitude of different types of activities women practiced within these

---

[23] The introduction of Sarti, Bellavitis, and Martini's *What is work?* as well as that of Bailey, Colwell, and Hotchin's *Women and work in premodern Europe* provide a good overview of the discussion about the modern and premodern definitions of work, as well as the transitions in the concept. See: Sarti, Bellavitis & Martini, 'Introduction. What Is Work?'; Bailey, Colwell & Hotchin, 'Approaching Women and Work in Premodern Europe'.

[24] Whittle, 'A Critique of Approaches to 'Domestic Work'', 62–3.

[25] Even if this study cannot apply Maria Ågren's 'verb-oriented method' due to the lack of systematic sources, her broad interpretation of work activities, and how to detect these, did inspire me in my interpretation of the sources. Especially in chapter 4, we will see how. See: Ågren, *Making a Living*.

market sectors aligns with the view of work as any activity that supported themselves and their families.[26]

The types of work women engaged in often corresponded with the types of women who appear in historical records. Some studies, such as Martha Howell's "Women, the Family Economy, and the Structures of Market Production", have focused on high-status work, in part because its evolution is more readily traceable in the sources. In contrast, most of the occupations examined in this book fall into what Howell categorized as "lower-skilled or less specialized work"—occupations that did not require access to raw materials or control over the distribution and consumption of commodities.[27] Small-scale trading has previously been identified as well-suited to the needs of single and widowed women, offering a potential income without requiring substantial initial investment.[28] Indeed, these are the labor activities where women's work is most visible in both Brabant and Biscay. The focus on 'low-status' activities allows for a clearer comparative view of the mechanisms defining the positions accessible to women and how women could operate within these occupations. After all, even in accessible positions, women still faced persistent limitations.

As we will see, not only the types of work shaped women's economic opportunities in Brabant and Biscay, so too did the type of market. In premodern towns, a substantial part of economic activity took place within the informal market. Economist Colin Williams defines the informal economy as:

> The informal economy is socially legitimate paid activity that is legal in all respects other than that it is not declared to, hidden from or unregistered with, the authorities for tax, social security and/or labour law purposes when it should be declared.[29]

However, this definition poses challenges when studying women's informal labor in premodern Brabant and Biscay. Although Williams adopts a broad and inclusive view of informal activity, his concept, rooted in twentieth-century anthropology, does not align with the market structures of

---

[26] Wiesner, *Women and Gender in Early Modern Europe*, 113.
[27] Howell, 'Women, the Family Economic, and the Structures of Market Production', 198–9.
[28] Honeyman & Goodman, 'Women's Work, Gender Conflict, and Labour Markets', 610; Montenach, 'Trades in Lyon', 20.
[29] Williams, *The Informal Economy*, 6.

premodern urban economies. In these contexts, the boundaries between formal and informal were far more fluid. Work was often unpaid, and those engaged in formal labor were not necessarily disconnected from informal activities. The informal market unfolded in the spaces between town ordinances, guild regulations, and formalized institutions. Rather than a clearly defined category, it functioned more as a spectrum—one that residents of Antwerp, Mechelen, and Biscay could skillfully navigate.

Informal work was an essential part of the urban economy. It was not necessarily hidden, illegal, or irregular, and interacted closely with formal economic structures.[30] One could argue that informal work can only be understood in relation to institutions with legal and organizational authority. This interpretation helps clarify why licensed work—such as that of saleswomen in Bilbao—did not always equate to formal work. Licensed informal traders often operated outside of institutions that had the legal competence to regulate labor. As Charlie Taverner has shown in his study of food hawkers, licenses were not instruments of formalization, but rather tools through which authorities integrated informal activity into the broader urban economy and asserted control over it.[31]

In this book, I treat informal work as a part of the institutional mechanisms shaping labor in the Brabantine and Biscayan towns—despite the paradox that it is defined precisely by the absence of institutional structures. This approach makes it possible to analyze how the informal market shaped women's work opportunities, and how various institutions and groups of urban residents interacted with informal sectors of the economy.

One clear conclusion in all studies about women and work is the importance of marital status and descent. Both within and outside guilds, women's work was often rooted in their responsibilities as household members, similar to men's work. For men, this typically meant balancing their household responsibilities with positions in other masculine and patriarchal institutions—something they could usually do without prompting social or cultural dilemmas.[32] For women, however, the legitimation of their economic activities was often tied to their family and

---

[30] Schmidt, *Prosecuting Women*, 249.
[31] Taverner, 'Licensing the Informal Economy in Early Modern Europe'.
[32] De Munck, *Guilds, Labour and the Urban Body Politic*, 196–7.

household roles.³³ Therefore, we need to distinguish between women of certain social standings (those with access to the types of work under study) and, within this group, between different marital statuses. In chapters 2 and 3, we will explore how the impact of marital status functioned and varied in Brabant and Biscay. It is evident that the archetypal household economic unit—centered around the nuclear couple and their household members—did not facilitate women's work to the extent often assumed, at least not for certain types of labor in Brabant and Biscay.³⁴ The interaction of the household with other factors, such as social and financial status and institutional organization, is more complex than commonly accepted.

The influence of institutions on women's labor positions plays a central role in this study. In the Brabantine case study, we see how guilds and the household were deeply embedded in the organization of work. In Bilbao, by contrast, the absence of such institutions did not translate into women's unrestricted access to all labor markets. In both regions, a patriarchal cultural framework shaped gendered expectations around work, and this framework was closely intertwined with the authorities that structured local labor markets.³⁵ Gender roles were rarely contested and were reinforced by prevailing patriarchal values. Thus, women in Brabant and Biscay lived in a society where their economic roles were defined not only by socioeconomic factors but also by "an enduring pattern of male hegemony based on structures and principles accepted as natural, and endorsed by custom, law, and divine authority."³⁶ Women were subject to cultural scrutiny and restraints. While institutions take center stage in this book's explanatory framework, the patriarchal values underpinning many of their gendered structures will frequently come to the fore in the following chapters. Sheilagh Ogilvie highlights a similar nuance about the importance of cultural values in relation to the impact of institutions: "It might be argued that these regulations expressed cultural

---

[33] See, among others: Carlier, 'The Household: An Introduction', 7–8; Fridrich, 'Women Working in Guild Crafts'; Howell, *Women, Production, and Patriarchy*, 9–20; Howell, 'Citizenship and Gender', 51–2. Anna Bellavitis showed this dynamic by using a quantitative method, in: Bellavitis, *Women's Work and Rights*, 32.

[34] Martha Howell describes a classic example of the functioning of this type of household structure in *Women, Production, and Patriarchy in Late Medieval Cities*. See: Howell, *Women, Production, and Patriarchy*, 9–21.

[35] For a strong conceptual overview on the patriarchal mechanisms in premodern society, I would like to refer to Judith Bennett's *History Matters*. See, Bennett, *History Matters*, 54–70.

[36] Capp, *When Gossips Meet*, 15–25, citation p20.

attitudes [...]. However, it is not evident that these cultural attitudes would have had much impact without community and state institutions to give them practical expression."[37]

Another layer of urban society shaping women's work was the legal framework. Both Biscay and Brabant were governed primarily by customary legal systems, which diverged from formal Roman law and evolved through practice, precedent, and local tradition. Although European legal systems are often divided into Roman and customary law, this binary categorization tends to oversimplify how such frameworks affected women's economic opportunities.

Customary law has long been considered more favorable to women's labor roles than Roman law. In many parts of northwestern Europe—including some towns in Brabant—inheritance customs granted sons and daughters equal shares. Upon marriage, spouses typically merged their assets into a communal estate, from which a widow could inherit a substantial portion while also retaining her original property. These arrangements not only protected widows but also encouraged women's participation in economic activity that benefited the household.[38] In Biscay, too, customary law defined legal identities and rights. The regional *fueros* (customary law texts) formally granted women independent legal capacity, allowing them to own and dispose of property and represent themselves in court regardless of marital status.[39] Unlike many other European regions where women needed to acquire a status such as *femme sole* to act independently, Biscayan women had these rights by default upon reaching adulthood.[40]

Yet while these legal frameworks appear to support women's economic agency, relying too strictly on legal texts to assess real-life opportunities is misleading. Depending on factors such as social status, marital status, and sector of employment, legal norms were frequently adapted or even disregarded in practice. Moreover, legal systems were often a complex mixture of Roman law and adapted customary laws.[41]

[37] Ogilvie, *A Bitter Living*, 339.

[38] Carlier, 'The Household: An Introduction', 2–3; Cappelle, "In de macht, plicht en momboorije van heuren man".

[39] Monreal Zia, *The Old Law of Bizkaia (1452)*, 23; Castrillo Casado, *Las mujeres vascas durante la baja edad media*, 101–14; Ratcliffe, "Matris et Munium...", 94.

[40] Van Aert, 'The Legal Possibilities of Antwerp Widows', 285–7; Cappelle, "In de macht, plicht en momboorije van heuren man", 61; De Longé, *Coutumes de la ville de Malines*, 62.

[41] See, among others: Bellavitis and Zucca Micheletto, 'Introduction. North versus South'.

In Biscay, for instance, notarial records reveal that even women entitled to act independently were required to obtain their husbands' consent.[42] Female linen merchants (*lenceras tratantes*) sometimes included explicit revocations of Roman legal restrictions in their contracts, illustrating the coexistence of multiple legal influences and the negotiation required in practice.[43]

This legal flexibility was not unique to Biscay. Scholars such as Andrea Bardyn, Shennan Hutton, and Kaat Cappelle have shown that Brabantine customary law was similarly adaptable in economic matters.[44] Municipal magistrates and councils did consider women's legal status in regulation and litigation, but they also responded pragmatically to shifting social and economic conditions. Laws could be selectively applied, reinterpreted, or even circumvented altogether when necessary.[45]

In addition to this legal flexibility, it is important to consider the underlying motivations behind these legal structures. As Maria Ågren has argued, it is anachronistic to view legal capacity and emancipation as the primary goal of historical women's rights. In patriarchal premodern societies, customary law often emerged to support household economies and communal stability rather than to promote individual rights. Its flexibility was not a flaw but a functional feature: it accommodated the practical needs of at least a part of the population it governed.[46] Thus, evaluating women's labor roles requires an approach that favors practice over prescription. This book will use the legal framework as the broadest framework shaping women's labor activities.

---

[42] This was, for instance, the case in the court case of the fishmonger Mayora de Iturribalzaga, which we will discuss throughout this book. AFB, Municipal, 0304/001/011.

[43] For women revoking their rights under Roman law, see, among others, AFB, JCR0560/052, 29 April 1562; AFB, JCR1191/119, 19 August 1568.

[44] Bardyn, 'Women's Fortunes', 57–60; Hutton, *Women and Economic Activities*; Cappelle, 'Law, Wives and the Marital Economy'.

[45] Hutton, 'Property, Family and Partnership', 172; Zucca Micheletto, 'Reconsidering the Southern Europe Model'; Van Aert, 'The Legal Possibilities of Antwerp Widows'; Wiesner, *Women and Gender in Early Modern Europe*, 130–1.

[46] Ågren, *Making a Living, Making a Difference*, 8–9.

3. A North-South Comparison

The longstanding debate about regional differences in women's positions across Europe lies at the heart of the research project behind this book. One of the most enduring paradigms in gender and women's history posits that women in northwestern Europe enjoyed greater economic opportunities than their counterparts in the south. This thesis was first articulated by John Hajnal and later reinforced by David Herlihy and Christiane Klapisch-Zuber's influential study of the 1427 *catasto* of Florence.[47] Their focus on Italy laid the foundation for a widespread scholarly narrative that emphasized the precarious position of women in southern Europe.[48] At the same time, many studies of premodern women in northwestern European towns have explicitly or implicitly supported the idea of their exceptional economic agency.[49] Yet, as Mark Bailey has noted, this body of research has often developed "in a tendency for econometricians and historians to talk past one another rather than to engage and to collaborate more closely."[50] As a result, the north-south distinction became not only a deeply embedded assumption but also a subject increasingly ripe for critical re-evaluation.

In recent years, critical voices have grown louder—and may now outweigh those still advocating for strong gendered differences between the regions. More and more studies have pointed to the wild generalizations of these studies claiming a north-south division. In one of the few actual empirical comparisons of gender in northern and southern Europe, Ellen Kittell pointed out that many of the differences in women's positions between the two regions can be attributed to differences in the scope of studies rather than to inherent regional disparities.[51] Scholars studying southern European case studies have been calling for a reassessment of

---

[47] Herlihy and Klapisch-Zuber, *Les Toscans et leurs familles*. I used the English translation for this study, see: Herlihy and Klapisch-Zuber, *Tuscans and Their Families*.

[48] Paolo Viazzo provides an excellent overview of those studies claiming the existence of the 'Mediterranean model'—a concept Hajnal earlier referred to as the southern European model—in: Viazzo, 'What's so Special about the Mediterranean?'.

[49] See, among others: De Moor & Van Zanden, 'Girl Power'; Honeyman & Goodman, 'Women's Work, Gender Conflict, and Labour Markets'; Howell, *Women, Production, and Patriarchy*; Schmidt, Devos, & Blondé. 'Introduction', 3–4.

[50] Bailey, 'The Black Death, Girl Power, and the Emergence of the European Marriage Pattern in England', 518.

[51] Kittell, 'Testaments of Two Cities'.

the paradigm, highlighting how conclusions were often based on comparisons across different social strata, occupational structures, and marital practices.[52] Michelle Armstrong-Partida and Susan McDonough's recent cutting-edge article on single women's positions in the Mediterranean region may well have delivered the final blow to Hajnal's north-south framework.[53]

At the same time, scholars focused on northwestern Europe have also begun to challenge the region's presumed 'exceptionalism.'[54] Mark Bailey, for example, has rightly questioned the conclusions drawn by historians about the economic effects of marriage patterns in England.[55] Earlier assumptions now face growing skepticism and require careful reconsideration. The 'North-South Paradigm' has—finally, one might say—been dethroned, making room for more nuanced and localized analyses of gendered socioeconomic roles.

Yet this welcome shift also carries a risk: undermining the call for regional comparisons that has been a hallmark of gender history over the past two decades. Nevertheless, the comparative method can teach us much about women's positions. An empirical comparison of regions is essential for understanding women's socioeconomic positions without falling into the trap of ranking regions as 'better' or 'worse.' The case studies presented in this book—Brabant and Biscay—could certainly stand on their own. However, viewed together through a comparative perspective, they offer deeper insights into how different societies structured gendered roles in the urban economy.

Anna Bellavitis has emphasized that different types of labor markets "should be studied in relation to each other because it is only their interpenetration that can account for the gendered reality of the urban economies of early modern Europe."[56] Her historiographical approach draws attention to the crucial role of institutions, particularly guilds,

---

[52] See, among others: Zucca Micheletto, 'Reconsidering the Southern Europe Model'; Zucca Micheletto, *Travail et propriété des femmes en temps de crise*; Bellavitis, *Women's Work and Rights*, 9; Bellavitis & Zucca Micheletto, 'Introduction. North versus South'; Wessell Lightfoot, *Women, Dowries and Agency*.

[53] Armstrong-Partida & McDonough, 'Singlewomen in the Late Medieval Mediterranean'.

[54] Edwards & Ogilvie, 'What Can We Learn from a Race with One Runner?'.

[55] Bailey, 'The Black Death, Girl Power, and the Emergence of the European Marriage Pattern in England'.

[56] Bellavitis, 'Urban Markets', 137.

and their ambiguous impact on women's work.[57] While case studies of individual towns have shed light on the guild effect, they have rarely been able to look beyond guild structures, as doing so requires comparisons across towns with different institutional and economic contexts. In *Commerce before Capitalism*, Martha Howell similarly underlines the value of comparative case studies, noting that similarities in labor conditions across regions often depended "on whether traditional practices in those areas resembled [one another, ed.]."[58] The strength of comparative methodology in deepening our understanding of institutional impacts is further demonstrated by Charlie Taverner's study of informal hawkers in sixteenth- to eighteenth-century London and Naples. Although Taverner's work does not primarily focus on gender, it effectively highlights the differing attitudes toward informal work depending on the presence or absence of formal competitors.[59]

A comparative analysis of women's work in small-scale trades in Bilbao, Antwerp, and Mechelen offers a fresh perspective on the mechanisms shaping women's labor opportunities in premodern towns. It challenges the dominant historiographical focus on guilds as the primary determinants of these opportunities. In towns where guilds regulated production, as we will see in the Brabantine cases, they were undeniably important actors in shaping women's access to work. However, the Biscayan case invites us to reconsider this emphasis. Bilbao, a thriving harbor town with a relatively small population, exemplifies the 'market-oriented' towns described by Howell, yet stands out due to the absence of guilds in everyday commodity trades. This absence allows us to reexamine the foundations of women's economic participation, offering a clearer view of the informal economy without interference from corporative structures. By placing Brabant and Biscay side by side, the comparison brings all factors influencing women's labor opportunities into sharper relief and opens new perspectives on the interplay between institutions, markets, and gendered work.

---

[57] *Ibidem*, 152–60.
[58] Howell, *Commerce before Capitalism in Europe, 1300–1600*, 4.
[59] Taverner, 'Licensing the Informal Economy in Early Modern Europe'.

4. Mapping the Terrain: Biscay and Brabant

While the three towns selected for this study cannot claim to represent all towns in either northern or southern Europe—can any town ever truly do so?—their distinct positioning within these broader regions offers a crucial comparative lens. This selection, while acknowledging its limits, highlights the challenges of using such comparisons to support a traditional north-south thesis. Yet it is precisely the divergence in socioeconomic contexts that makes this comparative approach so valuable for unpacking the mechanisms that shaped women's positions in the labor market. By examining these contrasting environments, this book reveals the complex and sometimes unexpected ways in which institutional, economic, and social factors interacted to create both opportunities and constraints for women.

Brabant and Biscay were markedly different regions in terms of demographics, urban development, economic activity, and political structure. Like many premodern regions, their markets catered both to local urban residents and to wider hinterlands, while also engaging in interregional trade. In both Antwerp and Bilbao—and to a lesser extent Mechelen—maritime commerce played a central role. The pronounced contrasts between the regions make it important to set the stage with some contextual background. The following section briefly situates the three towns within their broader regional and historical frameworks. The gendered dimensions of their labor markets, however, are the subject of the chapters to come.

Bilbao

Bilbao's economy was directed towards the sea. Its commerce, both from overseas and in connection with supplying northern Castile, made it a crucial node in the kingdom's commercial network. The town did have artisans, such as shoemakers and blacksmiths, but they mostly produced on a small scale, providing town residents with necessary commodities.[60] The inaccessible terrain around the town prevented its spatial growth but provided the raw materials—iron and wood—necessary for its maritime industry.[61] Iron production and trade were major drivers of the town's economy.[62]

---

[60] García Fernández, 'Las cofradías de oficios en el País Vasco'.
[61] O'Flanagan, *Port Cities of Atlantic Iberia*, 258–69.
[62] García de Cortázar et al., *Vizcaya en la edad media*, vol. 2.

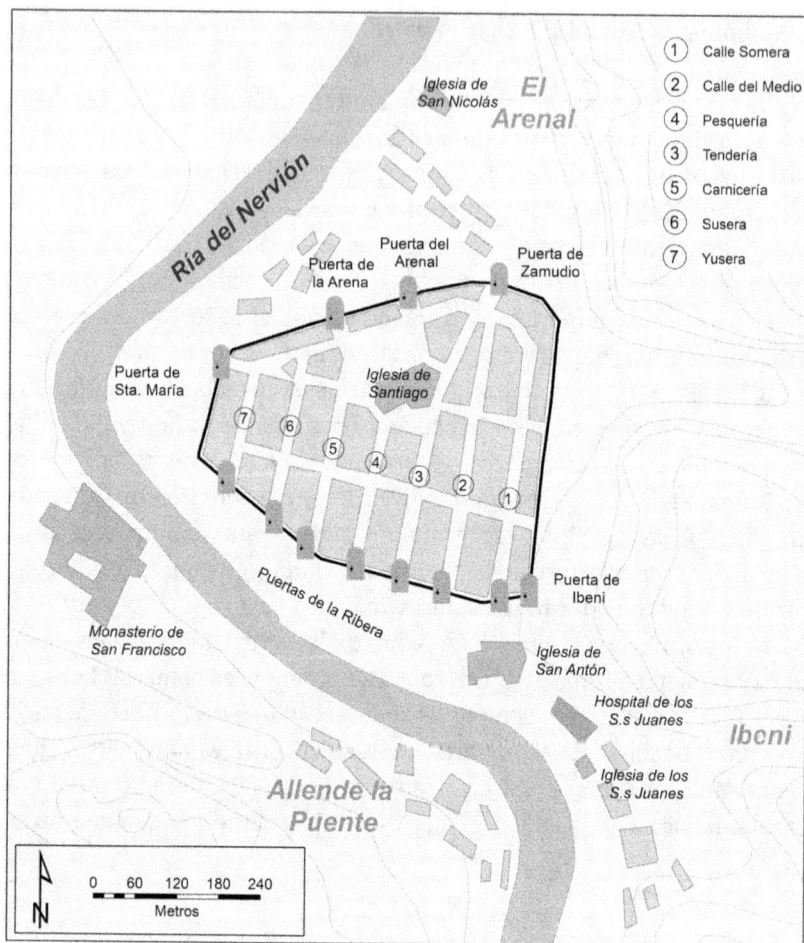

Figure 3. Map of Bilbao at the end of the fifteenth century.
Source: Jesús Ángel Solórzano Telechea.

Nevertheless, Bilbao was, first and foremost, a commercial town. In his well-known *Historia del Consulado de Bilbao*, Teófilo Guiard y Larrauri states that:

> Bilbao was a commercial settlement before it was a town. Its inhabitants were traders before they were citizens, paid trading levies before they paid urban taxes, and had mercantile judges to decide over trade conflicts before they had magistrates to decide over civil cases.[63]

Though economically important, Bilbao's population was small, and demographic growth was limited until the eighteenth century. In 1500, Bilbao had approximately 5,600 residents. This number rose sharply in the early sixteenth century, only to decline to the earlier figure by 1600.[64] As the town's economic importance increased, the number of streets and buildings also grew, but Bilbao remained a small settlement (see figure 3). The narrow streets and town walls allowed for little spatial expansion.[65] Most of the town's marketplaces, where women traded actively, were on the edge of town or even outside the walls.

The town council's ordinances reflect the importance of commerce and maritime activities. These ordinances were promulgated by a select group of councilors.[66] One mayor headed Bilbao's municipal government. The council contained two jurors, eight governors, two clerks, and six judges.[67] Some councilors came from elite Biscayan families, and some from the mercantile class. The overlap between these two groups steadily increased until a few prominent families had established an oligarchy in the Biscayan town by the sixteenth century.[68] The council of Bilbao was authorized to make and enforce laws governing urban life. The Bilbao town council controlled its own formation, economic policies, control mechanisms, and criminal courts.[69] Although its power diminished as the

---

[63] Guiard y Larrauri, *Historia del Consulado y Casa de Contratación de Bilbao y del comercio de la villa*, LXXXI–II.
[64] Catalán Martínez & Lanza García, 'Crecimiento demográfico en tiempos de crisis'.
[65] Bolumburu Arizaga & Martínez Martínez, *Atlas de villas medievales de Vasconia*, 53–106.
[66] Solórzano Telechea, 'Las voces del común en el mundo urbano'.
[67] Bolumburu Arizaga & Martínez Martínez, *Atlas de villas medievales de Vasconia*, 159–64.
[68] Ignacio Salazar, 'Gobierno local en el Bilbao bajomedieval'.
[69] García de Cortázar et al., *Vizcaya en la edad media*, vol. 4, 50–2.

kingdom centralized, the Biscayan commercial hub had a significant say in the organization of urban life.[70]

Antwerp

Throughout this book, we will see similar source material for Antwerp and Mechelen. When it came to women's positions in small-scale trade, they seem to have been rather similar in the two towns. Notwithstanding, the political and especially economic history of the two towns was quite distinct.

The well-studied history of premodern Antwerp is a narrative of increasing wealth and success, at least until the second half of the sixteenth century. Except for the period from 1357 until 1406, when the count of Flanders conquered and ruled Antwerp, the city belonged to the duchy of Brabant.[71] In the fifteenth century, Antwerp was one of the four principal Brabantine towns with juridical and economic hegemony over their hinterlands.[72] The town grew as a commercial center throughout the fifteenth century and achieved economic supremacy over surrounding regions at the century's end.

In 1400, Antwerp had a population of approximately 15,000, making it one of the middling towns of the Low Countries. Like the surrounding towns, Antwerp profited from its drapery.[73] However, in the fifteenth century, the town soon emerged as a center of trade rather than production. With access to Atlantic commerce and the Hanse towns, its location facilitated interregional trade.[74] Antwerp's growing economic allure is reflected in the growth of the population to 40,000 by the end of the fifteenth century.[75] Furthermore, the poverty rate in town declined.[76] While at the beginning of the sixteenth century, trade in Antwerp was still seasonal—bound to the fairs of Antwerp and the northern Brabantine town of Bergen-op-Zoom—by the mid-century, Antwerp had established itself as a permanent trading post for both northern and southern

---

[70] Irigoyen López, 'Characteristics of Castilian Cities', 301.
[71] Van Gerven, 'Antwerpen in de veertiende eeuw'.
[72] Limberger, *Sixteenth-Century Antwerp and Its Rural Surroundings*, 216–21.
[73] Prims, *Geschiedenis van Antwerpen. VI*, 2.
[74] Van Houtte, 'Anvers aux XVe et XVIe siècles', 251.
[75] Marnef, *Antwerpen in de tijd van de Reformatie*, 25.
[76] Bardyn, 'Women's Fortunes', 77.

European traders.[77] It maintained that position until the second half of the sixteenth century, when political instability drove international traders to Amsterdam.

Antwerp was first and foremost a commercial hub, but the town had industries as well. A large number of artisans supported and benefited from the town's trade.[78] As in other Brabantine towns, many of these occupations were organized in craft guilds or fell under a corporation's authority. Craft guilds in Antwerp acquired privileges relatively late in comparison to other Brabantine and Flemish towns. In the second half of the fourteenth century, thirty guilds gradually received privileges.[79] Their autonomy was limited. Craft guilds in Antwerp did not gain the right to participate formally in the city's government until the 1430s. The growth of their economic power gave them the ability to exert political pressure. In 1435, twenty-one craft guilds gained influence over the city's finances and the election of mayors.[80] One year later, they were granted formal participation in municipal government, though only in advisory positions.[81] Although the guilds in Antwerp had relatively little direct involvement in the town government, they were not powerless institutions. The corporations controlled the production of prestigious luxury items, as well as other sectors important to the town's economy. This authority gave them leverage in town politics.[82]

Mechelen

In the same manner as many towns in the late medieval southern Low Countries, Mechelen derived its economic power from the drapery industry, which emerged in the thirteenth century. In the fourteenth century, wool cloth from Mechelen circulated throughout western Europe.[83] In the fifteenth century, the town successfully shifted from mass production of

[77] Gelderblom, *Cities of Commerce*, 15–33.

[78] Marnef, *Antwerpen in de tijd van de Reformatie*, 23–4.

[79] Jacobs, 'De ambachten in Brabant en Mechelen', 560; Prims, *Geschiedenis van Antwerpen. VI*, 9–10.

[80] Prims, *Geschiedenis van Antwerpen. VI*, 106.

[81] Everaert, 'Macht in de metropool', 21–36.

[82] Ben Eersels has also shown the great impact of guilds without direct political representation on town governments in the eastern part of the southern Low Countries. See Eersels, 'The Craft Guilds Are the City'; De Munck, 'La qualité du corporatisme'.

[83] Van Uytven, *De geschiedenis van Mechelen*, 42–4.

average-grade wool cloth to the manufacture of luxury woolens—a move that secured its economic dominance over the surrounding hinterland, further reinforced by political favor from the dukes of Burgundy and the Habsburg regentess Margaret of Austria, who chose Mechelen as their principal seat in the Low Countries. Nevertheless, Mechelen's drapery steadily lost market share, limping along until the mid-sixteenth century, when production nearly ceased.[84] Other economic sectors that had blossomed in the fifteenth century—metal foundry, luxury production, and the construction industry—suffered drastic reductions in the political and economic crises of the mid-sixteenth century.[85]

The trend of rise and decline over the fifteenth and sixteenth centuries also shows in Mechelen's population numbers. At the end of the fourteenth century, Mechelen had approximately 15,000 inhabitants. By 1500, this number had grown to 25,000, and by 1565, the population peaked at roughly 30,000. But by the end of the sixteenth century, economic and political crises caused a steep decrease of population to 11,000.[86]

As in Antwerp, most occupations involving production or small-scale trade in Mechelen were organized in craft guilds. Although the number fluctuated throughout the century, there were approximately thirty-eight privileged craft guilds in Mechelen. Five of these guilds (bakers, brewers, butchers, tanners, and fishmongers), called the *hoofdambachten* (major craft guilds), were directly represented in the town's government.[87] Another seventeen guilds, the so-called *grote ambachten* (great craft guilds), were involved in the election of these representatives and could participate in the *Grote Raad* (Great Council) of Mechelen.[88] From the thirteenth century, the valuable woolen cloth industry and trade was organized in a merchant guild—the *lakengilde*.[89]

In contrast to Antwerp, the elites of the Mechelen craft guilds had a strong position in urban government. Official positions sitting on and appointed by both the magistracy and the *Buitenraad* (outer council) were

[84] Daems, 'De lakenindustrie in de stad Mechelen en in haar omgeving', 29–37.
[85] Mast, 'Politiek, prestige en vermogen', 5–11.
[86] Van Uytven, *De geschiedenis van Mechelen*, 83; Mast, 'Politiek, prestige en vermogen', 5.
[87] The guilds represented in the town government changed throughout the fifteenth century. The butchers, bakers, fishmongers, tanners, and brewers remained in the group of represented guilds, but the weavers were replaced by the dyers. Jacobs, 'De ambachten in Brabant en Mechelen', 572–3.
[88] Laenen, *Geschiedenis van Mechelen tot op het einde der middeleeuwen*, 278–9.
[89] Peeters, 'De produktiestructuur der Mechelse lakennijverheid en de ambachten van wevers en volders'.

held by a limited number of guild members and an even more limited number of local aristocrats. The magistracy regulated and controlled daily life in the city. They had to consider the views and requests of the outer council, comprised of approximately seventy representatives from the craft guilds. Throughout the late Middle Ages, there were changes in the number of craftsmen serving in town government, and craftsmen's seats eventually decreased in favor of the urban elite. Moreover, as elsewhere in the southern Low Countries, the town council's autonomy decreased after the end of the fifteenth century.[90]

5. Sources

A primary challenge in studying women's work in late medieval and early modern urban labor markets lies in the scarcity of clear, quantifiable sources that offer a comprehensive view of women's agency. In a comparative study like this one, the difficulty is compounded by the need for sources that are not only rich in detail but also sufficiently parallel across regions. This book draws on a diverse set of materials to reconstruct women's economic positions in Antwerp, Mechelen, and Bilbao over a period of roughly one hundred years. This timeframe is long enough to gather meaningful data yet narrow enough to avoid the disruptions caused by major religious, geopolitical, or economic transformations. Focusing on a limited number of towns also allows for an in-depth engagement with diverse local source types, making a broader regional comparison feasible. A small number of examples from nearby towns—particularly Portugalete in Biscay and Leuven in Brabant—complement the primary source base.

The study relies chiefly on the most comparable source type available: town ordinances. These texts articulate which economic activities were deemed appropriate for women by urban authorities, as well as by guilds in Brabant. While ordinances provide valuable insight into the intended structure of urban labor markets and the gendered assumptions underlying them, they offer only a limited view of actual practices. To counterbalance this normative perspective, I supplement the ordinances with sources such as tax registers, court cases, guild membership lists, and sentence books. These records allow for a more textured view of how

---

[90] Van Uytven, *De geschiedenis van Mechelen*, 97–125; Haemers, 'Ad Petitionem Burgensium'.

economic life unfolded in practice and how individual women navigated it. They also help uncover aspects of women's work that ordinances either misrepresent or omit altogether.

Recent scholarship has been critical of using normative texts like ordinances to study gender in the premodern period. As historians have pointed out, work regulations "did not embrace the whole world of urban work";[91] guild ordinances "were all written by men, of course, and there is some evidence that women had a stronger sense of work identity than male-authored sources suggest";[92] and written rules "not only may distort the picture of gender and work but often are completely silent on the topic."[93] These are just some of the pitfalls associated with relying on ordinances—yet they have formed the basis for many important earlier studies. Despite their limitations, ordinances remain indispensable for understanding how urban institutions envisioned and sought to regulate women's economic roles. They are uniquely well suited to showing "what is typical"—how authorities sought to shape the ideal daily practices of market life.[94] In this sense, ordinances are central to the comparative approach taken here.

While ordinances were not direct reflections of everyday behavior, scholars have long used them to infer social and economic realities. Ordinances "represent fairly *ad hoc* responses to existing economic and political contingencies."[95] Some of these *ad hoc* responses were made explicit by a *narratio* at the beginning of the ordinance. The documents from Bilbao contain particularly vivid descriptions of the daily practices that prompted the council to put each regulation in place. A close reading of these texts allows us to assess how municipal authorities interpreted women's labor, what kinds of behavior they aimed to encourage or suppress, and who influenced them in regulating the urban labor markets. The recurrence of certain regulations also reveals that many ordinances were routinely ignored—underscoring their character as reactive instruments rather than prescriptive blueprints.[96] As such, ordinances do reflect

---

[91] Bellavitis, *Women's Work and Rights*, 53.
[92] Wiesner, *Women and Gender in Early Modern Europe*, 117.
[93] Ågren, *Making a Living*, 6.
[94] Ogilvie, *A Bitter Living*, 23; Stabel, 'From the Market to the Shop', 53.
[95] Kittell & Queller, "Whether Man or Woman", 65.
[96] Stabel, 'Women at the Market', 267; Hutton, 'Women, Men, and Markets', 416.

daily practices, though at a generalized level that applies to categories of workers rather than individuals.

The analysis of guild membership lists, alongside evidence from town ordinances, deepens our understanding of women's roles within the premodern guild system in Brabant (see chapter 2). These sources reveal how some women participated in the economic life of Mechelen and Antwerp within guild structures. In contrast, there is no evidence of women's involvement in the few known brotherhoods of Bilbao. Women in Bilbao appear to have conducted their small-scale trade outside these predominantly male institutions.

In all three towns, the surviving judicial sources from the period are limited in number. Yet court cases and dispute settlements often reveal aspects of economic life not captured by normative sources. For instance, they shed light on tensions between guild members or conflicts involving informal market activity, which ordinances rarely address directly. Despite their scarcity, these records are crucial for understanding how economic regulations were experienced and contested in daily practice. As Howell's analysis of the Leiden *Correxieboeken* demonstrates, even small collections of such sources can yield significant insights into the practical realities of women's work.[97] Similarly, Daryl Hafter has shown the value of combining normative texts with court reports, as they demonstrate the flexibility of legislation and, in the case of towns with a guild structure, the guilds' flexibility "in defending their economic goals."[98]

Judicial records and sentence books from Mechelen, Antwerp, and Bilbao offer important perspectives on the institutional regulation of labor. They reveal not only the challenges authorities faced in controlling the economic activities of both men and women but also how individuals navigated or subverted these frameworks. Such sources expose the ingenuity with which urban residents, including women, interpreted rules and exploited loopholes to secure their livelihoods. While ordinances reflect the intended frameworks governing women's economic roles, and guild membership lists corroborate formal participation in trade, judicial documents provide a dynamic view of how these systems functioned in practice.

---

[97] Howell, *Women, Production, and Patriarchy*.
[98] Hafter, *Women at Work in Preindustrial France*, 20.

The final source type used in this study is the towns' tax levies. Building on earlier studies that employed taxation registers to investigate social status and identity, this study uses these records to assess women's financial standing—an important indicator of their economic autonomy. However, these registers present notable limitations. They generally list only household heads, making it difficult to trace the contributions of married women or women living in non-head-of-household roles, such as servants. Moreover, as Bellavitis has observed, they rarely include occupational details for either men or women.[99]

Nonetheless, as Darlene Abreu-Ferreira's work on seventeenth-century Portugal has shown, taxation records can still provide valuable insights into women's economic circumstances.[100] In Antwerp, Mechelen, and Bilbao, they help reconstruct the broader financial context in which women operated, complementing other source types in important ways. Taken together, these sources allow for a comparative analysis of women's economic experiences in different institutional and regional settings. They make it possible to link structural conditions—such as guild restrictions or municipal regulations—with individual experiences and economic practice across the regions under study.

*

The use of disparate yet comparable documents enables a more nuanced analysis of women's labor opportunities and the factors that shaped them. For Antwerp, 81 ordinances issued between 1331 and 1595 address women's work, with the majority concentrated between 1450 and 1550. Mechelen yields 66 ordinances on the same topic, likewise mostly from the same century. These regulations were primarily preserved in guild registers, which compiled statutes, privileges, and ordinances granted by local authorities or regional lords.

In contrast, Bilbao presents a different archival landscape. Until the mid-fifteenth century, the town was destabilized by intense political struggles between the *bandos*, the region's powerful noble factions. These conflicts prevented the formation of a consistent town council and hindered the development of a stable economic administration.[101] As a result,

---

[99] Bellavitis, *Women's Work and Rights*, 11–32.
[100] Abreu-Ferreira, 'A Status of Her Own'; Abreu-Ferreira, 'Fishmongers and Shipowners'.
[101] Guiard y Larrauri, *Historia del Consulado y Casa de Contratación de Bilbao*, 189–90.

documentation on trade and occupations is virtually absent before 1460. From 1458 to 1592, however, 143 ordinances regulating labor—including women's—have been preserved, offering a rich body of normative material for analysis.

Beyond ordinances, judicial sources provide valuable insight into actual practice and enforcement. The Antwerp correction books, which record verdicts issued by the town courts, occasionally include cases related to market offenses. Of the entries recorded between 1414 and 1568 in two extant correction books, eleven concern women's activities in the market. Additional rulings on women's employment can be found in other published registers of Antwerp's governmental institutions.[102] In Mechelen, judicial records survive only sporadically in the guild archives. However, the fishmongers' guild preserved a more consistent set of sentence books, documenting rulings issued between 1492 and 1561, involving both men's and women's economic activities. Similarly, the Antwerp mercers' guild maintained a shorter register with similar sentences. These judicial records provide critical insight into how guilds responded to women's work in specific contexts and offer evidence of irregular practices or transgressions.

In Bilbao, valuable judicial material is found not in local sources but in the records of the Royal Chancellery of Valladolid (*Real Chancillería de Valladolid*), a high court that adjudicated cases when litigants claimed the local courts could not offer impartial judgment. Several saleswomen from Bilbao brought disputes among themselves or with the town council before this court. The case reports give details of the women's appearances and include records of the elaborate arguments and testimonies presented and the evidence produced.[103]

Of the sources used in this study, only tax levies and guild membership lists allow for quantitative analysis. These materials are limited in scope, but they enrich our understanding of economic participation in the three towns. Table 1 presents an overview of the available membership and entrance lists for guilds in Antwerp and Mechelen related to small-scale trade and production. While most lists are fragmentary, the membership records from the Antwerp mercers' guild contain a relatively large number

---

[102] Most of the registers containing such conflicts and settlements are published in the *Antwerps Archievenblad*.

[103] Some parts of the section on sources and methodology can also be found in my publication; see Vandeweerdt, 'Women, Town Councils, and the Organisation of Work'.

of entries. Despite their limitations, these records offer useful reflections on the findings derived from the town ordinances. The available taxation registers include a 1470 tax list from Bilbao, a 1544 survey of house values from Mechelen, and two 1537 Antwerp lists recording property values in four urban districts (the 4th, 6th, 8th, and 11th). Chapter 1 provides a more detailed discussion of the origins and usage of these registers.

Table 1. Overview of the available entrance lists and membership lists for Antwerp and Mechelen ca. 1400–1600.

Town	Guild	List type	Period
Antwerp	Old clothes sellers	Membership list	ca. 1550
Antwerp	Mercers	Entrance list	1516-1555
Mechelen	Old clothes sellers	Entrance list	1566-1602
Mechelen	Shopkeepers	Entrance list	1404-1510 and 1554-1560
Mechelen	Gardeners	Entrance list	1478-1503 and 1521-1548
Mechelen	Glove makers	Membership list and entrance list	ca. 1550 – ca. 1580

Source: SAA, GA#4277; SAA, FA#22; SAA, 860#7761; SAM, Oudkleerkopersambacht 21; SAM, Kramersambacht 47; SAM, Hoveniers-, fruiteniers- en mandenmakersambacht 16; SAM, Hoveniers-, fruiteniers- en mandenmakersambacht 17; SAM, Handschoenmakers-, tesmakers-, riem(be)slagers-, wildeledermakers- en schedemakersambacht 554bis.

6. Chapter Organization

The chapters in this book reveal the complexities of women's labor in premodern urban economies, focusing on their roles in small-scale trade and production in Antwerp, Mechelen, and Bilbao during the fifteenth and sixteenth centuries. By tracing women's work activities and analyzing the institutional structures that shaped their labor environments, this study uncovers how gender, socioeconomic organization, and individual circumstances intersected in distinct regional contexts. These frameworks were not unchangeable; they were part of women's daily lives, who, in turn, wielded them with economic and judicial savvy. Bridging institutional frameworks and individual strategies, this book offers a comparative, source-based analysis of women's economic opportunities. The four chapters of this book guide the reader through the key steps necessary for understanding women's labor positions in late medieval and early modern urban contexts.

Chapter 1 lays the empirical foundation by mapping women's labor activities in small-scale trade and production across the three towns. Using a large body of mostly normative sources, particularly town ordinances, it identifies the labor tasks that women performed and the sectors in which they were active. This chapter also explores the social and economic backgrounds of these working women. Tax data, especially from Bilbao, show that many saleswomen belonged to the lower social strata, underlining the economic necessity of their work. This chapter establishes the groundwork for deeper institutional and experiential analysis.

Chapter 2 turns to the institutions that organized and influenced women's labor: the household economy, craft guilds, and the informal market. In the Brabantine towns of Antwerp and Mechelen, guilds and household structures played a dominant role, shaping access to labor and codifying acceptable forms of women's work. In contrast, Bilbao lacked a comparable guild structure in small-scale trade, leaving the informal market and the town council's oversight as the main frameworks for women's labor. This contrast is crucial to understanding regional variation in women's economic roles and opportunities.

Chapter 3 examines how these institutions not only organized but also constrained women's labor. Guilds in Antwerp and Mechelen, in particular, acted as masculine institutions that limited access to certain trades and enforced exclusionary practices. In all three towns, patriarchal values and concerns over economic control drove regulation. Yet the nature of the constraints differed: in the Brabantine towns, institutionalized guild systems imposed clear barriers, whereas in Bilbao, regulation stemmed more directly from municipal authority and was less centered on the exclusion of women. This comparative analysis highlights the different forms gendered restrictions could take, depending on the structure and power of local institutions.

Chapter 4 highlights women's capacity to shape their own labor opportunities and their strategies for navigating the institutional frameworks and limitations that governed their work. It explores two main avenues through which women influenced their economic environment. First, it examines their impact on the regulatory framework. Through petitions and informal influence, women occasionally modified or shaped existing rules, thereby shifting their labor positions. In Bilbao, where formal institutions were less dominant, saleswomen's influence on council regulations is especially evident. The second part of the chapter focuses on how women responded when confronted by urban authorities about their economic activities. In both regions, women employed resourceful—and at times similar—strategies to protect their work and income. This chapter also revisits the view of guilds as restrictive institutions. While many women were excluded from certain activities under guild regulations, the guild-based structure of the Brabantine economy also offered those within it access to protective mechanisms not available to women operating in Biscay's more informal labor market.

CHAPTER 1

Tracing Women's Work

During the fifteenth and sixteenth centuries, the women of Brabant and Biscay were far from mere bystanders in the urban economy; they were active and visible participants across a range of labor sectors. This point has been well established in the scholarship on premodern women and work. As Maria Ågren has put it, "The point of departure for research cannot be whether women worked but, rather, what they did for a living."[1] Yet even this now standard assertion only begins to address the complexity of women's economic lives. It leaves open critical questions about the specific types of labor women engaged in, the conditions under which they worked, and the varying socioeconomic profiles of those involved. These nuances are essential for understanding women's roles in premodern urban settings and form the foundation for the chapters that follow.

This chapter provides an overview of the labor sectors accessible to different groups of women in Bilbao, Antwerp, and Mechelen, drawing on empirical evidence. It also introduces the primary subjects of this book: the women active in these sectors during the fifteenth and sixteenth centuries. Starting with a comparative outline of the labor fields available to women, the chapter explores how opportunities varied across urban and institutional contexts. In Biscay, the informal nature of the labor market made women's work in small-scale trade particularly visible. In Bilbao, traditionally 'feminine' sectors remained dominated mainly by women throughout the period.[2] In contrast, Brabantine sources reveal a labor market more heavily shaped by the regulatory framework of craft guilds, even though women's economic contributions extended well beyond guild structures.

[1] Ågren, 'Introduction', 4.

[2] With 'traditional' feminine work, I refer to what scholars have defined as work that had often been in women's hands before 1400. This definition mainly meant "selling the kinds of goods that they had traditionally made [or procured, ed.] for domestic use," as stated by Martha Howell, or work that "required skills that most women would have acquired as housewives," as stated by Grethe Jacobsen. Howell, *Commerce before Capitalism*, 100–1; Jacobsen, 'Women's Work and Women's Role', 9. See also: McIntosh, *Working Women in English Society*, 250; Wiesner, *Women and Gender in Early Modern Europe*, 131.

The final part of this chapter turns to the financial and social status of women involved in these labor sectors. Women engaged in small-scale trade did not necessarily enjoy financial stability. Although the sources are fragmented and flawed, they allow for cautious conclusions about the economic positions of some women studied in this book. In Bilbao, several women can be traced to lower socioeconomic strata. In Mechelen and particularly in Antwerp, the available sources are less conclusive. However, connections to guild structures suggest that some of these women belonged to the urban middling groups.

1. Female Labor Sectors, Women's Work, and Town Ordinances

This chapter's overview of labor sectors relies primarily on town ordinances, which offer the most comprehensive perspective on formal labor structures in urban settings. In Bilbao, the town council held sole jurisdiction over the promulgation of ordinances. Unlike Brabant, where the craft guilds largely drove regulation, Bilbao's council focused on regulating commerce and daily trade, with minimal oversight of artisan occupations. Women appear prominently in these ordinances, reflecting their significant role in the town's everyday economic life, especially as informal sellers. Council intervention was often prompted by citizen complaints—some formal, others informal—as seen in ordinances citing "many citizens […] had complained, saying that many frauds had happened."[3] While the precise channels of communication remain uncertain, only the council held the authority to enact and enforce urban regulations. As such, female traders in Bilbao were subject to the council's control, and the frequency and specificity of regulations underscore the recognized and normalized presence of women in certain market sectors.

Brabantine ordinances, although issued by town councils, were frequently responses to craft guild initiatives. Given the guilds' prominent role in town governance, their interests often aligned with municipal policy. As a result, Brabantine regulations reflected guild concerns and institutional priorities. Masculine language typically referred to the collective body of guild members, while feminine terms were employed more

---

[3] Enríquez Fernández et al., *Ordenanzas municipales de Bilbao (1477–1520)*, fol. 281r–282r, 20 March 1510.

selectively to designate distinct groups of women working in or around formalized trades. This gendered distinction in language highlights the need to differentiate among various categories of working women in the Brabantine context—including formal and informal sellers, women from guild-affiliated families, and wage laborers.

In what follows, I will offer a brief overview of the roles women assumed in the key labor sectors examined in this book: the bread trade, fish trade, itinerant informal trading of daily commodities, merchant activity, and artisanal work. The final subsection will address the many women who remain invisible in the archival record—the hidden workforce that operated beyond the margins of formal documentation. Not all labor sectors provided equal opportunities for women across both regions, and it is precisely these differences that lie at the heart of this book's comparative analysis. This initial overview of women's participation in each sector provides a first building block toward understanding the broader patterns explored in the following chapters. A deeper investigation into the mechanisms that shaped these regional divergences for each labor sector will form the subject of subsequent chapters.

Bread Trade

The Brabantine urban organization of the bread trade fits squarely within the framework of studies on women and work in a guild context.[4] Town ordinances offer insights into the dynamics of bread production and trade, shedding light on the multiple actors involved in this sector. These regulations also reflect the town councils' nuanced approach to women's labor, particularly in how they categorized and addressed women's roles within the industry.

In the southern Low Countries, the production and sale of bread were typically overseen by a craft guild, specifically the bakers' guild. Membership required registration and the payment of an annual fee, and the guild was led by a (male) dean elected from among the privileged masters. A guild master and his wife usually ran their workshop with the assistance of children, servants, and apprentices. Bread was produced in the bread hall or the family workshop and sold in the market hall or

---

[4] See, among others: Hafter, *Women at Work*; Howell, *Women, Production, and Patriarchy*; Hutton, 'Women, Men, and Markets'.

on the streets.⁵ This arrangement functioned as a household production unit, with the male master occupying the formal and visible role in guild structures—and therefore in written sources—while the contributions of other household members, particularly women, largely escaped documentation.

Women's labor, though significant, mainly remained under the radar. In Antwerp, the town council only acknowledged women in the bread trade in connection with a male baker. In 1481, for instance, bakers had to swear an oath to sell bread only in public spaces—a vow they also swore on behalf of their household members.⁶ Women became more visible in the context of informal trade. On 'free market' days, non-guild members were permitted to sell bread.⁷ However, later that same year, the council banned any "baker's wife, or other women, or bakers, or male and female apprentices, or family members" from participating in the free market.⁸ This regulation specifically targeted the (female) members of bakers' households, reflecting the authorities' concern with informal competition. As will be shown throughout this book, town ordinances often engaged most directly with women's labor in the context of informal work—suggesting that informal economic activity was central to many women's livelihood strategies.

The Mechelen town ordinances pay more attention to women's independent work in the bakers' guild. Alongside references to female household members, the 1476 ordinance on bread excises explicitly mentions "male and female bakers"—a dyad also noted by Ellen Kittell and Kurt Queller in their work on Douai.⁹ Concerned about losing excise revenues, the Mechelen council addressed women engaged in all aspects of the bread trade. The ordinance required the payment of taxes on bread baked by both male and female bakers, regardless of whether production occurred on private property or in the bread hall.¹⁰ By 1535, the council had introduced new regulations on the composition of bread dough, explicitly addressing "bakers and female bakers that bake bread in the

---

⁵ Burm & De Munck, 'Het broodje gebakken?', 163.

⁶ SAA, PK#1394, 25 August 1481.

⁷ SAA, PK#913, fol. 68r–68v, 17 November 1481.

⁸ "Ende dat van nu voordane geenrehande backers vrouwen oft anderen noch oic backers knapen joncwyven oft huysgesinne [...]." SAA, PK#913, fol. 68r–68v, 17 November 1481.

⁹ Kittell & Queller, '"Whether Man or Woman"'.

¹⁰ SAM, Bakkers 2, 27 December 1476. Transcription by Paul Behets, *Rollen en aanvullende reglementen van de Mechelse ambachten. Deel I*, 31–3.

market hall."[11] Similarly, admission rules for the guild used gender-neutral language: "any person from inside or outside the said town" wishing to join the guild had to pay a set fee, while "children of free guild masters" were entitled to a reduced rate.[12] Even as guild structures predominated, the Mechelen regulations reveal a broader and more explicit acknowledgment of women's economic roles. At the same time, the ordinances in Mechelen, like those in Antwerp, continued to regulate women's labor within the context of household production.

What becomes most evident in both towns is the central authority of the bakers' guild in regulating the bread trade. Guild oversight permeated all aspects of bread production and sale, shaping how women's work was framed and recorded. As a result, women's labor in Brabant is primarily visible through the lens of guild authority—a pattern that, as the following pages will demonstrate, recurs across other market sectors. This guild-centric structure stands in stark contrast to the Biscayan case study, where women within the bread trade operated within a less formalized and more publicly visible framework.

*

In her study of late medieval Exeter, Maryanne Kowaleski found that bread production was often controlled by guild members, even though retail bread sales were carried out both by guild members and informal vendors.[13] Marjorie McIntosh, by contrast, describes a different situation in other English towns, where baking bread for sale was not regulated by a guild. Yet, due to the significant capital investment required to build an oven, most bakers were still men.[14] Just like the Brabantine examples, these English case studies reveal a bread trade dominated by formal structures and often skewed toward male participation. This context stands in sharp contrast to the situation in Bilbao, where both bread production and bread sales were in the hands of women.

---

[11] "[...] dat de backere oft backerssen ter hallen backen [...]." SAM, Bakkers 2, fol. 7r–8v, 17 January 1535.
[12] SAM, Bakkers 2, fol. 11r–12r, 9 November 1478.
[13] Kowaleski, 'Women's Work in a Market Town', 148.
[14] McIntosh, *Working Women in English Society*, 183.

Unlike in the Brabantine towns, the Bilbao town council did not have to navigate competing formal and informal market structures. The bread trade in Bilbao was informally divided into two distinct, women-dominated occupations: bread sellers (*panaderas*) and bread bakers (*horneras*). The *panaderas* prepared dough and sold the baked bread in the town's streets. Not all townspeople relied on their services—many households, particularly women such as housewives and servants, prepared their own dough as part of their daily subsistence labor.[15] For safety reasons, private ovens were prohibited within homes, and all baking had to be done in public ovens operated by the *horneras*.[16] These women ran the ovens for a fixed price set by the town council. At night, *horneras* and their female assistants prepared for the next day's work. Early each morning, *panaderas* and other women would gather near the ovens to have their dough baked.[17] A *hornera* could hire up to five other women to help manage the workload.[18]

Both *panaderas* and *horneras* were exclusively female professions, yet neither was formally institutionalized. There was no guild or corporate body overseeing their activities, nor did the work require the significant start-up capital often associated with male-dominated or higher-status trades. The *horneras* did not own the public ovens they operated, but worked them under the supervision—and at the discretion—of the town council. Regulation of the bread trade fell directly under the jurisdiction of the Bilbao town council, and the ordinances consistently addressed women—using gendered terms such as *mugeres, amas, moças, horneras,* and *panaderas*.[19] Only when regulating the supply of grain did the council's ordinances turn to male actors.

Besides bread production and sales, women in Bilbao were also active participants in the grain trade—a marked contrast to the situation in many towns of the southern Low Countries. In fourteenth-century Ghent, for instance, the wheat trade was entirely controlled by men, and women were explicitly barred from buying or selling in the Corn Market.[20] In Mechelen, town authorities prohibited the wives of wheat sellers from

---

[15] Enríquez Fernández et al., *Ordenanzas municipales de Bilbao (1477–1520)*, fol. 75v.
[16] Del Val Valdivieso, 'El trabajo de las mujeres', 70.
[17] Rivera Medina, 'Cuerpos de mujer en el mundo laboral bilbaíno'.
[18] Ayuso Sánchez, 'El mundo laboral femenino', 124.
[19] Translation: Women, housekeepers, servant girls, bread bakers, bread sellers.
[20] Hutton, 'Women, Men, and Markets'.

taking part in transactions.[21] Similarly, in Antwerp, household members of grain sellers were forbidden from entering the grain market on designated 'free Saturday market days.'[22] By contrast, no such restrictions existed in Bilbao, where women appeared more frequently in the ordinances regulating the grain trade.

A central concern of the Bilbao town council was to ensure a fair and reliable distribution of grain within the town and to prevent excess quantities from being diverted elsewhere. Additionally, the council was determined to safeguard excise revenues. To this end, they issued ordinances that addressed a wide range of actors involved in the grain trade. In 1482 (and again in 1501), for example, the council targeted *panaderas*, prohibiting them from purchasing more than one *fanega* of grain.[23] In 1495, *mesoneros* (male innkeepers or male and female innkeepers) were likewise banned from hosting merchants whose primary aim was to buy grain for export.[24] That same year, the council addressed "all citizens and foreigners," using masculine (or mixed) language.[25] In a comparable ordinance issued in 1500, the council made specific mention of servant girls and women employed in local households.[26] Over time, as new actors became involved in circumventing regulations, the council expanded its ordinances accordingly. Women engaged in a variety of roles within the grain trade, and while the council addressed them directly, it did not always distinguish them from male participants.

Although men and women operated under the same legal framework in the Bilbao grain trade, their roles were not necessarily identical. Alongside gender-neutral regulations, the council also issued ordinances targeting specifically female occupations within the grain economy. *Roderas* were tasked with transporting grain to the mills, where it was ground for the *panaderas* and other Biscayan residents. They also weighed the processed

[21] SAM, Magistraat (Ordonnantiën) – Serie III, nr.2, fol. 144r–147r; SAM, Magistraat (Ordonnantiën) – Serie III, nr.2, fol. 243r–244v, 27 November 1520.

[22] SAA, PK#913, fol. 3r, 10 March 1442.

[23] One *fanega* of grain contained 33.5 liters. Enríquez Fernández et al., *Ordenanzas municipales de Bilbao (1477–1520)*, fol. 17r–17v; Hamilton, *American Treasure and the Price Revolution in Spain*, 152–85.

[24] This ordinance was repeated in 1513. Enríquez Fernández et al., *Ordenanzas municipales de Bilbao (1477–1520)*, fol. 45r–45v, 23 January 1495; *Ibidem*, fol. 146v, 7 February 1513.

[25] *Ibidem*, fol. 47r–47v, 28 January 1495.

[26] *Ibidem*, fol. 47r–47v, 28 January 1495; Enríquez Fernández, Hidalgo de Cisneros Amestoy & Martínez Lahidalga, *Colección documental del archivo histórico de Bilbao (1473–1500)*, fol. 5r–5v, 18 March 1500.

grain, although this activity was increasingly contested throughout the sixteenth century.[27] *Cojedoras* functioned as intermediaries, connecting grain suppliers (the *mulateros*) with potential buyers. These women played a vital role in facilitating bulk trade. Nonetheless, the control of grain and wholesale commerce remained largely in male hands. Given the strategic importance of grain to the town's sustenance and stability, the council exerted stricter oversight over women's involvement in this sector than in less vital trades. I will examine this control—and the varied forms of women's participation in the grain trade—in more detail in chapters 3 and 4.

Fish Trade

The fish trade was an important means of distributing a key subsistence product for premodern urban dwellers. The accessibility and abundance of fish in urban markets make it a compelling case study for comparing women's labor and the attitudes of institutions towards their work in this market field. Other scholars, such as Danielle van den Heuvel for eighteenth-century Amsterdam and Darlene Abreu-Ferreira for seventeenth-century Porto, have already turned their attention to female fishmongers in premodern Europe. They found a group of women with a consolidated occupational identity, even if not formally organized.[28]

Throughout this book, I discuss the impact of institutions on women's opportunities in the fish trade, as well as women's strategies for dealing with the institutional framework. As we will see, the case of the Bilbao fishmongers aligns to some extent with previous case studies, such as those of Porto and Amsterdam.[29] The Brabantine case studies, particularly that of Mechelen, present a more nuanced picture due to the pronounced role of the fishmongers' guild. This section introduces the structure of the fish trade in both regions and the roles women played within it.

---

[27] Enríquez Fernández et al., *Libro de acuerdos y decretos municipales*, fol. 71r, 31 August 1509. Janire Castrillo Casado gives a more detailed description of the *roderas*' activities in: Castrillo Casado, *Las mujeres vascas durante la baja edad media*, 280–1

[28] Abreu-Ferreira, 'Fishmongers and Shipowners'; Abreu-Ferreira, 'Neighbors and Traders'; Van den Heuvel, 'The Multiple Identities'; Van den Heuvel, 'Partners in Marriage and Business?', 225–7.

[29] Other studies focusing on or including the premodern female fishmongers can also be found. See, among others: Coomans, 'Policing Female Food Vendors'; Harmsen & Hubers, "En Zij Verkocht de Vis ..."; Jacobsen, 'Women's Work and Women's Role'; Vicente, 'Images and Realities of Work'.

The ordinances for the fish trade in Mechelen and Antwerp show how both councils dealt with a formal and informal portion of the trade. While the ordinances do not always offer a complete picture of daily practices, they give a good idea of the different actors involved in the Brabantine fish trade. The activities of (female) fishmongers are especially visible in Mechelen, likely because of the town's fourteenth- and fifteenth-century staple rights on the fish trade. These rights required any trader bringing fish into Mechelen's territory to offer their goods for sale at the Mechelen market. The revenue from excise duties on the fish trade was a major source of income for Mechelen and led to repeated conflicts with neighboring towns such as Antwerp and Brussels.[30] The economic importance of staple rights is likely a key factor in the abundance of sources related to the fish trade.

Although women in Brabant could still operate in the fish trade in their own names, the town ordinances of Mechelen and Antwerp tended to exclude them from formal recognition. In Mechelen, only around eleven percent of fishmonger regulations were directed towards women. The regulations governing the formal trade within the fishmongers' guild focused almost exclusively on men. The guild's entrance rules mention women only twice. In 1454 and again in 1508, the town government decreed that "the son of a free fishmonger's daughter" could enter the guild at half the usual fee—a privilege also extended to illegitimate sons and sons of guild masters.[31] This phrasing suggests that the fishmonger's daughter was not eligible for guild membership on her own. However, she could still pass on benefits to her sons, whether or not she remained active in the trade. This arrangement served to strengthen the guild's exclusivity.[32]

The masculine character of the Mechelen fishmongers' guild is reflected in its language, which overwhelmingly addressed only male actors involved in the formal trade. Membership records in the guild's

---

[30] Schoeffer, *Historische aanteekeningen rakende de kerken, de kloosters, de ambachten en andere stichten der stad Mechelen*, 126–7.

[31] "Item, die een yegelic wettich zoon van eens vrije visschers dochter van der voirscreven stad ende een yegelic bastaertzoon van eenen vrijen visscher die int voirscreven ambacht sal willen comen ende gevrijde zijn sculdich sal sijn te gevene voir sijn incompst int voirscreven ambacht twee pond grote vlaams gelds te bekeeren in drijen gelijc voirscreven staet." SAM, Visverkopers 14, 26 July 1454; SAM, Visverkopers 23, 16 October 1508.

[32] Similar inheritance mechanisms can be found in other guilds and locations throughout premodern Europe. See, among others: Burm & De Munck, 'Het Broodje gebakken?'; Jacobsen, 'Women's Work and Women's Role', 14–6; Montenach, 'Creating a Space for Themselves', 55.

account books from 1466 to 1579 confirm this gendered exclusivity: no female names appear on these lists, not even those of widows known to have been active in the trade during this period.[33] Official guild membership, therefore, remained strictly male. Yet, when we read the normative ordinances alongside the guild's account books and sentencing records, it becomes clear that women contributed significantly to the fish trade in Mechelen—even if their roles were not formally acknowledged.

In the ordinances of the Mechelen fishmongers, the majority of decisions using feminine or gender-neutral language were directed at female members of guild masters' households. In 1454, for instance, the Mechelen council decreed that "every member of the aforesaid guild [the fishmongers' guild, ed.] may have only one market stall for himself and his wife to practice his trade."[34] This phrasing explicitly situates women's labor within the framework of household participation rather than independent professional activity. This pattern appears not only in Mechelen but also in Antwerp's fishmonger regulations.

Antwerp's fish trade regulations similarly demonstrate women's access to guild work through household connections. As we will explore further in chapter 3, the Antwerp council adopted an ambivalent stance toward fishmongers' wives: they were granted certain privileges denied to outsiders, yet also faced restrictions that reinforced their status as non-members. For example, these women were allowed to sell fish in and around the market area—but only in their husbands' absence.[35] Like the widows absent from the Mechelen fishmongers' membership lists, they could step in as substitutes, but they were not recognized as full and independent participants in the trade. Their labor was permitted only insofar as it supported the household economy, not as a standalone economic force.

Although the Mechelen fishmongers' guild, which was formally restricted to men, exercised considerable control over the fish trade, it did not enjoy a total monopoly. Ordinances and records of daily practice reveal that women, particularly in the herring trade, participated independently of the guild. These *harincvrouwen*, or 'herring women,' operated at the

---

[33] SAM, Visverkopers 462a, fol. 14v–15r; SAM, Visverkopers 462b (first 12 pages, no foliation); SAM, Visverkopers 462c (first 4 pages, no foliation).

[34] "Item, dat nyement van den voirscreven ambachte van den visschers en sal mogen hebben mair een banc op te vischmerct voir hem ende voir sijn wijf om sine neringe dairop te doene." SAM, Visverkopers 14, 26 July 1454.

[35] SAA, GA#4363, 6–11, 17 November 1452; SAA, GA#4369, 3r, 9 September 1422.

margins of the formal trade. They were authorized to sell herring without being guild members, and the regulation of their activity focused mainly on product quality and designated selling locations. Unlike guild members who sold in the official fish market, herring women were confined to adjacent backstreets.[36]

This pattern finds parallels in other trades. In Leuven, for example, *pensvrouwen* sold sausages and other meat products under similarly informal conditions. Both groups—*harincvrouwen* and *pensvrouwen*—engaged in trades tied to daily subsistence and often perceived as traditionally feminine labor. While the formal guild economy sought to regulate access, it also accommodated informal female competition, particularly when such activity was rooted in custom and met subsistence needs. These women were typically butchers' or fishmongers' wives, or independent traders whose relationship to the guild was defined more by monetary exchange than by institutional affiliation.[37]

Unlike ordinances for the formal fishmongers, regulations regarding the inclusion or exclusion of the Mechelen herring sellers are scarce. This lack of detailed regulation is characteristic of informally organized segments of urban markets, a theme that will be further explored throughout this book. The herring women's right to trade stemmed not from guild membership but from long-established local customs. A 1454 ordinance, for instance, affirmed their position based on "old habits," highlighting the legitimacy of customary practice in shaping market participation.[38]

Evidence from the Mechelen fishmongers' guild's sentence books further shows how the *harincvrouwen* were recognized as independent traders. Five sentences refer specifically to herring sellers, indicating that they could be held individually accountable.[39] As in other premodern European trades, the most profitable segments—wholesale and

---

[36] SAM, C. Magistraat (Ordonnantiën) – Serie III, nr.2, fol. 21r–23v, 26 July 1454; SAM, Visverkopers 23, 16 October 1508.

[37] SAM, C. Magistraat (Ordonnantiën) – Serie III, nr.2, fol. 217v–221v, 29 January 1510; SAM, C. Magistraat (Ordonnantiën) – Serie V, nr. 1, fol. 99r–101v, 6 February 1533; Vandeweerdt, "Van den vleeschouweren oft pensvrouwen". For broader research on these traditionally feminine food trades, see, among others: Pilorget, 'Circulations féminines et encadrement de l'espace urbain'; Crowston, 'Women, Gender, and Guilds', 28; Gold, 'On the Streets and in the Markets', 36–37; Montenach, 'Trades in Lyon'.

[38] "[...] de vrouwen die dat gewoonlic sijn te doene die selen nair der ouder coustumen alsulken haring ende boxhoren mogen vercoopen ende penneweerden [...]." SAM, Visverkopers 14, 26 July 1454.

[39] SAM, Visverkopers 320; SAM, Visverkopers 321; SAM, Visverkopers 322.

long-distance sales—remained dominated by men, typically interregional merchants or local guild members.[40] Still, the presence of the herring sellers in Mechelen's organization of the fish trade was undeniable. They were addressed as a distinct occupational group in the ordinances, granted permission to trade by the town authorities, and carried out their work parallel to the guild, though never formally part of it.

*

As in most Iberian coastal towns, fish in Bilbao was sold in small quantities by *pescaderas* (female fishmongers) and *sardineras* (sardine sellers).[41] While men controlled the more lucrative wholesale trade, a few women—mostly widows—also participated at that level. One such woman was Isabel de Sabugal, a resident of Portugalete, a town near Bilbao. She became embroiled in a dispute with a Galician trader over five *millares* and twelve barrels of sardines she sought to purchase. Isabel clearly operated as a well-established merchant.[42]

Most women involved in Bilbao's fish trade, however, did not handle goods in bulk. The town's *pescaderas* typically acquired small amounts of fish from public nets or from merchants, while town officials weighed, inspected, secured, and distributed the fish. Not all fish arrived from overseas fishermen; inhabitants of nearby coastal towns—*mugeres, moços e moças e omes*—also brought fish to Bilbao by mule or carried it on their heads. Upon arrival, the council inspected the goods.[43] Similarly, *pescaderas* from other Biscayan coastal towns such as Portugalete, Bermeo, and Laredo transported fish in small boats, called *pinazas*, to Bilbao for retail sale.[44] In this context, Bilbao's women fishmongers were part of a wider network of fishermen (and women), interregional traders, retailers, and customers.

The *pescaderas* and *sardineras* sold their goods in the streets, in shops, or at market tables. The *pescaderas* primarily sold fresh fish, while the *sardineras* formed a specialized subgroup of the town's *regateras* (female

---

[40] Honeyman & Goodman, 'Women's Work, Gender Conflict, and Labour Markets', 611; Bennett, "History That Stands Still", 274; Jacobsen, 'Women's Work and Women's Role', 11.

[41] Abreu-Ferreira, 'Fishmongers and Shipowners'; Vicente, 'Images and Realities of Work', 129–30; Iziz & Iziz, *Historia de las mujeres en Euskal Herria*, 259.

[42] ARChV, Sala de Vizcaya, Caja 79,1, 1552.

[43] Enríquez Fernández et al., *Ordenanzas municipales de Bilbao (1477–1520)*, fol. 36v–37r, 17 December 1488.

[44] Javier Enríquez Fernández et al., *Libro de acuerdos y decretos municipales*, fol. 26v, 5 March 1509.

retailers). The council authorized them to sell sardines and other dried or salted fish.[45] As we will explore in a later chapter, *sardineras* often worked closely with other fishmongers and were regularly addressed together in municipal bylaws. One published collection of ordinances from Bilbao includes fifty-six regulations concerning fish sales. While not all targeted female fishmongers, those that did focused primarily on the quality, pricing, and weight of the fish they sold. Additional regulations addressed sales locations, informal trade, and organizational issues within the fish trade.[46] The prominent attention to women fish sellers in these ordinances likely reflects their centrality in Bilbao's small-scale food distribution system— making them both highly visible and more vulnerable to male control.

Local authorities prioritized the regulation of market space as a strategy for controlling trade practices.[47] It may have proven difficult for the council to monitor and regulate women engaged in small-scale retail. Although Bilbao lacked enclosed food halls, as seen in other premodern European towns, the fair distribution of food and the control of designated market spaces remained just as crucial.[48] This situation helps explain the town council's repeated interventions to limit the locations where women could trade. In 1497, for instance, it ruled that "no retail women nor other persons" from within or outside Bilbao were permitted to sell fish in shops or houses; instead, they were required to do so at the square and the Portal de Zamudio—the two official sites for trading fish in the town.[49]

To further consolidate control over the market space, the council designed meticulous regulations about Bilbao's fish trade. In 1510, it constructed a shelter or marked area for fishmongers' stalls and introduced a system for assigning these spaces. According to town ordinances, the nineteen *pescaderas* and *sardineras* selling fish at the square in Bilbao would rotate weekly through the most desirable market stalls at the entrance of the square, thereby ensuring that "they would all enjoy the entrance of the quay and the façade of the council's house," where the market was

---

[45] Del Val Valdivieso, 'El trabajo de las mujeres', 74.

[46] Enríquez Fernández et al., *Ordenanzas municipales de Bilbao (1477–1520)*.

[47] See also: Stabel, 'From the Market to the Shop'; Hutton, 'Women, Men, and Markets'.

[48] *Ibidem*, 90; Schöts, 'Female Traders and Practices of Illicit Exchange', 136; Montenach, 'Legal Trade and Black Markets', 26; Davis, *A History of Shopping*, 74; Stabel, 'From the Market to the Shop'.

[49] The square that the council referred to was located in the Calle Barrencalle. García de Cortázar et al., *Vizcaya en la edad media*, 1:346–7; Enríquez Fernández et al., *Ordenanzas municipales de Bilbao (1477–1520)*, fol. 85v, 13 February 1497.

located.⁵⁰ In the same ordinance, the council required the women to clean the square weekly and limited the areas in which they could operate to reduce waste and nuisance.⁵¹

Although the council's regulation of fishmongers may have aimed to control their commercial practices (see chapter 3), its push for spatial ordering did not fundamentally alter the gendered nature of the marketplace. In contrast to the meat halls of Brabant and Flanders—enclosed spaces often designed to emphasize traders' masculinity—the newly delineated fish market in Bilbao remained unmistakably female.⁵²

Itinerant Informal Traders

Informal, itinerant small-scale trade in daily provisions—including occupations such as peddling and street vending—was a market sector in which women played a highly visible role in towns across premodern Europe. Sources relating to these trades often specifically focus on female traders, as is the case for certain occupations in Bilbao. While itinerant trade remained largely informal in both Brabant and Biscay, mechanisms of control were nevertheless present, and they varied significantly between the two regions. A key difference lay in the presence or absence of formal competitors and the institutions holding authority over occupational organization.

In Bilbao, itinerant female traders featured prominently in municipal ordinances, underscoring their central role in the town's small-scale food distribution system. Besides the *pescaderas* and *sardineras*, the town's *regateras* (female retailers) formed the second most frequently addressed occupational group in the regulations. These women sold a wide range of daily provisions—including candles, fruit, vegetables, and oil—and were often addressed collectively with the fishmongers in town bylaws.

---

⁵⁰ "[...] E asy echadas las dichas suertes e declarados quienes avian de estar en la dicha delantera, en la entrada en el dicho conçejo aza la casa del conçejo, e dende en renque fasta la esquina que esta pegada a las dichas escalleras, que estan junto con la dicha puente e vaxan de la dicha Plaça; e luego los dichos sennores acordaron e mandaron que de semana en semana se muden las de vn cabo a la otra por su orden por sienpre jamas, porque todos gozen ygoalmente de la entrada del dicho cay e delantera de en derecho de la dicha casa del conçejo." Enríquez Fernández et al., *Ordenanzas municipales de Bilbao (1477–1520)*, fol. 276r–279r, 2 October 1510.

⁵¹ *Ibidem*.

⁵² Hutton, 'Women, Men, and Markets'; Vandeweerdt, "Van den vleeschouweren oft pensvrouwen".

Most retailers in Bilbao were women running their own businesses.[53] They were not organized into formal institutions and answered directly to the town council. Some occupations, such as *candeleras* (candle sellers) and *aceiteras* (oil sellers), operated under a licensing system and were required to maintain consistent supplies of their goods, thereby ensuring access to essential commodities.[54] This system enabled the council to control both the number and selection of traders—a regulatory approach echoed in other non-guild towns such as Amiens, where the council similarly oversaw female itinerant traders.[55]

Although many retailers—especially those selling fruits, vegetables, nuts, or poultry—were not formally licensed, their work was nevertheless subject to scrutiny and town regulations. Between 1463 and 1515, the council issued fourteen ordinances regulating this sector. These measures focused on pricing, the use of market space, and the permitted hours and days for buying and selling. Even in the absence of formal competition from guild-based traders—a factor that eased the path for women's involvement in food distribution—the *regateras* remained firmly under the influence of the town council's control.

The council's close regulation of *regateras* aimed to prevent malpractice and ensure the steady provision of everyday goods. For example, retailers were required to wait until residents had purchased directly from bulk traders before acquiring goods for resale. Yet the council struggled to enforce such regulations. Between 1487 and 1513, it reiterated the rule concerning the timing of stock purchases no fewer than four times.[56] In 1496, following citizen complaints, candle sellers were given ten days to correct undersized candles.[57] In 1497, a town official was appointed to prevent *fruteras* (fruit sellers) from trading at the Puerta d'Artecalle.[58] The absence of formal organization among the *regateras* likely complicated

---

[53] Rivera Medina, 'Superando fronteras', 24; Del Val Valdivieso, 'El trabajo de las mujeres', 73.

[54] Javier Enríquez Fernández et al., *Libro de acuerdos y decretos municipales*, fol. 21r–21v, 21 February 1509; *Ibidem*, fol. 27v–28v, 7 March 1509; *Ibidem*, fol. 98r–99r, 28 November 1509.

[55] Pilorget, 'Circulations féminines et encadrement de l'espace urbain', 24.

[56] Enríquez Fernández et al., *Ordenanzas municipales de Bilbao (1477–1520)*, fol. 25r–26v, 19 September 1487; *Ibidem*, fol. 35r–35v, 24 September 1488; *Ibidem*, fol. 52r–52v, 5 June 1495; *Ibidem*, fol. 109v–110r, 11 January 1503; *Ibidem*, fol. 146r–146v, 18 February 1513; Javier Enríquez Fernández et al., *Libro de acuerdos y decretos municipales*, fol. 42r, 18 May 1509.

[57] Enríquez Fernández et al., *Ordenanzas municipales de Bilbao (1477–1520)*, fol. 72v–73v, 13 January 1496.

[58] *Ibidem*, fol. 83v–84r, 11 January 1497.

the council's efforts at oversight. However, this informality also allowed the council to intervene directly and penalize transgressions without the potential contestation by a competing governing (socioeconomic) institution.

*

The visibility of itinerant female traders was lower in Brabantine towns than in Bilbao. Aside from the *harincvrouwen*, few groups of informal female merchants appear in the Brabantine town ordinances. Unlike in Bilbao, where fruit, vegetables, wax and oil, dairy products, and candles were often traded informally, these goods were typically regulated through guild structures in towns like Antwerp and Mechelen. While women could formally join such guilds, their presence remained limited. The membership records of Mechelen's gardeners' guild, for instance, reveal that relatively few women became official members.[59]

Nevertheless, guild ordinances did occasionally address women affiliated with the guild, both as independent members and as widows or relatives of guild masters. In addition to regulating formal guild activities, the ordinances of Mechelen's gardeners and fruit sellers also mentioned female wage earners. However, these women's roles are not described in as much detail as those of the itinerant fruit and vegetable sellers in Bilbao. A 1491 ordinance, for example, aimed to curtail competition within the guild, stating that "no member of the guild may employ the employees of his fellow guildsmen, whether men or women, without his permission."[60]

Although women are quite visible in the regulations of the fruit and vegetable sellers' guild, the trade did not seem to have the same informal character as its Biscayan counterpart. Informal competition did exist on 'free market days,' when any resident of the town was allowed to sell produce from their own property. This was the case in Antwerp's fruit and vegetable trade, where the council allowed citizens to sell a certain amount of their own produce without owing anything to the guild.[61] There

---

[59] SAM, Hoveniers-, fruiteniers- en mandenmakersambacht 16; SAM, Hoveniers-, fruiteniers- en mandenmakersambacht 17.

[60] "[...] nyemande vanden voerscreve ambachte, wye die zij, georloeft wesen en sal zijns mede ambachtsman wercklyden, weder die mannen oft vrouwen zijn die hij te wercken gestelt heeft, te ontsmeken oft te onderhueren sonder sinen oirlof [...]." SAM, Fruiteniers 7, 12 December 1491.

[61] Bisschops, 'Oudt register, mette berderen, 1336–1439 (Vervolg)' vol. 28, fol. 127v, 27 June 1428.

was also constant informal competition in Antwerp. In 1452, for instance, the council addressed "women and others who are not members of the guild," setting out the payments they owed the guild to conduct trade.[62] No similar evidence of this regulatory approach survives for Mechelen.

In Mechelen, the clearest signs of tension between formal and informal trade are found in the case of the female herring sellers previously discussed. In Antwerp, the *uitdraagsters* (literally "female carriers") offer a particularly telling example of informal itinerant commerce. These women competed directly with the established guild of secondhand dealers, the old clothes sellers. Like guild members, the *uitdraagsters* sold secondhand goods on commission for a fixed fee. However, their activities were more narrowly defined, as only guild members could purchase and resell items at public auctions, estimate goods' values, and utilize certain marketplaces—some key privileges denied to the *uitdraagsters*.

With some exceptions, previous studies have paid limited attention to saleswomen in Brabant and the wider southern Low Countries, largely because their activities were overshadowed by those of the officially organized old clothes sellers. In Antwerp, *uitdraagsters* were required to swear an annual oath to the dean of the old clothes sellers' guild and were held accountable to the guild in cases of misconduct or fraud.[63] Though not formally organized into a separate economic institution, they were addressed collectively in town ordinances as a distinct group of women working under the same regulations. Through this regulatory attention, both the town government and the guild acknowledged them as legitimate economic actors.

Authorities paid particular attention to the *uitdraagsters* because their work did not take place within a (guild-)regulated household workshop and, like the saleswomen of Bilbao, they operated without a formal institutional structure to govern their trade. However, unlike in Bilbao, the regulation of the *uitdraagsters* was primarily geared toward ensuring the guild's control over their labor. No ordinances defined the eligibility criteria for becoming an *uitdraagster*. The question of inclusion or exclusion was not addressed by the Antwerp council when dealing with this group of itinerant female traders.

---

[62] SAA, GA#4650, fol. 99r–101r, 20 December 1452.
[63] "Item, dat de dekens van den voorscreven ambachte jaerlicx zullen moghen hebben eenen eedt van elcken uuytdraechsteren weder zij inneecoopen oft niet [...]." Geudens, *Dit raect het oude cleercoopers ambacht*, 6–7.

Ordinances concerning the *uitdraagsters* focused especially on the spatial organization of their work. Market access was a key concern for the Antwerp council. Compared to their guild-affiliated counterparts, the *uitdraagsters* faced more strict regulations: they were limited to itinerant trade and explicitly prohibited from establishing permanent shops, as set out in regulations from 1436 and 1550.[64] In 1547, the council further regulated their work by defining the spaces where guild members and *uitdraagsters* could sell goods during the Thursday, Friday, and Saturday markets. This ordinance, which applied to both groups, aimed to address complaints about congestion on market days. Yet it maintained a clear distinction: guild members were permitted to occupy designated stalls, while *uitdraagsters* continued to be denied fixed selling spaces.[65]

This situation highlights a first key contrast between itinerant traders in Brabant and those in Biscay. While the Bilbao council sought to centralize informal trade, as seen with the fishmongers' designated space, the Antwerp authorities pursued the opposite approach. In the Scheldt town, the right to consolidate secondhand trade in a specific market location remained a privilege of the male-dominated old clothes sellers' guild. This status marks an initial insight into the mechanisms we will discuss further in chapter 3, which shaped regional differences in the governance of informal female labor.

While *uitdraagsters* are most prominently documented in Antwerp, evidence of their presence also appears in Mechelen and Leuven. As in Antwerp, Mechelen's *uitdraagsters* faced restrictions on both the type and origin of goods they were permitted to sell. They were barred from trading goods from their homes—a regulation also enforced in Antwerp—and prohibited from selling items obtained from *sterfhuizen* (deceased's estates), a privilege reserved for guild members.[66] Furthermore, guild ordinances forbade them from being hired by guild members to sell goods on their behalf. Instead, they could only be contracted by private citizens to sell on commission, and, as specified in a 1577 ordinance, "they cannot bring more goods to the market than they can carry around their necks."[67]

---

[64] SAA, GA#4001, fol. 30r–32r, 10 November 1436; SAA, GA#4273, fol. 7v–13v, 19 January 1550.

[65] SAA, PK#915, fo. 80v–82r, May 1547.

[66] SAM, Oudekleerkopersambacht 1, fol. 1r–29v, 16 December 1577; SAM, C. Magistraat (Ordonnantiën) – Serie III, nr.2, fol. 13r–13v, 3 October 1457.

[67] SAM, Oudekleerkopersambacht 1, fol. 1r–29v, 16 December 1577.

The relationship between guild members and informal *uitdraagsters* reveals a similar dynamic across the Brabant towns: while these women lacked formal institutional backing, their collective regulation suggests a shared occupational identity. As will be further explored in chapter 4, this echoes the kind of group coherence observed among certain informal saleswomen in Bilbao. Although the broader dynamics of female trade differed between Brabant and Biscay, the *uitdraagsters* may represent the closest point of comparison between the two regions.

Merchants

The overall focus of this book is women's positions in small-scale trade—occupations that contrast with the high-status commercial roles studied by Martha Howell. Even so, archival sources from Mechelen, Antwerp, and Bilbao unsurprisingly reveal women's presence in these higher-status occupations as well. Although such roles fall outside the central scope of this study, they cannot be ignored: the line between low- and high-status work was often blurred. In some sectors, urban residents from different social backgrounds worked side by side, and in most cases, sources attest to interactions across social strata. While they are not the same market sectors in the two regions, I will briefly discuss some of the groups of merchants and their professional contexts in Brabant and Biscay.

In Mechelen and Antwerp, membership lists from the influential mercers' guilds offer valuable insight—these are further discussed in the next chapter. Like many occupations considered here, the Brabantine mercers were organized in a guild. Unlike some other guilds, women could formally become members in their own right, though their representation remained limited. The extant membership lists reflect only a small number of women and exclude female family members of guild masters, who were often involved in guild-related labor but not formally recorded.[68] The Antwerp mercers' guild was a powerful and wide-reaching institution, encompassing more than twenty-four occupations.[69] Between 1516 and 1555, most members were registered as oil workers, poultry and dairy vendors, shopkeepers, grocers, or tinsmiths. In Mechelen, by contrast, the mercers' guild was restricted to shopkeepers who sold a range of primarily luxury goods, such as gold and silver accessories, silk and cotton yarns, knitted

[68] For a more detailed analysis of the mercers' membership lists, see Chapter 2.
[69] Van Aert, 'Van appelen tot zeemleer', 117–8.

gloves, hats, sleeves, and socks.[70] Oil, poultry, and dairy sellers in Mechelen belonged instead to a separate guild, the so-called oil workers' guild.

The town councils of Mechelen and Antwerp regularly issued regulations that explicitly addressed women working in the mercers', shopkeepers', and oil workers' guilds. These ordinances did not limit women's opportunities in these trades. Significantly, even the male-dominated guilds did not attempt to exclude women from these activities. On the contrary, various council decisions explicitly addressed both male and female sellers, referring to "the male and female vendors of dairy, whether oil workers or others selling butter, eggs, cheese, or similar alimentary goods."[71] Although most formal guild members were men, the language of the ordinances reflects a broader recognition of women's commercial roles. They mention women not only as wives and widows of guild members, but also as independent traders—*voercoopsters* (female vendors) and *cremeressen* (female shopkeepers).

In particular, the poultry and small game trade reveals a striking use of inclusive language. Much like the Bilbao council's decisions concerning the *regateras*, the Mechelen council's regulations focused on issues such as pricing, quality, and permitted times for sale. Women selling grease products and poultry were addressed as individual sellers and as part of household economic units, operating in both formal and informal contexts. For instance, in 1523, the Mechelen council issued an ordinance specifying the locations where "all *voircooperen* and *voircoopperssen* of poultry and game meat residing within the town" were allowed to pluck and prepare their goods.[72] This gender-inclusive phrasing appears throughout the 1523 ordinance governing the trade in poultry and small game and can be found again in the 1533 ordinance about poultry and game sales, highlighting the authorities' recognition of women's active role in this branch of commerce.[73]

*

[70] SAM, Kramers 4, 1 September 1561. Transcription by Paul Behets, *Rollen en aanvullende reglementen van de Mechelse ambachten. Deel II*, 274–82.

[71] "[...] vercooperen, vercooperessen van suivele het zij vetwariers oft dier gelike het zij boter, eyere, kase oft dier gelike proviande." SAA, GA#4001, fol. 72r–73r, 20 December 1484.

[72] "[...] dat alle voircooperen ende voircoopperssen van gevoghelte ende wiltbrade woonachtich bynnen der stadt ende vrijheyt van Mechelen [...]." SAM, C. Magistraat (Ordonnantiën) – Serie V, nr. 1, 1r–5r, 12 January 1523.

[73] SAM, C. Magistraat (Ordonnantiën) – Serie V, nr. 1, fol. 101v–105r, 6 February 1533.

Beyond the distribution of foodstuffs and other everyday goods, women in Bilbao were also active in the production and trade of linen fabrics. Most linen produced locally was of lower quality than the imported varieties, and while much of it was destined for regional consumption, exports to other parts of the kingdom were steadily increasing. Linen production appears to have taken place primarily in the surrounding rural areas. In Bilbao itself, a group of women, known as *lenceras*, were engaged in selling linen cloth from shops in the town. These *lenceras* operated at various economic levels, as evidenced by a 1509 ordinance. Concerned about potential fraud and tax evasion, the town council ordered all linen sellers to relocate their businesses to shops in the town center within six days.[74] A week later, on 12 February 1509, two *lenceras*, Joana de Carryaso and Milia, appeared before the council to request an extension, citing poverty as the reason they could not comply immediately. The council granted them a postponement until Easter.[75] Their case suggests that they ran modest businesses, likely trading linen on a small scale. However, archival records such as debt declarations, commercial contracts, and conflict resolutions show that not all *lenceras* operated so modestly. Some conducted large-scale trade, extending their activities beyond the region.[76]

Not all cloth merchants in Bilbao were locals, and several supporting occupations—many of them held by women—facilitated the town's textile trade. Among these were the *plumeras*, *corredoras*, and *huespedas*. The *huespedas*, or hostesses, managed inns and boarding houses for merchants, particularly women, who traveled to Bilbao to purchase goods. Although the council attempted to restrict the commercial roles of these hostesses, enforcement proved difficult.[77] In 1521, and again in 1534 and 1549, new ordinances tried to limit their involvement in brokerage

---

[74] Enríquez Fernández et al., *Libro de acuerdos y decretos municipales*, fol. 16v, 5 February 1509.

[75] *Ibidem*, fol. 19r, 12 February 1509. Chapter 4 will go into more detail about the use of the 'poverty argument'.

[76] This will be discussed in chapters 2 and 4. See, for example: ARChV, Pleitos Civiles, Pérez Alonso (F), Caja 991,3, 1538; ARChV, Registro de ejecutorias, Caja 810,31, 1554; Enríquez Fernández, Hidalgo de Cisneros Amestoy & Martínez Lahidalga, *Colección documental del archivo histórico de Bilbao (1514–1520)*, 1553-4, 10 July 1517.

[77] Enríquez Fernández et al., *Ordenanzas municipales de Bilbao (1477–1520)*, fol. 33r–33v, 11 July 1488; Enríquez Fernández et al., fol. 130v–131r, 5 March 1509.

activities, particularly their work as intermediaries between the *plumeras* and Bilbao's cloth merchants.[78]

The *plumeras* were women from the Biscayan countryside who traveled to Bilbao to purchase linen cloth, possibly for use in producing padded goods such as mattresses and pillows, which they then resold.[79] In council ordinances, they were described as a type of merchant, since they arrived from outside the city to procure goods for (regional) export.[80]

Brokerage, while prohibited to hostesses, was a permitted activity for *corredoras*. These women guided foreign merchants and *plumeras* to local linen sellers' homes and negotiated deals on their behalf in exchange for a fee. While they played a valuable role in facilitating commerce, they were not considered essential. As a result, the town council imposed strict limits on the fees *corredoras* could charge. The repeated issuance of such regulations suggests, however, that enforcement was difficult, and that *corredoras* frequently exceeded the authorized limits.[81] The town council's struggles to regulate female brokers will be a recurring theme in this book, as these women played roles not only in the textile trade but also in the grain sector.

Artisan Workers

Women's roles in urban economies extended beyond market stalls and itinerant trade. In the artisan sector, they participated in the production and sale of goods across numerous trades, often navigating the regulatory frameworks of the craft guilds. Their presence, though rarely central in guild statutes, is nonetheless visible in a wide range of occupations. In Brabant, most artisan activities were formally organized into craft guilds. These guilds contended with informal competitors, including women, and also addressed women's access to artisan work through male guild members.

---

[78] I will elaborate on these conflicts in a later chapter. See: ARChV, Registro de ejecutorias, Caja 359,65, 1521; ARChV, Sala de Vizcaya, Caja 4368,4, 1534; AFB, Municipal, 0031/002/0010, 27 May 1549.

[79] Castrillo Casado, *Las mujeres vascas*, 292.

[80] In the ordinance of 28 June 1499, the council would first address the *plumeras* but later identify them more generally as *mercaderas* (female merchants). Enríquez Fernández et al., *Ordenanzas municipales de Bilbao (1477–1520)*, fol. 98r–100v, 28 June 1499.

[81] *Ibidem*, fol. 33r–33v, 11 July 1488; *Ibidem*, fol. 59v–60r, 25 May 1492; *Ibidem*, fol. 98r–100v, 28 June 1499; Enríquez Fernández, Hidalgo de Cisneros Amestoy & Martínez Lahidalga, *Colección documental del archivo histórico de Bilbao (1514–1520)*, 1553–4, 10 July 1517.

Ordinances regulating women's labor in artisan occupations do not focus on a single trade; rather, mentions of women's work appear across various artisan sectors and are not consistently presented as problematic. For instance, a 1428 Antwerp ordinance concerning furriers stipulates that anyone, "whether they are male or female," wishing to work as a furrier without guild membership must pay a small annual fee.[82] Similarly, in 1437, the council issued an ordinance stating that only "male or female citizens and guild members" could wear guild robes.[83] Regulations about or including women's work are found in nearly all artisan occupations in Mechelen and Antwerp. Women were involved in a diverse range of trades. The precise nature of their operation within guilds and how these powerful institutions addressed women's work will be explored in subsequent chapters.

The craft guilds, although masculine, left room for women to operate within or on the margins of their organization. Occasionally, craft guilds instituted regulations about another group of women: that of wage workers. When women's labor was needed, craft guilds expanded the female wage workforce—so long as it did not threaten their grip on the labor sector. As Jane Humphries and Carmen Sarasúa have argued in other contexts within early modern Europe, these women were not privileged guild members. They worked with limited protections and typically earned lower wages than their male counterparts or formally recognized guild workers.[84] Nevertheless, guilds relied on these female wage workers, which created a need for regulations to safeguard their working conditions. A 1493 ordinance issued by the Mechelen hatters stipulated that "if any *steeckeressen* or female worker comes to make any complaint about her master to the aforesaid dean and jurors of the said craft guild," the guild authorities were to investigate the matter and instruct the master to respond accordingly. If the wage worker chose to leave her employment as a result, she was permitted to do so. Additionally, the ordinance included a clause protecting female employees from retaliation: a master could not insult or defame a worker who had filed a complaint.[85] Female wage workers were not merely tolerated but were acknowledged as an integral

---

[82] Bisschops, 'Oudt register, mette berderen, 1336–1439', vol 27, 469–70.
[83] SAA, GA#4001, fol. 37v–39r, 4 March 1437.
[84] Humphries & Sarasúa, 'The Feminization of the Labor Force and Five Associated Myths', 175.
[85] "Item, dat als eenighe steeckerssen oft werckvrouwen over haren meester daerse wrachte clachtich quame aen den voirscreven deken en de geswoornen van den voirscreven ambachte van

part of the artisan workforce. Their position was such that, at times, their interests could align with those of both the guild and the town authorities.

*

In Bilbao, the town council paid much attention in their ordinances to the provisioning trades. The prominent role of women in these informally organized trades makes for a high level of visibility for women's work in the Biscayan commercial hub. Artisan occupations appear less frequently and are almost exclusively addressed to men in Biscay. Limitations on who could participate in work were not common, though not nonexistent.

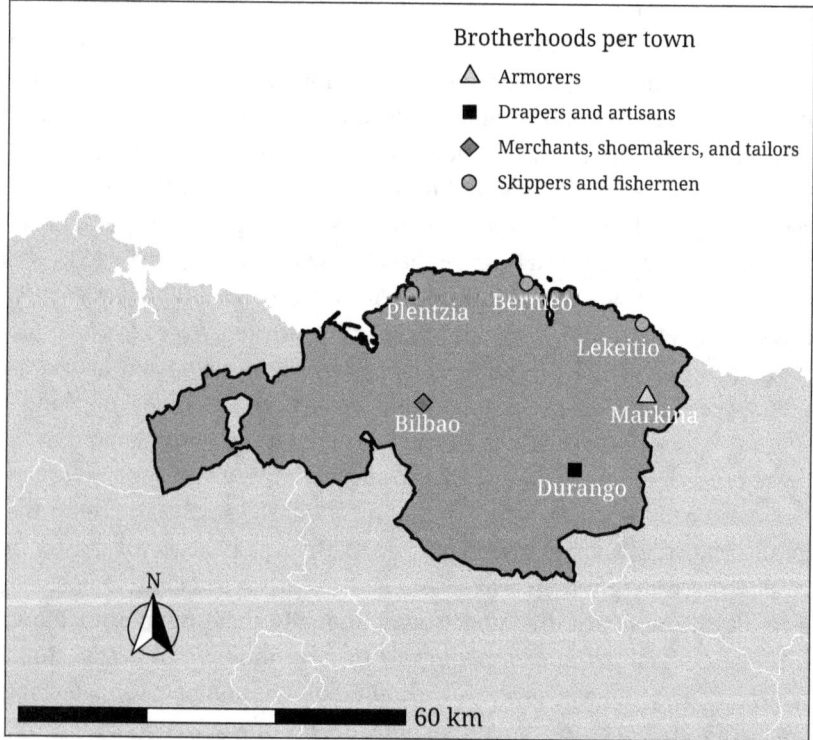

Figure 4. Map of the existing occupational brotherhoods in premodern Biscayan towns.[86]

quader betalinghen, quaden loone, quaden ghereetscape van garen ende vilten te gheven [...]." SAM, Hoedenmakersambacht 1, fol. 1r–8v, 12 November 1493.

[86] This map is based on the results of Ernesto García Fernández's study of premodern Basque brotherhoods. See: García Fernández, 'Las cofradías de mercaderes', 15.

As guilds were rare in Biscay (see figure 4) and did not have political power in Bilbao, there were few regulations concerning who could participate in certain trades. The informal organization of work characterized the commercial hub of Biscay and possibly other neighboring Atlantic seaports as well.[87] Official participation in artisan occupations seems to have been reserved for men, although Ana Iziz, Rosa Iziz, and Janire Castrillo Casado found evidence of women working with their husbands or fathers in other Basque towns. There is also evidence of a widow's right to continue her late husband's trade in nearby towns, where artisan organization is more visible in the sources.[88] For Bilbao, however, there is no evidence of women's activities in these artisan occupations.

The Hidden Workforce

The written documents from both regions—particularly the town ordinances that form the basis of this chapter—offer only a partial view of women's economic roles. Town councils typically issued ordinances in response to specific concerns, meaning that certain forms of women's labor may have been considered customary, regulated informally, or simply overlooked. For instance, Mechelen's ordinances concerning the fish trade make minimal reference to female household members or informal traders, even though the guild's sentence books, discussed in the next chapters, reveal their involvement. Moreover, gendered language in ordinances may not accurately reflect gendered economic practices. While useful, these normative sources reflect town officials' concerns more than the full scope of daily economic life.

In Brabant, ordinances frequently omit large segments of the female workforce active in market sectors. Scholars have shown that the widespread presence of women in guild life is often underrepresented in the normative documents. Guild masters were routinely supported by their wives, children, and other household members, and widows commonly succeeded their husbands in guild positions.[89] Many women also operated

---

[87] Abreu-Ferreira, 'Neighbors and Traders'; Cruchaga Calvin, 'La mujer en las villas portuarias del Cantábrico'.

[88] Iziz & Iziz, *Historia de las mujeres en Euskal Herria. 1*, 258; Castrillo Casado, *Las mujeres vascas*, 261–71.

[89] Harmsen & Hubers, "'En zij verkocht de vis ...'", 33; Schmidt & van Nederveen Meerkerk, "Reconsidering the 'Firstmale-Breadwinner Economy'", 75.

outside the formal guild structure, participating in the informal economy that coexisted alongside institutionalized trades.[90] Despite this, references to women appear only sporadically in Brabantine ordinances, leaving much of their economic activity, like that of many men, absent from the official record.

In Biscay, the visibility of women in certain occupations does not mean they were absent from others, even if those roles went unacknowledged in official regulations. As in Brabant, married women in Bilbao likely contributed to household workshops, though ordinances primarily addressed male heads of household. Alternative sources—particularly legal disputes adjudicated by the Royal Chancellery in Valladolid—reveal women's broader involvement in commercial life. For example, while ordinances concerning hostellers were directed mainly at men, court cases show that female hostellers played active roles in the town's drapery sector. As in other regions, women's economic roles extended well beyond what the bylaws of Bilbao explicitly recorded.

The overview presented in this chapter does not claim to represent the full scope of women's labor or the complexity of their economic positions. Rather, it provides a foundational framework for the chapters that follow. Despite their limitations, the silences in the town ordinances, especially when compared across regions, reveal much about institutional attitudes toward gendered labor. These silences, as much as the regulations themselves, lay the groundwork for the comparative analyses in the next three chapters.

2. Women's Financial Status

The town councils of Antwerp, Mechelen, and Bilbao issued several ordinances concerning women's labor. Certain tasks were considered to carry a more "female" character, while others were deemed inappropriate or illicit for women, prompting regulatory interventions. However, these ordinances rarely offer details about the social backgrounds of the women involved in these activities. For the period 1450-1550, only a limited number of sources allow for such analysis. Yet scholars have long emphasized the importance of social status in shaping women's labor opportunities.[91]

---

[90] Lambert, 'Merchants on the Margins', 238–9.
[91] See, among others: Castrillo Casado, 'Participación de las mujeres', 214; Hafter, *Women at Work in Preindustrial France*, 56; Hutton, 'Women, Men, and Markets', 424.

By examining fiscal records from Antwerp, Mechelen, and Bilbao, this chapter provides context on the economic standing of women household heads listed as taxpayers. These sources reveal that, particularly in Bilbao, the assessed wealth of these women was often modest—at least among those who headed their own households. This financial context sheds light on the motivations of the women who, in later chapters, appear as workers, rule-breakers, and litigants. Limited resources, after all, create one of the strongest incentives for labor: necessity.

The analysis of women's wealth and its distribution in Brabant relies on two tax surveys: a partial house rent levy from Antwerp in 1537 and a complete one from Mechelen in 1544.[92] For Bilbao, the data comes from a direct taxation register from 1470, supplemented by the hearth count of 1492.[93] As in Brabant, most of the municipal revenue in Biscay came from excise taxes on consumables. However, when debts rose—as in 1470—the town resorted to direct taxes.[94] Bilbao's census differs from those of Antwerp and Mechelen: it registered more individuals, as taxes were levied on both movable and immovable property. According to Javier Enríquez Fernández and colleagues, tax officials did not assess individual assets for most citizens. While wealthier residents' estates were evaluated, most others paid a pre-set sum based on their "quality as citizens"—likely a mix of social standing, household size, and general wealth.[95]

---

[92] In 1537, Charles V requested an *aide* of 400,000 guilders from the Estates of Brabant to finance his war against France. To pay for the *aide*, the Antwerp craft guilds suggested levying a one-time direct tax on top of the usual indirect excise taxes. This project provided the impetus for the Antwerp tax survey. However, the town did not collect enough money from this direct tax and decided to increase the beer and wine excises instead. The City Archives of Antwerp still holds the estimates for the sixth, eighth, eleventh, and part of the fourth neighborhoods of the town, a valuable source for information about the housing values and ratios of owners to leaseholders. See: Limberger, 'The Making of the Urban Fiscal System of Antwerp until 1800', 141; Masure, 'De stadsfinanciën van Antwerpen, 1531–1571', 218–9. Source: SAA, HN#103.

The tax survey for Mechelen was made for a tenth and twentieth penny tax on the housing value of Mechelen inhabitants. Using a method similar to that used in Antwerp, authorities registered the value of houses in the city center and the outer streets. Furthermore, the household head was identified as owner-tenant or leaseholder. See: Van Dijck, 'Towards an Economic Interpretation of Justice?', 78; Mast, 'Politiek, prestige en vermogen', 66–7. Source: SAM, K. Geldwezen, IV. Belastingen op de huizen, Serie I, nr. 1, 1544.

[93] Source: Enríquez Fernández et al., *Repartimientos y foguera-vecindario de Bilbao (1464–1492)*.

[94] Rivera Medina, "E tobimos por bien echar sisa", 427–43.

[95] Enríquez Fernández et al., *Repartimientos y foguera-vecindario de Bilbao (1464–1492)*.

Many urban inhabitants were not recorded in these surveys. In 1544 Mechelen, which had an estimated population of 28,000, only 4,563 taxpayers were registered (see table 2).[96] Clerics, the poor, and nobles were often exempt from direct taxes and thus absent from most lists.[97] Marleen Mast calculated that around 18 percent of Mechelen's population was excluded from the levy due to poverty or legal exemptions.[98] Still, some exempt and poor residents do appear: 55 households were registered as tax-exempt, and 139 people were listed as poor, of whom 16 paid nothing. Even so, most exempt individuals were not recorded by the enumerators.

Table 2. Total number and percentage of taxpayers by demographic category and marital status (for both men and women) in the house rent levies of Mechelen (1544) and Antwerp (1537), along with median tax amounts in stuivers (st) for each group.

Demographic category	Mechelen			Antwerp		
	#	%	Median tax amount (st)	#	%	Median tax amount (st)
Man	3639	79.8	24	1084	87.2	720
Unknown	3637	79.7	24	/	/	/
Widower	2		15,5	/	/	/
Woman	869	19	16	151	12.3	300
Married	1	0	49	1	0.1	1020
Single	/	/	/	1	0.1	480
Widow	480	10.5	20	82	6.7	675
Unknown	388	8.5	12	67	5.4	150
Married couple	/	/	/	1	0.1	120
Widow and heirs	/	/	/	1	0.1	3000
Heirs	/	/	/	4	0.3	1267.5
Others	52	1.1	35.5	1	0.1	120
Unknown	3	0.1	4	/	/	/
Total	4563	100	21	1242	100	600

Source: SAM, K. Geldwezen, IV, Serie I, nr. 1, 1544; SAA, HN#103, 1537.

[96] Van Uytven, *De geschiedenis van Mechelen*, 119.

[97] Hanus, *Affluence and Inequality in the Low Countries*, 300–3; Ryckbosch, 'Economic Inequality and Growth before the Industrial Revolution', 7.

[98] Mast, 'Politiek, prestige en vermogen', 64.

Comparable calculations for Antwerp are impossible due to the fragmentary nature of the 1537 house rent levy. Only 1,242 inhabitants from four neighborhoods were registered (see table 2),[99] a small fraction of the town's estimated 55,000 to 84,000 residents.[100] On their own, the Antwerp figures would not suffice to draw meaningful conclusions about women's social status. However, the similarities between the Antwerp and Mechelen tax data lend credibility to the available Antwerp lists.

Table 3. Total number and percentage of taxpayers by demographic category and marital status (for both men and women) in the tax register of Bilbao (1470), along with median tax amounts in maravedís (mrs) for each group.

Demographic category	Bilbao		
	#	%	Median tax amount (mrs)
Man	1320	63.6	187
Married	11	0.5	125
Unknown	1309	63.1	187
Woman	446	21.5	31
Married	35	1.7	62
Single	36	1.7	31
Widow	31	1.5	62
Unknown	344	16.6	31
Widow and heirs	168	8.1	293
Heirs	121	5.8	169
Married couple	17	0.8	62
Other	3	0.1	31
Total	2075	100	156

Source: Enríquez Fernández et. al., *Repartimientos y foguera-vecindario de Bilbao*.

The Bilbao taxation list captured a larger share of the population than the Mechelen records. In a town of approximately 5,600 inhabitants, more than one third were registered as taxpayers in 1470 (see table 3).[101] Due

[99] The taxation list contained 1,269 entries, but the 27 entries without a registered tax amount are not included in the calculations.
[100] Marnef, *Antwerpen in de tijd van de Reformatie*, 24–6.
[101] Solórzano Telechea, 'The Politics of the Urban Commons', 185.

to Bilbao's rapid population growth, multiple households often shared a single house.[102] The 1492 hearth count recorded 573 houses and 1,257 hearths, showing that most buildings housed more than one domestic unit.[103] Around 85 percent of households shared a residence with at least one other adult besides a spouse. The 1470 tax list included 2,075 individual taxpayers—almost double the number of hearths—because each adult household head, who could be multiple per hearth, was taxed. This finding means that the financial status of a broader segment of the population is visible in Bilbao than in Antwerp or Mechelen.

This broader registration also extended to working women. Bilbao's tax list includes a higher proportion of women with occupational identifiers (see table 4), enabling a more detailed analysis of their financial positions. However, the overall share of women in the Bilbao register is not substantially higher than in Mechelen. Across all three towns, many inhabitants, particularly women, were not individually recorded in the tax registers. Those who were not household heads, such as wives, servants, children, and other cohabitants, were generally omitted. Married women typically appeared under their husbands' names. The women listed in the house rent levies of Antwerp, Mechelen, and Bilbao were usually household heads or lived independently. Although the number of female taxpayers was limited (see tables 2 and 3), it aligns with earlier findings. In early modern Dutch tax registers, Ariadne Schmidt and Elise van Nederveen Meerkerk noted that "only 15-30 percent of all household heads were women."[104] Similar low figures appear across other regions and time periods.[105]

*

Without a doubt, the taxation lists reveal significant inequality between male and female taxpayers in all three case studies. The most pronounced discrepancy appears in Bilbao, where female household heads were

---

[102] O'Flanagan, *Port Cities of Atlantic Iberia, C. 1500–1900*, 269.

[103] Enríquez Fernández et al., *Repartimientos y foguera-vecindario de Bilbao (1464–1492)*.

[104] Schmidt & van Nederveen Meerkerk, 'Reconsidering the 'Firstmale-Breadwinner Economy'', 73.

[105] For Portugal, Amélia Polónia found that 18 percent of the taxpayers on a taxation register from 1568 from the Vila do Conde were female. In the German town of Stuttgart in 1545, that number was even lower: 14.5 percent. Some centuries later, in 1735, 22 percent of the taxpayers in Grenoble were women, as Anne Montenach has shown. See: Polónia, 'Women's Participation in Labour and Business', 7; Bellavitis, *Women's Work and Rights*, 32; Montenach, 'Creating a Space for Themselves', 50.

clustered among the town's least wealthy residents. The median tax paid by these women was 31 *maravedís*—the lowest standard taxation rate. This median was 80 percent lower than the median amount paid by male taxpaying household heads (see table 3). In Antwerp and Mechelen, women also tended to pay the lowest tax rates. In Mechelen, the median house rent levy for female taxpayers was 30 percent below that of men. In Antwerp, the difference was even greater, with women paying a median 60 percent less than male taxpayers (see table 2). The disparity in Antwerp may partly result from the smaller sample size or different registration methods used in the surviving records.

These findings confirm earlier research: female taxpayers in all three towns possessed, on average, less wealth than male taxpayers.[106] Even considering that many male taxpayers likely represented larger household units, a marked gender disparity in individual wealth remains, especially in Bilbao. Non-married women working outside the framework of a collaborative household economy often had to survive with fewer financial resources than either their male counterparts or women embedded in larger family units.

Of course, these tax payments do not represent the wealth of all women. As expected, marital status played an important role. In both Brabantine towns, just over half of the female taxpayers were widows—a reflection of the broader social norm that recognized widows as legitimate heads of household.[107] Widows tended to hold more wealth than never-married women. Their status as household heads often reflected a transfer of shared property through inheritance or usufruct rights. Consequently, in Antwerp and Mechelen, widows' median tax contributions approached those of men (see table 2). Their relatively higher wealth aligns with their prominent place in local ordinances and urban economic life.

In Bilbao, most women were not identified by marital status. Of the 446 women on the list, only 31 were recorded as widows. As table 3 shows, these widows paid a median of 62 *maravedís*—twice the amount paid by the 344 women of unknown marital status (31 *maravedís*). While widows in Bilbao were better off than most single women, their wealth was still modest, with their median placing them in the lowest quarter of the

---

[106] Fontaine, 'Makeshift, Women and Capability', 59; Marfany, 'Family and Welfare in Early Modern Europe', 125; Montenach, 'Creating a Space for Themselves'; Comas-Via, 'Widowhood and Economic Difficulties', 94.

[107] Fontaine, 'Makeshift, Women and Capability', 60.

taxation list. As later chapters will show, widowed saleswomen in Bilbao often referenced their limited means when appearing in court. Their work may have been driven primarily by the need to generate income.

However, a second group of widows appears in the Bilbao taxation list: those registered together with other heirs (8.1 percent of all taxpayers listed). This group paid a median tax of 293 *maravedís*—more than the median for male household heads. These women likely belonged to more affluent family networks and had retained access to shared property and social capital from their marriages. The separate classification of these widows in the tax register suggests that town officials themselves distinguished between less affluent and more privileged widows.

Table 4. Women's occupations in the taxation survey of Bilbao (1470), ordered by median tax amount in maravedís (mrs).

Occupation	#	Median tax amount (mrs)
Sardine seller (f)	2	31
Fruit seller (f)	3	31
Retailer (f)	11	31
Servant (f)	12	31
Housekeeper (f)	15	31
Seamstress	23	31
Unknown	366	31
Bread seller (f)	5	33
Laundress	6	47
Shopkeeper	1	62
Linen seller (f)	2	125
Total	446	31

Source: Enríquez Fernández et al., *Repartimientos y foguera-vecindario de Bilbao*.

Occupational identifiers for women appeared more frequently in the Bilbao taxation lists than in those from the Brabantine towns. In Bilbao, 32 percent of male taxpayers and 17.9 percent of female taxpayers were recorded with an occupation (see table 4). Most of the men identified by occupation worked in the town's artisan sectors—trades that are notably absent from other Biscayan source types. Common occupations included shoemaker, blacksmith, carpenter, rope maker, and butcher. Service was also one of the most frequent occupational designations for both men and women. In Bilbao, servants were typically young and unmarried, but there were also *amas de casa* (housekeepers) who had turned domestic service into a long-term career.[108] As Deborah Simonton has shown in her study of eighteenth-century Nordic Europe, such lifelong service was not unique to Bilbao but a broader phenomenon in premodern Europe.[109]

Eighty women in the Bilbao register were identified by occupation. Some held typically female roles, such as seamstress or laundress. Notably, twenty-one of them worked in the town's retail and food trades—those sectors where women were dominant, as discussed above. While the presence of these occupational identifiers is not surprising, their inclusion in the taxation registers is a crucial element in assessing these women's economic roles throughout this book.

There was little diversity in the financial standing of these occupationally identified women. Of the eighty, only fourteen paid more than the minimum tax of 31 *maravedís*—and five of those paid just slightly more, at 33 *maravedís*. Retailers and food sellers were central to Bilbao's everyday commerce, particularly in provisioning the town. Yet, as Carol Gold observes in her study of early modern Copenhagen: "Widowed, single or married, they sold small amounts of food and clothing, most of which they did not produce themselves, but rather had bought for resale. These women were not at the very bottom of the social structure, but only slightly above it."[110] This description seems to fit the position of many Bilbao women in similar trades.

In Brabant, occupational identifiers were even less common, though women with listed occupations showed more variation in tax levels than their Bilbao counterparts (see table 5). The Mechelen house rent levy recorded occupational data for only 2.6 percent of women and 4.9 percent of men. While most of the identified female occupations likely belonged to the "low-status, low-pay" categories, some women practiced skilled or guild-based trades (with the exception of the mercers' trade) and appeared among the wealthier taxpayers. In line with previous findings, occupational identifiers were less frequently assigned to women, suggesting that

---

[108] Del Val Valdivieso, 'El trabajo de las mujeres en el Bilbao tardomedieval', 84; Rivera Medina, 'Superando fronteras', 28.
[109] Simonton, "Birds of Passage' or 'Career' Women?', 207–25.
[110] Gold, 'On the Streets and in the Markets', 36.

they may not have declared a profession or did not strongly identify with one.[111] This was also true for most men. Or, as Anna Bellavitis has stated, "a professional identity was a privilege relatively few people in society possessed."[112]

Table 5. Women's occupations in the house rent levies of Mechelen (1544) and Antwerp (1537), organized by median tax amount in stuivers *(st)*.

Mechelen			Antwerp		
Occupation	#	Median tax amount (st)	Occupation	#	Median tax amount (st)
Beggar	1	0	Shopkeeper	1	150
Stud worker (f)	1	0	Unknown	146	300
Midwife	2	8	Laundress	1	300
Wheelbarrower	1	8	Seamstress	1	390
Spinner	1	10	Pastry seller (f)	1	720
Lateres	2	11	Midwife	1	840
Flax worker	1	12	Total	151	300
Laundress	5	12			
Seamstress	3	14			
Shopkeeper	1	15			
Unknown	846	16			
Teacher	1	18			
Postmaster	1	23			
Baker	1	24			
Wet nurse	2	33			
Total	869	16			

Source: SAM, K. Geldwezen, IV, Serie I, nr. 1, 1544; SAA, HN#103, 1537.

*

[111] Schmidt & van Nederveen Meerkerk, 'Reconsidering the 'Firstmale-Breadwinner Economy'', 73; Sarasúa, 'Women's Work and Structural Change', 492; Humphries & Sarasúa, 'Off the Record', 46.
[112] Bellavitis, *Women's Work and Rights*, 31.

The greatest challenge in using the taxation lists of the three towns lies in their lack of comparability. Since the sources do not explain how tax amounts were calculated, it is difficult to directly compare the specific figures or levels of wealth held by women in Bilbao, Antwerp, and Mechelen. To enable a more meaningful comparison, I have grouped taxation amounts into deciles—ten equal categories containing 10 percent of taxpayers each, ranked from highest to lowest based on tax amount or housing value. Figure 5 (p. 80) presents the overall distribution of wealth between male and female taxpayers in the three towns.

The contrast between the Brabantine and Biscayan towns is striking. In all three towns, most women taxpayers fell into the lower deciles. In other words, single women were consistently concentrated in the lowest financial tiers—but this position was most pronounced in Bilbao. There, the number of women in the two lowest deciles even exceeded the number of men. In Antwerp and Mechelen, while female taxpayers were similarly overrepresented in the lower end of the wealth spectrum, they never outnumbered men in those same deciles.

Although scholars agree that single women generally held a lower socioeconomic status in premodern Europe, not all women in the lowest deciles were destitute. As Jord Hanus has pointed out, "among the 'poorest' 40% of taxpayers, the majority were actually small-scale households, often numbering only one adult." Single women—whether living alone or cohabiting with other single adults—did not require the same level of income as larger households. Nevertheless, their resources were often insufficient to support dependents or to operate a more substantial household.[113]

We can tentatively conclude that a substantial group of women in Bilbao lived and worked independently. The occupational identifiers accompanying some of these women's names (see table 4) suggest that many belonged to the category of single traders who supplied Bilbao's inhabitants with daily commodities—precisely the group under study in this book. These same women frequently invoked their need for income when their economic activities were obstructed. While the 'poverty argument' they presented in court (see chapter 4) may have been a strategic legal tool, it likely also reflected genuine financial hardship. Some women may have turned to irregular economic practices out of necessity. At the

---

[113] Hanus, *Affluence and Inequality in the Low Countries*, 156–60.

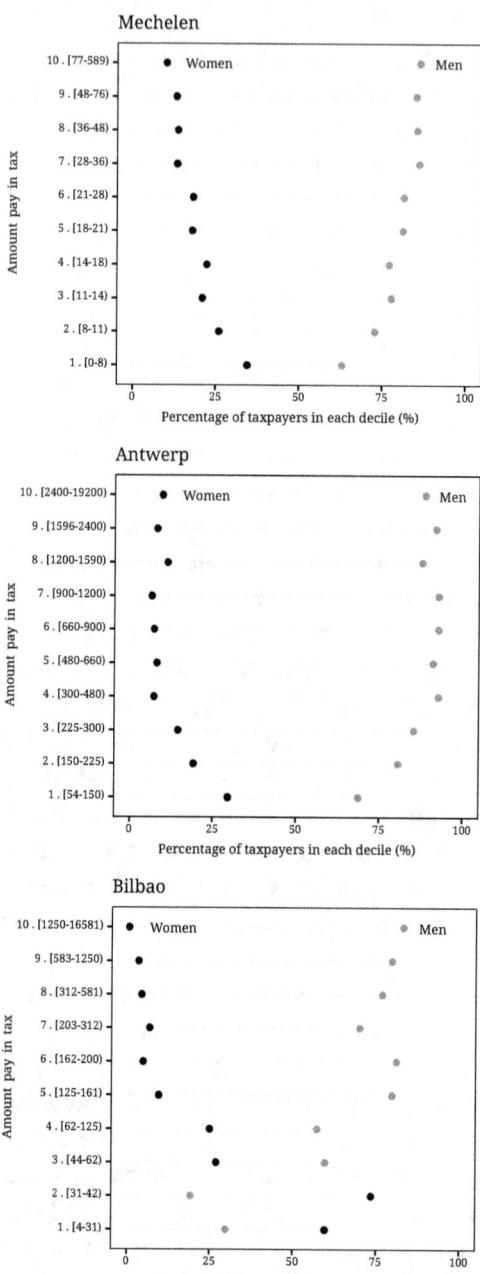

Figure 5. Deciles of taxpayers by amount of tax paid in the registers of Bilbao (1470), Antwerp (1537), and Mechelen (1544), showing the percentage of women and men in each decile. Tax amounts are given in maravedís *(Bilbao) and* stuivers *(Antwerp and Mechelen).*
Source: See tables 4 and 5.

same time, those who pursued cases at the Chancellery in Valladolid must have possessed at least some financial resources or social support, since taking a case to a higher court involved considerable cost. Thus, although the 1470 Bilbao tax register attests to the low social status of many female sellers at that time, we cannot assume the same for all women involved in sixteenth-century legal disputes, even if they held similar occupations. These women likely had greater access to resources or networks that enabled them to act.

In the Brabantine towns, the group of women who lived and worked independently—most often found in the lowest deciles of the taxation lists—remains largely invisible in other archival sources. Moreover, many of the Brabantine women under study in this book are absent from these tax lists altogether. Women's work in Antwerp and Mechelen was more often documented in connection with husbands or male relatives. The women who worked independently, such as Antwerp's *uitdraagsters*, Mechelen's *harincvrouwen*, and the numerous informal sellers who do not appear in the official records, were not necessarily single, but those who were may have lived lives similar to Bilbao's single tradeswomen.

While the taxation lists provide a valuable overview of women's financial standing in Brabant, other sources offer some nuanced glimpses into the financial status of specific groups of women. For instance, five sentences from the Antwerp *Correctieboeken* provide qualitative evidence of the economic circumstances of women engaged in informal trade (see chapter 3). In these cases, women who violated trade regulations were given the option to pay a fine or complete a pilgrimage as penance. All five women returned with letters confirming that they had completed their pilgrimages, which may indicate that they lacked the financial means to pay the fines.[114] This supports the idea that they belonged to the lower economic strata of urban society, as depicted in figure 5.

In contrast, the *Correctieboeken* also include cases of women affiliated with craft guilds who similarly violated trade rules.[115] Unlike the informal traders, these women more frequently opted to pay the fines, suggesting that they had access to more financial resources. Affiliation with a guild may have offered these women some protection—or it may indicate that they belonged to a more financially stable, 'middling' group from the

---

[114] Van Herwaarden, *Opgelegde bedevaarten*, 18–21.
[115] E.g. Melis-Taeymans, 123, 17 August 1437; Melis-Taeymans, 8, 11 February 1415.

outset.[116] These cases, while anecdotal, reinforce the broader patterns seen in the taxation data: women's financial circumstances were diverse and shaped by complex, context-specific factors. In both Brabant and Biscay, single and working women occupied various layers of the urban socioeconomic fabric. As the following chapters will demonstrate, their position was influenced not only by personal status or occupation but also by institutional connections, legal frameworks, and the specific urban environments in which they lived and worked.

3. Conclusion

The ordinances from Antwerp, Mechelen, and Bilbao offer a glimpse into the work activities available to women in these towns. They state, for example: "No female host hosting merchants, men or women, especially the *plumeras*, is allowed to bring the linen drapes of citizens, men or women, to her house to broker";[117] "women accustomed to do this, can sell and retail herring and buckling;"[118] or "purse or glove makers' wives, their children or grandchildren can work as the old habits allow them."[119] These patriarchal documents capture only part of the economic life in premodern towns. Yet they are invaluable in identifying a broad range of activities open to women. The overview offered in this chapter lays the groundwork for the chapters that follow, which will explore the socioeconomic, cultural, and institutional structures shaping women's labor roles in greater depth.

The taxation lists from Antwerp, Bilbao, and Mechelen add an essential dimension to this analysis by revealing gendered disparities in wealth. Women living and working independently—outside a household headed by men—consistently paid lower taxes than their male counterparts. This finding confirms the structural inequality of the period, while also exposing key differences between the two regions. In Bilbao, a distinct group of lower-status women, including fishmongers, retailers, and bread sellers, can be clearly identified. In contrast, although the tax records of Brabant

[116] See also: Vandeweerdt, 'Women, Town Councils, and the Organisation of Work'.
[117] Enríquez Fernández et al., *Ordenanzas municipales de Bilbao (1477–1520)*, fol. 33r–33v, 11 July 1488.
[118] SAM, Visverkopers 14, 26 July 1454.
[119] Génard, 'Register van den dachvaerden', 400–1.

also point to a considerable number of lower-income women, their specific work activities are harder to trace. Moreover, in Brabantine towns, a larger share of the urban population, particularly women, remained hidden behind male household heads. The Bilbao data, supported by complementary sources, allows for a more detailed understanding of women's financial status.

While direct insight into individual women's experiences remains a challenge, this chapter has highlighted two initial elements that shaped women's labor opportunities: normative frameworks and wealth. Social status, marital status, and access to networks influenced women's economic opportunities in both regions. The tax registers from Antwerp, Bilbao, and Mechelen offer important indications of the socioeconomic status of the women whose activities appear in the ordinances. Meanwhile, the normative frameworks provide a first glimpse into how labor was organized in the three towns and what opportunities were available to women. Together, these two elements help us understand the institutional context in which these women operated. Our next chapter builds on this foundation by analyzing how institutional structures more directly shaped the economic activities of the women introduced in this chapter.

CHAPTER 2

Shaping the Framework

In the fifteenth- and sixteenth-century towns of Biscay and Brabant, women's work opportunities were largely determined by gendered divisions of labor and power, a cultural context reinforced by the institutions that organized economic practices. As noted in the book's introduction, institutions are groups of actors that establish formal and informal norms to structure interactions.[1] Specifically, small-scale sales and artisan production were organized in three key socioeconomic institutions: the household production unit, the predominantly male craft guilds, and the informal market.

This chapter analyzes how each of these institutions gave shape to women's work opportunities in Antwerp, Mechelen, and Bilbao. Archival documents reveal the strong influence of household production and craft guilds in the Brabantine towns, while Bilbao's small-scale trade centered more prominently on the informal market. The absence of craft guilds in Bilbao's relevant market sectors—possibly linked to the diminished role of household production—highlights the distinct position of Bilbao's saleswomen. Ordinances, guild membership lists, and judicial sources, reflecting the perspectives of municipal governments and legislative institutions, illuminate the organization of women's work, albeit with limitations in capturing daily practices.

The household economic unit, craft guilds, and informal markets did not operate in isolation; rather, they frequently intersected, interacted, complemented, and contradicted each other. For example, guild structures were intrinsically linked to the significance of the household economy in guild-dominated regions.[2] Recognizing the interconnectedness of these institutions is crucial for understanding their role in shaping women's work opportunities. Furthermore, factors such as marital status, social standing, networks, and local socioeconomic structures influenced women's work. As a result, institutional organization did not affect all women

---

[1] Ogilvie, "Whatever Is, Is Right'?', 650; Hunt & Shepard, 'Introduction. Producing Change', 8.
[2] Hafter, *Women at Work in Preindustrial France*, 24.

in the same way. The interplay between different institutions, as well as between institutions and individual circumstances, presents further challenges for this study. This chapter lays the foundation for understanding these dynamics before exploring institutional restrictions and women's individual interactions with these systems in chapters 3 and 4.

1. The Household Economy in Brabant and Biscay

The work opportunities of female members of a guild master's household production unit have been the subject of a number of studies. In 1995, Merry Wiesner argued that "girls and women [worked] alongside the journeymen and apprentices in many capacities, but their ability to do so was not officially recognized or discussed in guild ordinances."[3] Martha Howell noted, "Women, we can surmise, first entered market production via the family production unit, where market production often began."[4] The household has always been central to the study of premodern women's economic activities. In premodern society, women's access to market-oriented work was closely tied to their roles within the household economic unit, which served as a key institution for organizing labor at the individual level. Customary law, town regulations, and guild structures all reinforced its importance. As the smallest and most widespread entity of labor organization, the household economic unit is undeniably significant. This section analyzes the role of the household economy in shaping women's work in Antwerp, Mechelen, and Bilbao.

The importance of cooperation among household members, particularly within Brabantine guild culture, is evident. Although women's work within the household unit was seldom formally acknowledged, the participation of guild masters' family members in workshop activities was often permitted and even expected. Regulations rarely prohibited women from engaging in (parts of) their husbands' trades. Overall, the Brabantine case studies largely support the findings of earlier scholarship.[5] Yet the household economic unit remains a subject of ongoing research. The market-oriented nature of the labor fields examined in this

---

[3] Wiesner, 'Gender and the Worlds of Work', 222.
[4] Howell, 'Women, the Family Economic, and the Structures of Market Production', 215.
[5] See, among others: Power and Postan, *Medieval Women*; Gilissen, 'Le statut de la femme dans l'ancien droit Belge'; Nicholas, *The Domestic Life of a Medieval City*; McNamara & Wemple, 'The Power

book—often distinct from commodity production—invites a re-evaluation of the household's role. Biscay, in particular, presents a divergent case that challenges the typical patterns of household collaboration emphasized in historical research. Furthermore, as I will argue in chapter 3, the allowances granted to household members within the Brabantine guild framework should not be generalized.

This study adopts a broad definition of 'household,' drawing on the work of Myriam Carlier, Tine De Moor, and Jan Luiten van Zanden, among others. A household is defined as a group of individuals residing under a single roof or within the same establishment. As Carlier has stated, "This living together may or may not involve members of one family."[6] In fact, most households included more than one (nuclear) family, and their members did not have to be related by blood. Servants, journeymen, and apprentices might live with their employers and be part of the household, at least temporarily.[7] The prevalence of remarriage further complicated household composition, creating blended families and contributing to the multi-nuclear nature of these dwellings.[8] Moreover, several households often lived together under the same roof, making the composition of the household even more complex.[9]

This complexity is evident in historical records, such as the 1492 hearth count of Bilbao, where a significant portion of households contained multiple taxpaying citizens, indicating the presence of multiple family units or unrelated individuals living together. Specifically, of the 575 houses in Bilbao in 1492, only 205 were houses with a single family unit. Houses were divided into different hearths, each of which could again hold multiple family units, highlighting the prevalence of complex households.[10] Moreover, the household was not a static entity; its composition and dynamics shifted frequently due to life cycle changes, the arrival and departure of members, and fluctuating labor opportunities, particularly for women.[11]

---

of Women through the Family'; Dillard, *Daughters of the Reconquest*; Howell, *Women, Production, and Patriarchy*.

[6] Carlier, 'The Household: An Introduction', 3.

[7] De Munck, *Guilds, Labour and the Urban Body Politic*, 196; Hafter, *Women at Work in Preindustrial France*, 24; Whittle, 'A Critique of Approaches to 'Domestic Work'', 39.

[8] Howell, *Commerce before Capitalism*, 105–7.

[9] Hanus, *Affluence and Inequality in the Low Countries*, 72; Howell, *Commerce before Capitalism*, 97.

[10] Enríquez Fernández et al., *Repartimientos y foguera-vecindario de Bilbao (1464–1492)*.

[11] Tomkins and King, 'Conclusion', 265.

Widows

The death of a spouse was an especially crucial moment for a woman's household. When her husband died, a widow became the (temporary) head of the household in many premodern European towns. This custom meant that widows held an exceptional status. As they took over their husbands' positions, widows had access to positions not generally open to women.[12] In the Brabantine towns, a guild master's widow took over her husband's economic functions in the guild after his death. Under this 'widow's right,' widows could become guild mistresses until they remarried or an adult son took over.[13] There is evidence of the temporary position of widows in the guilds in Brabantine regulations about guilds' poor boxes. The Mechelen glove makers decided that only guild masters, not their wives, had the right to financial aid from the guild's poor box. However, they also decided that "a widow that is lying sick will receive the poor box money."[14] In a similar fashion, the Antwerp tanners and shoemakers required widows to pay the same amount as other guild masters to the guild's poor box.[15]

As Ellen Kittell and Kurt Queller have argued, the death of one spouse did not cause complete dissolution of the household unit. "The unit continued," although the surviving spouse had to change his or her position in the household.[16] In Bilbao, this shift is visible in widows' many debt conflicts with their husbands' creditors. In 1550, for example, Marina Sáenz de Marquina, a widow, and Pedro de Bermeo appeared before the judges of the *Sala de Vizcaya* in the Royal Chancellery of Valladolid. Marina's husband had owed Pedro a debt of 333 *ducados* for grain he had purchased on credit. During his lifetime, Marina's husband had not repaid Pedro. Two years after her husband's death, the judges ordered Marina to pay Pedro, as she had inherited both her husband's property and his debts.[17]

---

[12] Castrillo Casado, 'Las mujeres del común y la sociedad política', 516; Wiesner, 'Gender and the Worlds of Work', 222.

[13] Schmidt, 'Contested Authority', 219; Wiesner, 'Guilds, Male Bonding and Women's Work', 126–7; Hafter, *Women at Work in Preindustrial France*, 68.

[14] "Item, een weduwe die sieck leghet van natuerlijcker sieckten die sal de busse hebben." SAM, Handschoenmakers-, tesmakers-, riem(be)slagers-, witledermakers- en schedemakersambacht 554bis, fol. 6v–7r.

[15] SAA, GA#4001, fol. 183v–185v, 28 July 1557.

[16] Kittell & Queller, 'Wives and Widows in Medieval Flanders', 451.

[17] ARChV, Sala de Vizcaya, Caja 2939, 11, 1550.

Examples of a widow dealing with conflict because of her responsibility to stand in for her husband are not only found in the Biscayan town. In 1539, the widow of Jan Wouters, a member of the Antwerp mercers' guild, was ordered by the guild deans and jurors to pay off her husband's apprentice. Since neither she nor her son was willing to take over his training after her husband's death, the contract was terminated.[18]

Widows in both regions assumed the position of household head from their husbands after they died. As the examples show, these widows took on responsibilities beyond carrying out their husbands' occupations. The administration of property and other tasks previously performed by the husband had now become the widow's concern.

The crucial role of widows in managing the household economy is particularly evident in Brabant. In 1566, the annual accounts of the Mechelen glove makers' guild were submitted not by the current dean, Hendrick de Leeuw, but by the widow of his predecessor, Daneel de Coninck. De Coninck, who had served as dean at the beginning of the administrative year, died prematurely. Consequently, de Leeuw was appointed as his successor. At the year's end, when the guild sought to collect the corporation's financial records, de Leeuw was compelled to collaborate with de Coninck's widow. As the new administrator of the 'de Coninck household,' she possessed access to her late husband's files and was deemed competent to assess his administrative conduct.[19] While her level of direct governance likely differed from her husband's, she was entrusted with the responsibility of settling his outstanding guild business after his death.

Taking up the position of household head did not necessarily mean that widows in Brabant and Biscay were part of a collaborative household economic unit. A widow's unique position lay not in her responsibility to provide for the household, but in her assumption of both spousal roles. As such, previous conclusions about widows' positions apply only if spousal cooperation had previously existed. In Bilbao, many widows provided for themselves and their households without necessarily continuing a spouse's

---

[18] "Den 14en meey anno 1539 is gheappointeert bij deekens ende oudermans van der mersen hoedat de weduwe wijlen Jan Wouters, onsen ouderman was, dat sij Heynen, huerren leercnape, soude betaellen naer advenant den tijt dat hij henlieden ghedient hadde ende laten hem ghaen. Ende dat overmits dat deselve Heyne, haer cnape, met harren soene, Jacoppen, niet volleere en woude ende hij gheen ghebreck oft achterdeel van delselve Jacop Wouters en wiste." SAA, GA#4212, fol. 224r, 14 May 1539.

[19] SAM, Handschoenmakers-, tesmakers-, riem(be)slagers-, witledermakers- en schedemakersambacht 557, fol. 50v.

occupation. For example, the *cojedora* Marina de Gardea explained her role in a court case, stating, "she had been married, but her husband had died, and because of dire need, she had gone to the *plaza* to guard grain."[20] Marina is a compelling example of a widow excluded from socioeconomic institutional protections. It is likely that she belonged to a lower social class during her marriage, which precluded her from inheriting from the marital estate or assuming her deceased husband's lucrative position.[21] While traditional spousal cooperation did exist in premodern Bilbao, the repeated appearance of vulnerable widows is a first indication that the household production unit was not a firmly established organizational unit in certain labor sectors.

Spousal Cooperation

In 1547, the married couple Sancho de Salinillas and Teresa de Molinar registered a debt to the linen seller María Ibáñez de Jáuregui, wife of the silversmith Juan de Larrea, with the *Corregidor* of Biscay. They owed the couple 3553 *maravedís* after having bought several *varas* of linen from them.[22] The letter of obligation would be the first in an extensive series of transactions involving María and Juan. In theory, in Biscay, women "whether single, married, or widowed—were legally capable of acquiring and disposing of their own properties, movable or immovable." Moreover, after reaching legal adulthood, women could litigate by themselves in court regardless of their marital status.[23] Nevertheless, matrimony resulted in a system of 'absolute community property,' motivating the married couple to make decisions together about household assets. As such, we can see the married couple undertaking economic transactions together.

Property was communal—though not as exclusively as in some Brabantine towns. In Biscay, both spouses were allowed to enter transactions involving their property. Women could extend this permission quite far, as a complaint from the husband of Catalina de Uribarri from

---

[20] "[...] que ella estaba casada e se le fue su marido e asy por la mucha necesidad se fue a la plaça a cojer trigo [...]." ARChV, Sala de Vizcaya, Caja 3467, 5, 14r.

[21] Fontaine, 'Makeshift, Women and Capability', 59; Comas-Via, 'Widowhood and Economic Difficulties'; Montenach, 'Creating a Space for Themselves on the Urban Market', 52.

[22] AFB, JCR2232/084, 7 July 1547.

[23] Monreal Zia, *The Old Law of Bizkaia (1452)*, 23; Castrillo Casado, *Las mujeres vascas durante la baja edad media*, 101–4; Ratcliffe, "Matris et Munium...': Marriage and Marriage Law', 94.

1516 shows. Catalina's husband, Ochoa de Libarrona, appeared before the mayor of Bilbao, complaining that his wife "wandered out of the house and his company, stealing communal goods and property to buy sardines, clothes, and iron" for resale. Even though Ochoa accused his wife of damaging the couple's conjugal property, the mayor of Bilbao—and later the *Corregidor* of Biscay and the judges of the Royal Chancellery at Valladolid—supported Catalina, who denied her husband's allegations.[24]

If we return to María Ibáñez de Jáuregui, we find that she appears in twenty-nine contracts, declaring debts that others owed her in her own name. Most debts were made by buying linen goods from her. The contracts involving María registered with the *Corregidor* of Biscay show María to be a high-level linen seller who engaged in transactions independently of her husband. However, some information is missing from these contracts. Fifteen more contracts registering debts because of linen sales were signed only by Juan de Larrea, María's husband. Even if Juan was a silversmith, he was clearly deeply involved in his wife's business—one could even argue that it was the couple's business rather than María's.[25] One of those debt declarations specifically refers to both spouses selling linen to the debtors.

There is no denying the close spousal economic cooperation between María and Juan. Juan's work as a silversmith is not as well documented as the couple's involvement in linen sales. In 1562, the church of Santa María de Lezama recorded a debt owed to him for a cross and an incense burner he had made.[26] The scarcity of sources explicitly referring to his craft reflects the broader lack of documentation on productive occupations in sixteenth-century Bilbao. In other transactions he signed, Juan appears clearly engaged in his wife's business and that of the de Jáuregui family.[27] María and Juan, wealthy residents of Bilbao, exemplify a pattern of close spousal cooperation that is most often observed among affluent households in the Biscayan source material. Notably, however, despite this cooperation, María's direct involvement in Juan's silversmithing remains

---

[24] "[...] le andaba ausentada de su casa y conpannia, robándole quantos bienes y haçienda tenía y que con los dineros de ellos compraba sardina e panno e azero [...]." ARChV, Registro de Ejecutorias, Caja 308, 31, 29 March 1516.

[25] "que por razon de resto, e alcance, e feneçimiento de todas cuentas, e dadas e tomados que con bos e con María Bannes de Jáureguy, lençera, vuestra muger, hemos abido e tenido asta oy día." AFB, JCR1191/119, 19 August 1568.

[26] AFB, JCR1544/050, 7 January 1562.

[27] AFB, JCR2659/493, 19 May 1563; AFB, JCR2643/014, 4 January 1567; AFB, N0484/0256, 8 July 1569.

undocumented.[28] Their case contrasts sharply with that of fishmongers, retailers, and other informal traders in Bilbao, for whom evidence of household-based economic collaboration is largely absent from both normative ordinances and judicial records.

There are a few exceptions to this general silence regarding spousal cooperation in the occupational groups studied. In 1508, the town council decreed "that from this day on, no householders (f), servants (f) nor servants (m), nor *cojedoras* shall be allowed to set the price of grain, except for honorable married women."[29] This ordinance is one of the rare instances in which the Bilbao council explicitly legitimized women's economic roles based on marital status. It remains unclear why only married women were granted this privilege—or which married women qualified. In 1515, Yñigo de Olabarria was appointed the town's official grain weigher, and both he and his wife were required to swear an oath for the position.[30] Yñigo's wife likely played an active role in his new duties and may have been among the "honorable married women" permitted to participate in price setting. Similarly, the council allowed the wives of grain weighers to carry out their husbands' responsibilities, while excluding other women from such roles. The council specified that only the grain weigher "and the people from their household" could perform the task.[31] In certain occupations, then, spouses clearly collaborated—either by sharing responsibilities or by engaging in complementary work within the same sector.

Another example of this dynamic appears in a conflict settlement between the town council and a married couple, both identified as innkeepers. Andrés de Vilela and his wife, María López de Novia, operated a hostel for merchants. In 1541, they came into conflict with the Bilbao council for organizing trade on behalf of their guests and acting as sales

---

[28] A note on the source corpus regarding María Ibáñez de Jáuregui's transactions is warranted. In the summaries of four 1554 transcripts in the *Archivo Foral de Bizkaia*'s digital catalog, she is incorrectly identified as the widow of Juan de Larrea. However, the documents themselves, as well as later records, consistently refer to her as the 'wife of' Juan de Larrea.

[29] "[...] que de oy dia en adelante ningunas nin algunas amas, moças nin moços nin cojedoras aparejadas non sean o(roto) de poner preçio ninguno en los trigos, saluo onb(roto) mugeres casadas [...]." Enríquez Fernández et al., *Ordenanzas municipales de Bilbao (1477–1520)*, fol. 127r.

[30] Enríquez Fernández et al., *Libro de acuerdos y decretos municipales de la villa de Bilbao: 1509–1515*, fol. 38v and 43v.

[31] "[...] saluo ellos, los mismos que tienen los dichos pesos e las personas de sus casas [...]." Enríquez Fernández et al., *Libro de acuerdos y decretos municipales de la villa de Bilbao: 1509–1515*, fol. 27v–28r, 5 March 1509.

intermediaries—activities prohibited by local regulations. Both were summoned before the council and penalized, after which they appealed the case to the *Real Chancillería* in Valladolid. The documentation reveals that the council primarily held María responsible for the illicit activities conducted in the hostel. When the couple's procurator defended their case, he stated that María had been penalized due to an earlier conflict with "the women innkeepers, [...] against whom the foresaid process had been [...]," omitting any mention of her husband's role.[32] Although the couple jointly managed the hostel, it appears that each spouse undertook distinct responsibilities. The informal trade activities for which they were persecuted seem to have been chiefly under María's control.

While the Bilbao sources rarely offer explicit references to spousal cooperation, scattered cases such as this suggest both its existence and its occasional recognition by local authorities. Biscayan customary law acknowledged the strong position of married couples, while also granting married women room to operate with a degree of independence. Nevertheless, for women engaged in small-scale trade, town ordinances and judicial records remain largely silent on their economic collaboration with spouses within household units.

*

There is ample evidence of spousal cooperation in the Brabantine towns. Wives and other women living with guild masters were often exempt from certain prohibitions directed at non-guild members. In these male-dominated guilds, men were expected to assume the role of household head, but they also relied heavily on the support of their spouses. This support could take various forms, illustrating the integral role women played within the household and the broader economic framework.

In her study of the household economy in early modern Dutch food trades, Danielle van den Heuvel distinguished several forms of spousal cooperation. These same forms can be found in the Brabantine sources. First, two spouses could complement each other's work. Artisans would supply their wives with goods to sell or products to finish. In the Leiden meat trade, craftsmen's wives could sell byproducts from their husbands'

[32] "[...] contra las mesoneras lo que toca a la dicha Mari Lopez mi parte syn incorporar ni poner en ello cosa alguna tocante a las otras personas contra quieren el dicho proceso se hizo [...]." ARChV, Sala de Vizcaya, Caja 4368, 4, 1541.

production. Butchers' wives in the Dutch town sold tripe and other meat byproducts.[33] Similarly, in Antwerp, fishmongers' wives were allowed to sit "outside of the fish market's gate" and sell fish, whereas other non-guild members ("woman or man") could only do so if they had caught the fish themselves or had brought it from outside the town's territory.[34] The wives of the Mechelen fishmongers, who worked as herring sellers, as introduced in chapter 1, also belong to this category.

Ordinances allowing craftsmen's wives to do certain tasks of their husbands' crafts often refer to this type of cooperation, exempting guild members' wives (and children) from prohibitions against other outsiders. A 1474 ordinance of the Antwerp glove and purse makers provides a clear example of this distinction. While female wage workers were obstructed by the guild, wives and other female members of the household economic unit were permitted to continue performing these typically female tasks, as will be discussed in greater depth in the next chapter.[35] The work of household women relieved the craftsmen of tasks, thereby creating the opportunity to produce more. In this way, all members would contribute to the household's income.

Although several ordinances describe complementary spousal cooperation in the Brabantine guilds, it is harder to find evidence of it in sources of daily practice. Most artisans' wives worked without recognition or formalization, leaving little evidence of their work behind. A few exceptions exist, such as the conflict between Liesbeth Maes and the old clothes sellers' guild brought before the Antwerp town council in 1435. The guild members complained that Liesbeth "should not work in the guild anymore since she had married a man from another guild."[36] Jan Godens, Liesbeth's husband, was a tanner. There are no surviving written regulations from the Antwerp old clothes sellers dictating that women had to leave the

---

[33] Van den Heuvel, 'Partners in Marriage and Business?', 222–3.

[34] "Dat van nu voerdane gheenrehande persone, wijf noch man, buyten der vischmerct porten sitten en zelen met vische te coepe noch daer visch vercoopen, uuytgenomen deghene die selve visch vangen oft van buyten der vrijheyt van der stad bringen, dat die haeren visch aldair zullen mogen vercoepen ende venten, gelijc van outs gewoonlic is, ende uutgenomen der vischcoepers wive, opdatter eenige sitten willen, dat zij dat zelen mogen doen ende visch vercoepen." SAA, GA#4369, fol. 2r, 17 July 1422.

[35] Génard, 'Register van den dachvaerden', 20, 400–1.

[36] "[...] dat zy haere ambacht niet meer hanteren en soude mids dat zy eenen man van eenen anderen ambachte genomen hadde [...]." Bisschops, 'Oudt register, mette berderen, 1336–1439 (Vervolg)", 29, 3–4.

guild after marriage. However, other guilds in neighboring Brabantine towns prohibited women from remaining in a guild upon (re)marriage.[37] Possibly, this custom was also applied by the Antwerp old clothes sellers' guild. Nevertheless, Liesbeth Maes did not agree. She argued that she had paid the old clothes sellers' entrance fee and should, therefore, be able to work under guild privileges. The aldermen of Antwerp agreed with her but wanted to ensure that her husband would not be too involved in his wife's occupation. Therefore, they decided that "Jan, her husband, could not buy or sell, but that he could only help her transport and guard her trade commodities and clothing, without buying and selling them himself."[38]

The guild and the aldermen were clearly aware that there was a good chance that Liesbeth's marriage would result in the two spouses' close cooperation. Jan Godens would not enter the guild but perform complementary tasks for Liesbeth's occupation while pursuing his own. Liesbeth might do the same for his occupation in return. As long as guild members' spouses did only certain tasks of the guild, this arrangement posed no problem to the town government, however.

Assistance provided by women to their husbands was accepted and encouraged by both local governments and guilds. The patriarchal guilds did not allow the opposite as easily, as the conflict between the old clothes sellers and Liesbeth Maes shows. Although a wife could help her husband without paying a guild membership fee, a husband could not do the same for his wife, as it was not in accordance with the patriarchal hierarchy. On the other hand, Liesbeth and Jan themselves did not problematize their separate occupational affiliations and even defended their cooperation before the Antwerp aldermen.[39] Possibly, as Anna Fridrich has argued, the couple "saw no reason to disguise workshop or any other work of their wives because it was perceived as a matter of course and perfectly legitimate due to her role in the household economy."[40] Thus, guilds, town governments, and citizens might struggle with the conflict between their economic and patriarchal values.

---

[37] Van Gerven, 'Vrouwen, arbeid en sociale positie', 952–6.

[38] "[...] Behoudelic dien, dat de voirs. Jan, hoer man, coepen noch vereoepen en soude, maer dat hy haer soude moegen helpen, haer goet ende cleederen af ende aen dragen ende dat helpen verwaeren, sonder selve yet te coepene of te vercoepene." Bisschops, 'Oudt register, mette berderen, 1336–1439 (Vervolg)', 3–4.

[39] Capp, *When Gossips Meet*, 24.

[40] Fridrich, 'Women Working in Guild Crafts', 138–39.

In a second type of spousal cooperation described by Van den Heuvel, "husband and wives appeared to have performed identical roles: they both worked as salespersons in a market booth."[41] Traditional cooperation took a different form in guilds that focused on trade rather than production. The Brabantine ordinances involving several guilds allowed husband and wife to run one market stall together. This was the case for the Antwerp retailers' guild, which in 1422, and again in 1452 and 1481, obliged their members to share a market stall between husband and wife, thus forcing them to take up the same role rather than complement each other's work. In other guilds, such as that of the Leuven butchers, wives were only allowed to take over their husbands' stalls if they were ill or out of town.[42] Further examples of these regulations can be found for the fishmongers of Mechelen, the Antwerp bakers, sock makers, and fishmongers.[43]

Evidence for this shared business can be found in normative sources, but is also confirmed in decisions made by urban and guild governments. This was, for example, the case with Willem de Bruyne and his wife, Kateline Dierix, who sold fish oil in the Cradewijck (the present-day Kraaiwijk) in the center of Antwerp. The council declared that because "the place where they conduct their occupation would be left with a heavy air and unusual smell", Willem and Kateline must move their shop to the Slijkpoort, the northernmost gate of Antwerp. The couple clearly ran the business together. What is more, the council of Antwerp clarified that the ruling was valid for the couple and all their descendants.[44] They assumed that the couple's business would be continued by their offspring.

The household unit was a common structure in Brabantine towns, encompassing both guild-affiliated and non-guild citizens. Craft guilds permitted spousal cooperation but also sought to curb any competitive advantage such cooperation might yield. Ordinances requiring spouses to share a market stall, for instance, aimed to prevent a single household from gaining an edge over other (single) craft members. Similarly, a 1487 regulation issued by the Antwerp sock makers prohibited family members from selling goods on designated free market days.[45] On days

[41] Van den Heuvel, 'Partners in Marriage and Business?', 225.
[42] SAA, GA#4211, 18 April 1422; SAL, 1527, 1593.
[43] SAM, Visverkopers 14, 26 July 1454; SAA, PK#1394, 25 August 1481; SAA, GA#4017, fol. 268r–277v, 17 September 1487; SAA, GA#4363, 6–11, 17 November 1452.
[44] Bisschops, 'Het 2e oudt register, in 't perkament gebonden 1438–1459 (Vervolg)', 30, 41–2.
[45] SAA, GA#4017, fol. 268r–277v, 17 September 1487.

when craft masters were barred from selling, their household members were likewise restricted. These rules suggest that wives were not intended to function as substitutes for their husbands within the market sphere. Nevertheless, spousal cooperation continued to offer a distinct advantage: "two spouses could support themselves and those close to them in a way that sole providers could not."[46] While guilds and town governments attempted to regulate these advantages and limit independent trade by members' wives, they also introduced exemptions to protect spouses' labor opportunities. Such instances reflect a delicate balancing act between patriarchal norms and the economic pragmatism required to sustain household livelihoods.

Although spousal cooperation was crucial to many households, not all married women in the Brabantine towns worked exclusively in the same occupation as their husbands did. As discussed in a later section, the Brabantine mercers' guilds accepted women regardless of their marital status. Under the status of *femme sole*, Brabantine women managed businesses separately from their husbands.[47] However, even without this status, spousal cooperation was not the only way for women to participate in some trades. For example, the women herring sellers of Mechelen were not all fishmongers' spouses. In 1545, a small group of citizens of Mechelen had a dispute with the fishmongers' guild. The citizens were selling herring, which, according to the guild, was only permitted for guild members and the 'herring women' working in the town. Two of the witnesses testifying about herring sales claimed that they were "aware that several women citizens—not members of the foresaid fishmongers' guild, among them Johanne Vermoesen, the wife of a barrel maker, and Mrs. Reynken, the wife of a shoemaker—have sold herring, dried and wet, by the piece."[48] Johanne Vermoesen and Mrs. Reynken were married to members of other craft guilds. Even though they might also have worked in their husbands' workshops, their herring sales would provide extra income for their families.

---

[46] Ling et al., 'Marriage and Work', 80.

[47] Van Aert, 'Tussen norm en praktijk'.

[48] "Verclaerende voorts hem oick wel kennelijck te zijne dat diverssche poirters vrouwen nyet wesende int ambacht van den visschers voorscreven als te weten Johanne Vermoesen een cuypers huysvrouwe, vrouw reynken, een schoenmakers huysvrouwe, vercocht hebben harinck drooghen ende natten metten stucke." SAM, Visverkopers 670, 1545–1549.

The work of wives likely represents the most discernible aspect of female participation within Brabantine guilds. Though mostly viewed through a limited normative lens, their contributions to the household economy encompassed a diverse range of roles. The specific activities undertaken by wives within Brabantine guilds depended largely on the nature of guild-organized work. Trade-focused occupations tended toward controlled tasks, whereas craft guilds involved in production adhered more closely to a structured household economy model. Incorporating the differentiation between labor sectors into women's opportunities in Brabantine towns adds an important nuance to the frequently cited significance of the household economic unit. We will revisit this theme in the next chapter.

Never-Married Household Members

Beyond married spouses, the household economic unit also depended on the contributions of servants, apprentices, children, and other family members.[49] These individuals are the least visible in the written record, largely due to their limited responsibilities and legal capacities. Even so, select examples from the Brabantine and Biscayan case studies reveal their participation in the urban labor force. In particular, the involvement of female minors underscores the broader managerial role played by wives and widows within the household. Although the evidence on unmarried household members in both Brabant and Biscay is too scarce to support firm conclusions about their specific labor roles, sources from Brabant occasionally attest to the cohesiveness of the household economic unit and the diverse contributions made by its members.

The inclusion of minor household members in economic activity, though rarely formalized, was generally accepted by guilds and town governments as a practical extension of the household economic unit. A 1403 ordinance from the Leuven purse makers, which excluded women from practicing the trade, nonetheless made exceptions not only for guild masters' wives but also for other women residing in their households.[50] Similarly, several guild ordinances from Antwerp and Mechelen

---

[49] See, among others: Howell, *Women, Production, and Patriarchy*, 9–26; Carlier, 'The Household', 7; Von Heusinger, 'Vater, Mutter, Kind'.

[50] SAL, 1523, fol. 207r–210v, 22 August 1403.

explicitly addressed the roles of daughters and servants.[51] The Mechelen fishmongers, for instance, specified that "neither he [the fishmonger, ed.], nor his wife, nor his children" could work if the master had violated the rules and was temporarily banned from the guild—underscoring once more that household members were not intended to act as substitutes for a punished guild member. In addressing informal competition from other urban residents, the Antwerp fishmongers acknowledged the reality of household-based cooperation. A 1464 ordinance allowed citizens to sell freshwater fish themselves, or to have it "sold and retailed by their wives or by their children or by those that live and room and board with him."[52] Such regulations reveal the acceptance of broader household participation in market-oriented work.

Different members of a household economic unit cooperating in the household workshop also appear in the Mechelen fishmongers' sentence books. Guild masters were prosecuted for allowing various household members—servants, daughters, apprentices, wives, mothers, and nieces—to sell fish. Additionally, five sentences punished women directly for this offense. For example, the widow Venne, likely a fishmonger's widow, was sentenced to a pilgrimage in 1518 for permitting her servant to sell fish.[53] Ten years prior, Rombout Venne's wife (possibly the same woman) had been penalized for the same transgression.[54] These cases demonstrate that both partners in the marriage could be held responsible for the informal participation of other household members. As I will argue in the next chapter, prosecutions for household cooperation were limited to specific situations.

*

[51] The Antwerp old clothes sellers, for example, issued regulations about the entrance fees of guild masters' children. SAA, GA#4001, 30r–32r, 10 November 1436. In the Antwerp grain trade, too, the town government saw the need to specify regulations about the work of male and female servants, wives, and other household members. SAA, PK#913, 3r, 10 March 1442.

[52] "[…] als dat sij selve die visschen sullen moghen vercoopen oft doen vercoopen ende penninckwaerden bij heuren wijven ofte heuren kinderen oft dengenen die in heuren aete ende drancke sijn." SAA, GA#4363, 20–1, 30 October 1464.

[53] SAM, Visverkopers 321, fol. 87v, 1518.

[54] SAM, Visverkopers 321, fol. 53v, 1508.

In Bilbao, evidence regarding never-married women's activities within the household economic unit primarily points to the participation of female servants. For instance, in 1509, the council granted women retailers selling candles and oil a trade monopoly, explicitly stating that "no other person, man or woman, nor servant [boy or girl, ed.], was allowed to sell [...]."55 Similar ordinances regulating the involvement of servants and children are found across various small-scale trades in Bilbao. Furthermore, ordinances reveal collaboration between Bilbao tradeswomen and servant girls. In 1548, the council, aiming to protect the town's food supply, prohibited the export of fish from Bilbao—a recurring regulation. This ordinance specifically barred the *sardineras* and *pescaderas* of Bilbao from taking fish out of the town or sending it with servant girls.56 While it remains unclear whether these servants were employed by the tradeswomen or potential buyers, these regulations highlight the young women's role in the economic activities of Bilbao's tradeswomen.

In 1544, the Bilbao town council confronted two citizens of nearby Portugalete who had dispatched their female servants to Bilbao to purchase grain. These women had exported more grain than allowed under the town's bylaws.57 Their involvement suggests that women's exclusion from certain market roles was likely not due to a lack of skill or capacity. Earlier, in 1500, the council fined the official grain weigher, Juan Saes de Çurbaran, for allowing his female servant to carry out his duties. According to the council, Bilbao citizens had complained that the involvement of servants in weighing grain led to fraud and irregularities.58 Apparently, the prohibition against letting servants work as grain weighers did not resonate with everyone. Grain weighers continued to delegate tasks to their servants, possibly viewing this informal labor as a convenient way to boost profits. They may have viewed these young women as capable workers within the household workshop, entrusting them with such tasks despite official restrictions.

---

55 "[...] e que otra persona ninguna, honbre nin muger, nin moço nin moça, non sea hosada de dar e bender en la dicha billa por librras de azeyte nin candela, saluo las regateras que estan obligadas en el conçejo, so pena de quinientos maravedis a cada vno por cada bez." Enríquez Fernández et al., *Libro de acuerdos y decretos municipales de la villa de Bilbao: 1509–1515*, 27v–28v, 7 March 1509.

56 Rodriguez Herrero, *Ordenanzas de Bilbao. Siglos XV y XVI*, 46–7.

57 AFB, Municipal 0034/001/008, 15 December 1551.

58 Enríquez Fernández et al., *Ordenanzas municipales de Bilbao (1477–1520)*, fol. 181r–182r.

Shifting Away from the Household Paradigm

Evidence of traditional household cooperation between spouses and their children is largely absent from the Bilbao source material. As in the Brabantine towns, documentation from Bilbao does identify men as the heads of household. A 1509 town council ordinance prohibited poor residents and beggar monastics from entering the area around the public ovens, where bread bakers, sellers, and other women worked. The council justified the regulation by claiming that "the women, and *amas* [householders] and servant girls who go to the ovens to prepare dough hurt their husbands and employers and act without their permission [...]."[59] This statement reinforces the dominant role of men as household heads or economic overseers. By contrast, the council's silence regarding female bread sellers—who likely managed their own businesses and supervised activity at the ovens—suggests that these women exercised considerable autonomy. Such silences are common in the sources concerning female small-scale traders in Bilbao, pointing to a pattern that contrasts with the more explicitly collaborative household model found in the Brabantine case studies.

Bilbao's ordinances on trade rarely distinguished between married, single, or widowed women, and other regional sources reflect a similar lack of concern for women's marital status in regulating economic activity. While many of these women undoubtedly contributed to the welfare of their households, their individual work seems to have operated largely independently of other household members. This distinction does not mean the household unit was irrelevant. Married women in Bilbao still benefited from communal property arrangements: in the event of separation or widowhood, a wife was entitled to half of the jointly acquired movable goods and usufruct rights over immovable property.[60] Nevertheless, to fully grasp the significance of the household economy in Bilbao, it is essential to account for social stratification. As Anna Fridrich has argued in her study of early modern Laufen, the importance and visibility of household economic units varied considerably across social groups.[61]

---

[59] "[...] que dan en los dichos hornos las mugeres e amas e moças e criadas que a los dichos hornos ban a amasar, en dapno de sus maridos e amos e syn su liçençia dellos [...]." Enríquez Fernández et al., *Libro de acuerdos y decretos municipales*, fol. 50r.

[60] Heath Dillard has also found this situation for other Castilian regions in the High Middle Ages. See: Dillard, *Daughters of the Reconquest*, 70.

[61] Fridrich, 'Women Working in Guild Crafts', 135–6.

In 1510, nineteen female fishmongers from Bilbao petitioned the town council to revise an ordinance enacted two weeks earlier.[62] These women represented "all the fishmongers and sardine sellers currently operating in the town square."[63] Although they were not the only fish vendors in Bilbao—the trade also took place at Calle de Barrencalle and Portal de Zamudio[64]—their central location likely marked them as the town's most prominent. None of the women was identified by marital status; they appeared before the council as *sardineras* and *pescaderas*, their occupational titles serving as their primary identifiers. This pattern also applies to the women retailing oil and candle wax. Two 1509 ordinances regulating their trade addressed fifteen women by name, of whom only one was identified as married and another (likely) as never-married.[65]

Earlier studies on women's work in Biscay and the Basque Country have often assumed that urban female occupations were primarily carried out by widows and never-married women.[66] However, the records of Bilbao's town council disputes with female traders suggest a more complex picture. These sources document women of varying marital statuses working across a range of occupations. A particularly illustrative case is the long-running legal conflict between the council and the *cojedoras*, which began in 1525. During this ten-year dispute, thirteen women testified about their work: six were married, three widowed, and four not identified by marital status.

Toda de Larrea, one of the *cojedoras*, was first mentioned in 1509, when the Bilbao council authorized four women to collect the grain tax from incoming merchants.[67] At that time, she was listed without title or refer-

---

[62] The nineteen women were: Catalina d'Otannes, Catalina de Bedia, Catalina Nafarra, donna Elvira de Gaxmuri, Joana de Gaxmuri, Joana de Larrea, Mayora de Iturribalzaga, Mari Fernandis de Salzedo, Mari Martines de Mendieta, Mari Peres de Çurvaran, Mari Saes de Maruri, Mari Saes de Susunaga, Mari Saes de Vasoçabala, Mari Saes de Aguero, Mari Peres de Vermeo, Sancha de Anunçibay, Teresa de Galdames, Teresa de Musquis, and Toda de Avando.

[63] "[...] a todas las pescaderas e sardineras que al presente residen en la Plaça de la dicha villa [...]." Enríquez Fernández et al., *Ordenanzas municipales de Bilbao (1477–1520)*, fol. 276r–279r.

[64] Enríquez Fernández et al., fol. 85v, 13 February 1497.

[65] Enríquez Fernández et al., *Libro de acuerdos y decretos municipales de la villa de Bilbao: 1509–1515*, 21 February 1509, fol. 21r–21v; Enríquez Fernández et al., 28 November 1509, fol. 98r–99r.

[66] Rivera Medina, 'Superando fronteras. Mujer y cultura laboral', 22; Iziz & Iziz, *Historia de las mujeres en Euskal Herria*, 258; Castrillo Casado, 'Participación de las mujeres en la economía urbana del País Vasco', 214.

[67] Enríquez Fernández et al., *Libro de acuerdos y decretos municipales de la villa de Bilbao: 1509–1515*, fol. 18r, 9 February 1509.

ence to marital status. By 1525, when the *cojedoras* appealed the council's prohibition of their occupation to the higher courts in Valladolid, she was referred to as Lady Toda de Larrea, wife of Martín de Camiruaga. Despite her marriage, Toda continued her occupation and testified in 1531 that "she and her husband rented the town's weights," a responsibility she had fulfilled since 1509. Ongoing war had forced the couple into debt, compelling them to sell their house and forcing Toda to rely again on her earnings as a *cojedora*.[68] While they had previously worked together, poverty ultimately compelled her to operate independently. At the time of her testimony, she had recently been widowed and claimed to possess less than 200 *maravedís*.[69] Toda de Larrea's story was not one of success; nonetheless, she had worked continuously as a *cojedora* throughout her adult life.

Toda de Larrea was not alone in continuing her work regardless of marital status. Mayora de Iturribalzaga, one of the 1510 fishmongers, remained active in the trade after her marriage to Fernando de Aguero.[70] As Darlene Abreu-Ferreira has also shown in her study of women's labor in northern Portuguese coastal towns, in Bilbao, marital status did not necessarily alter the work patterns of female street vendors.[71] While these women were also responsible for their households, those households did not function as economic units in the same way they did in Brabant. Rather than organizing their work collectively through the household, women in Bilbao typically pursued their trades independently, regardless of marital ties.

*

Arnaldo Sousa Melo, in his study of women's work in the late medieval Porto household economy, found a similar lack of evidence regarding spousal cooperation and women working in household workshops as observed in Bilbao. He attributed this silence to the assertion that women's

---

[68] "[...] que ella e su marido después tomaron en rrenta los pezos della villa e con las guerras pasadas ovieron grand perdida e asy el concejo los vendio por la renta la caseria qua tenían e una huerta esta no dexar les ninguna cosa de que se pudiese mantener e asy se gue al regimiento a pedir les licencia pues beyan como ella no tenia de que mantenerse [...]." ARChV, Sala de Vizcaya, Caja 3467, 5, 27 June 1536.

[69] "Segund, que he seido e soy viuda que en todo mi caudal no ay bienes que balgan dozientos maravedís [...]." ARChV, Sala de Vizcaya, Caja 3467, 5, 27 June 1536.

[70] AFB, Municipal, 0304/001/011, 1532.

[71] Abreu-Ferreira, 'Neighbors and Traders', 581–87.

work would only appear in written documents if it occurred outside the household.[72] However, in Mechelen and Antwerp, the significance of the household economy is reflected in various source types, including normative ordinances. This documentation suggests that other factors may have contributed to the absence of a prominent household economy in Bilbao. I have explored two potential influences: Bilbao's system of work organization and the town's maritime orientation.

Studies have demonstrated a close relationship between urban household economic units and guild systems. When guilds structured the context for work, women's labor opportunities were often confined to the household economy.[73] Or, the other way around, Daryl Hafter posited that "guilds developed naturally from the domestic production of urban families."[74] The absence of either institution in Bilbao makes it difficult to pinpoint the cause of this dynamic. However, the result is that retail and food trades were not organized into (masculine) guilds in Bilbao, and women's work did not align with the household organization prevalent elsewhere in Europe for these trades. Instead, these two institutions appear to have been supplanted by a deeply ingrained informal trade network.

In Bilbao, women had access to certain occupations in their own names. In most cases, these occupations were related to trade and organized informally. There is little evidence of women participating in productive occupations (such as shoemaking and blacksmithing), either in their own names or as part of a household workshop. There is one exception in Bilbao. In 1546-1547, Francisco de Melgar and Juan Ochoa de Larrea, two overseers of the Bilbao candlemakers, examined four new candidate candlemakers. One was a widowed woman, two were married women, and one was a man. All were citizens of Bilbao and were accepted as candlemakers after successfully completing their tests.[75]

In other Biscayan towns, such as Plentzia and Bermeo, regulations for the fishmongers' and butchers' guilds attest to the participation of wives and widows in these trades. In Plentzia, butchers' wives were prohibited from cutting meat, while in Bermeo, fishmongers' wives and children were

---

[72] Sousa Melo, 'Women and Work in the Household Economy'.
[73] Schmidt, Devos & Blondé, 'Introduction. Single and the City', 6; Stabel, 'Workplace Cultures', 97.
[74] Hafter, *Women at Work in Preindustrial France*, 24.
[75] AFB, Notarial, 0486/0020, 10 December 1547; AFB, Notarial, 0486/0019, 22 June 1547; AFB, Notarial, 0486/0005, 22 October 1547; AFB, Notarial, 0486/0006, 20 October 1546.

permitted to sell certain fish types.[76] As Rosa and Ana Iziz have suggested, in Basque towns, guild members' widows were allowed to practice their late husbands' occupations for a year after their deaths.[77] Similar to other European towns, including Brabantine Antwerp and Mechelen, these Biscayan guilds did not always maintain smooth relations with women active in the towns. In Plentzia, for instance, the fishmongers' guild complained about women selling fish at the town gates and requested a general ban on non-guild member women selling fish.[78] Biscayan guilds also attempted to restrict women's involvement. At the same time, guilds provided opportunities for women to participate in guild labor through domestic workshops.[79] Had Bilbao's occupations been organized into guilds, more women might have worked within a household economic unit. Conversely, many fishmongers and retail women selling on Bilbao's streets might have experienced a decrease in their work opportunities.

The limited influence of guilds in Bilbao may have allowed women to access trades that were more restricted in other towns dominated by powerful craft corporations. However, this openness was not a sign of gender equality. More likely, it reflected the limited options available to women in precarious financial circumstances. As discussed in chapter 1, women with occupational titles appear at the bottom of Bilbao's 1470 taxation list (see table 4, p. X), indicating their modest financial status. The informal work of the *cojedoras* likely ranked even lower in social standing than formal retail. Most women involved in the 1525 court case between the town council and the *cojedoras*, including Toda de Larrea, described their occupation as a response to economic hardship. Women of all marital statuses turned to these market activities as accessible means of survival in the absence of more secure opportunities.

---

[76] Castrillo Casado, 'Participación de las mujeres en la economía urbana', 214; Largacha Rubio et al., *Colección documental del archivo de la cofradía de pescadores de la villa de Lequeitio (1325–1520)*, 86r–88v, 2 December 1496.

[77] Iziz & Iziz, *Historia de las mujeres en Euskal Herria*, 258. In the neighboring region of Navarra, craft members' widows could also apply for the right to continue their husbands' trade in the first year after their death. As Amaia Nausia Pimoulier has shown in her research, throughout the sixteenth and seventeenth centuries, more than three hundred cases of such applications can be found. See: Nausia Pimoulier, 'El usufructo de viudedad Navarro'.

[78] Rivera Medina, 'Superando fronteras. Mujer y cultura laboral', 25.

[79] Stabel, 'Workplace Cultures', 97; Jacobsen, 'Women's Work and Women's Role'; Van den Heuvel, 'Partners in Marriage and Business?'; Bennett, *Ale, Beer, and Brewsters in England*.

Bilbao's maritime orientation and economic structure further help explain the overwhelming absence of spousal cooperation in the historical records. Unlike the Brabantine towns, in Bilbao, widows, married women, and never-married women frequently appear as independent small-scale traders. Many of the married women engaged in these trades appear to have been unable to rely on their husbands' contributions, particularly during times of crisis. The town's dependence on seafaring meant that many men were absent for extended periods, leaving their wives to fend for themselves.[80]

This context is evident in the 1525 testimonies of the *cojedoras* during their legal conflict with the Bilbao town council. Although some of them were married, their testimonies reveal that they could not count on their husbands' income or participation in a joint household workshop. When asked why she continued to work as a *cojedora* despite the town's ban on the practice, Ibañez de Regoita replied: "Because I have five young children, the oldest not yet seven years old, and this way, I do not have to beg from the town's wealthy; and because her husband left her nothing to spend."[81] Another *cojedora*, Ochanda de Zamudio, stated that she had asked permission from local authorities to pursue the trade because her husband was away.[82]

The absence of formal economic structures, such as guilds, gave women room to enter certain market sectors. Yet it was the absence of financial security possibly combined with an absent husband—that compelled many women to turn to small-scale trade. These occupations offered neither protection nor prestige, but they did provide a necessary income for themselves and their families.

2. Craft Guilds: The Stronghold of the Brabantine Urban Economy

Guilds have played a leading role in the analysis of women's work opportunities in the towns of the Low Countries and European towns in general.[83] These corporations, integral to the urban economy, wielded

---

[80] Castrillo Casado, 'Mujeres, negocio y mercaduría', 307.

[81] "[...] dixo por causa de la grand necesidad que tenia por quanto tenia cinco criaturas chiquitas que la maior no llegaba a mas de syete anos e por no andar a pedir e mantenerse entre buenos en el pueblo porque su marido no le abia dexado que gastar ni le avia ynbrado nada e a esta causa usaba del dicho oficio [...]." ARChV, Sala de Vizcaya, Caja 3467, 5, 27 June 1536.

[82] ARChV, Sala de Vizcaya, Caja 3467, 5, 27 June 1536.

[83] In 2008, Claire Crowston provided an insightful overview of this in her 'Women, Gender, and Guilds' journal article. Since then, more studies have focused on women's work in the elusive guilds.

significant economic, political, and cultural influence. For Brabantine women, guilds represented a source of stable work and income as well as a masculine institution that often excluded them. A woman's economic activities within the guild system were contingent upon factors such as marital status, lineage, social standing, and occupation.

Before examining these effects, it is important to understand which women participated in guild work and how they gained access. The previous section focused on one group: household members of guild masters. It is likely that most women entered guild occupations through this route because, within the patriarchal structure, guild masters were also husbands and fathers. Marriage was not a status expected only of women. In fact, studies have shown that in early modern urban Europe, widowers often remarried faster and more often than widows.[84] In traditional guilds like those of the fishmongers and butchers, at least one woman per household was involved in guild activities under the household economy's rules.[85] However, being a female member of a household economic unit did not guarantee inclusion in guild activities. As will be discussed in the next chapter, guilds also limited these work opportunities, although female household members were almost certainly involved in some capacity.

Beyond household members of guild masters, a small number of women joined guilds in their own names. Including these women provides a more complete view of women's work in the Antwerp and Mechelen guilds, particularly those that admitted female members. While 'traditional' corporations like the fishmongers and butchers recognized women's work, female guild members were notably absent from these guilds with traditional household economy structures, as noted by Kristien Harmsen and Helene Hubers for the early modern Antwerp and Utrecht fishmongers, and my own findings in the Mechelen fishmongers' account books from 1466 to 1543.[86] As far as the limitations of guild membership lists allow this analysis, they reveal that the same mechanisms influencing women's work in household production—parentage and marital

See, among others: Crowston, 'Women, Gender, and Guilds'; Fridrich, 'Women Working in Guild Crafts'; Montenach, 'Trades in Lyon'; Van den Heuvel, 'Guilds, Gender Policies and Economic Opportunities'.

[84] See, among others: Hardwick, *The Practice of Patriarchy*, 130–1; Schmidt, *Overleven na de dood*, 212–20; Wyffels, 'Women and Work in Early Modern Printing Houses', 127–32.

[85] De Munck, *Guilds, Labour and the Urban Body Politic*, 179–211; Hafter, *Women at Work in Preindustrial France*, 24–5.

[86] Harmsen & Hubers, "En zij verkocht de vis", 33; SAM, Visverkopers 462a; SAM, Visverkopers 462b.

Table 6. Number and percentage of men and women in the available entrance lists and membership lists from Mechelen and Antwerp.

	Men		Women		Total	
	#	%	#	%	#	%
Shopkeepers Mechelen (1404-1510)	288	90	32	10	320	100
Shopkeepers Mechelen (1554-1560)	63	97	2	3	65	100
Gardeners Mechelen (1478-1503)	190	96	7	4	197	100
Gardeners Mechelen (1521-1549)	210	93	16	7	226	100
Glove makers Mechelen	91	97	3	3	94	100
Old clothes sellers Mechelen	79	100	0	0	79	100
Old clothes sellers Antwerp	63	94	4	6	67	100
Mercers Antwerp (1516-1555)	3598	94	236	6	3834	100

Source: See Table 1.

status—also affected their access to guild membership. Ultimately, guilds and the household economy were two integral components of the same economic system.

For fifteenth- and early sixteenth-century Antwerp and Mechelen, only a handful of membership lists and account books documenting the registration of new female guild members have survived (see table 6). A major challenge lies in the lack of identifying information for most of the individuals listed. Beyond confirming guild affiliation and occasionally revealing family ties to other members, these sources often provide no further details about the new entrants. As a result, any generalizations about female guild membership based on these lists must be made with great caution.

The account books of the Mechelen gardeners and mercers do contain enough contextual information to allow for more confident interpretation. However, the most informative source is the entrance register of the Antwerp mercers' guild, which Laura Van Aert has also analyzed in her detailed study of the guild in a slightly later period.[87] The list is extensive because of the complex organization of this corporation. More than two hundred occupations—encompassing both trade and production—fell under the mercers' 'nation' in Antwerp. Most members were involved in

---

[87] Van Aert, 'Tot 'leven of overleven'?'.

retail, particularly the small-scale trade of everyday goods. Nearly half of the new members admitted between 1516 and 1555 were *kramers* (shopkeepers) or *vettewariers* (oil workers). Other common occupations within the guild included *kruideniers* (grocers), cheese sellers, and tinsmiths (see table 8 for an overview of the most frequent occupations in the Antwerp mercers' guild).

Table 6 shows that some guilds admitted a small number of women. Even the glove makers' guild—which upheld patriarchal norms in its statutes and regulations (as discussed in the next chapter)—included a minor percentage of female members.[88] As expected, the mercers' guilds of Mechelen and Antwerp admitted the highest proportion of women. Yet the average percentage of female entrants in any guild never exceeded ten percent. This pattern aligns with findings from other studies on the Low Countries during this period, which also emphasize the limited formal inclusion of women in guilds.[89]

Most women who did gain access belonged to guilds focused on trade rather than production. Guilds associated with production typically required formal apprenticeships—an entry route often restricted to men in those corporations with strong traditions of male exclusivity.[90] A brief apprenticeship list from the Antwerp mercers for 1516 and 1517 confirms this condition: all recorded apprentices were male and trained in production-related occupations. By contrast, nearly all women who entered the mercers' guild did so as traders, while many male members were admitted for production roles (see table 8, p. 114).

Women's membership in a guild was influenced by two major elements: marital status and family relations. The influence of marital status—particularly widowhood—is evident when comparing Brabantine guild entrance lists with membership lists. No women appear as new entrants on the Mechelen glove makers' entrance list.[91] However, two women, iden-

---

[88] The female occupational titles present in the mercers' entrance list are: *cremeresse, kaaskoperesse, kamverkoopster, koekverkoopster, kruidenierster, lijmverkoperesse, olijfverkoopster, pluimverkoopster, stijfstelverkoopster, vettewarierster,* and *zeepziedster*.

[89] Van Aert, 'The Legal Possibilities of Antwerp Widows', 290; Van den Heuvel, 'Guilds, Gender Policies and Economic Opportunities for Women', 128; Howell, *Women, Production, and Patriarchy*.

[90] De Munck, De Kerf & De Bie, 'Apprenticeship in the Southern Netherlands, c. 1400–c. 1800', 234.

[91] The year in which this document was written is unclear, but might be close to 1550, as the entrance list written in the same document was from this period. SAM, Handschoenmakers-, tesmakers-, riem(be)slagers-, witledermakers- en schedemakersambacht 554bis; SAM, Handschoenmakers-, tesmakers-, riem(be)slagers-, witledermakers- en schedemakersambacht 557.

tified as the Widow Vrijers and the Widow Conincks, are recorded among the registered members.[92] A similar pattern appears in the old clothes sellers' guilds of Antwerp and Mechelen. While no women are listed on Mechelen's entrance list, four are recorded as registered members in Antwerp, three of whom were widows.[93] The absence of these women from entrance lists, combined with their appearance in membership records, suggests that the widows had gained guild status by inheriting their late husbands' positions. In these cases, they were not considered 'new' entrants but rather placeholders of occupational continuity.[94] While they could competently take over the trade, their role was often seen as temporary—sustaining the business until a son or a, according to the guild, more suitable male journeyman could assume control.

Widows thus had a certain advantage in exclusive craft guilds. However, not all female guild members entered through marriage. In retail-focused guilds, women could join under their own names. The Antwerp mercers and the Mechelen shopkeepers, for example, admitted female members independently of marital status. Although women still represented a small minority—the highest number is found in the Mechelen shopkeepers' entrance lists and is only ten percent—their admission was not primarily tied to marital status. Unlike the dominance of widows in the glove makers' and old clothes sellers' records, most women on retail guild entrance lists were not identified as widows.

Only two women on the Antwerp mercers' entrance list are clearly recorded as married: they were listed under their husbands' names (wives of Jan Beuckelaers and Jan Simpas). This designation reflects broader legal norms. Both single and married women were generally required to have a male legal guardian for formal transactions.[95] If a married woman wished to enter the guild independently, she had to assume the legal status of *femme sole*.[96] The flexibility of retail made it a practical occupation for married women not engaged full-time in a household workshop. While clerks explicitly identified only two women as married, others on the list

---

[92] Only one other woman appears on this list. Lijne van Loven is registered only by her own name with no marital status.

[93] SAM, Oudkleerkopersambacht 21; SAA, GA#4277.

[94] Among others, Anne Montenach states this. See: Montenach, 'Trades in Lyon', 21–2; Montenach, 'Creating a Space for Themselves on the Urban Market', 53.

[95] Godding, *Le droit privé dans les Pays-Bas Méridionaux*, 77–81.

[96] Van Aert, 'Tot 'leven of overleven'?', 73.

may well have been married but not categorized as such. Daryl Hafter has linked the low numbers of independently registered women in guilds to the structure of the household economy. For a woman to join a guild in her own right typically meant her work diverged from her husband's.[97] Even among shopkeepers, the percentage of women remained low, as might be expected in an urban economy dominated by the household economy.

In addition to marital status, parentage influenced women's opportunities to enter or participate in guild work formally. Some Brabantine guilds, such as the butchers and fishmongers, only allowed masters' children (often a synonym for sons) to obtain master status.[98] As the Mechelen regulation providing for the sons of fishmongers' daughters demonstrates, other guilds gave preference to all guild members' offspring. Many studies have explored the claim of masters' sons to the guild title and the role of widows in this transmission.[99] Although it is not new, the idea that daughters inherited the trade is less accepted.[100] Ellen Burm and Bert De Munck have shown the contribution of master bakers' daughters to the continuity of the Antwerp bakers' guild at the end of the eighteenth century. Not only did daughters play a key role in finding and marrying suitable successors, but they could also take over the family workshops.[101] Marjolein van Dekken found similar activities among brewers' daughters in the early modern northern Low Countries.[102] While lacking definitive evidence, certain guild membership lists contain enough detail to support the claim that family ties played a significant role in women's admission to guilds, even if the specific activities of the registered women do not appear on these lists. These details come from records of the entrance fees that new members had to pay.

Although it might have been more difficult for women to enter the Antwerp mercers' guild than for men, in theory, the corporation only slightly favored masters' children of either sex. A minority of new guild members benefited from the reduced entrance fee given to artisans' children. According to De Munck, an average of twenty to thirty percent

---

[97] Hafter, *Women at Work in Preindustrial France*, 83.
[98] De Munck, *Guilds, Labour and the Urban Body Politic*, 194.
[99] Simonton, 'Widows and Wenches', 21-2.
[100] Hafter, *Women at Work in Preindustrial France*, 24; Hutton, 'Women, Men, and Markets', 428; Von Heusinger, 'Vater, Mutter, Kind', 170-2.
[101] Lanza, *From Wives to Widows in Early Modern Paris*, 93-4; Cavallo, *Artisans of the Body in Early Modern Italy*, 160-1.
[102] Van Dekken, *Brouwen, branden & bedienen*, 102-4.

Table 7. Number and percentage of new members, by fee category, in the entrance register of the Antwerp mercers' guild (1516–1555). The categories include full entrance fee, half entrance fee, and unknown.

New members	#	%
Men	3600	94
Full entrance fee	2448	68
Half entrance fee	700	19
Unknown	452	13
Women	236	6
Full entrance fee	145	61
Half entrance fee	64	27
Unknown	27	11
Total	3836	100

Source: SAA, FA#22; SAA, 860#7761.

of the new guild members in eighteenth-century Antwerp were sons of masters, who only paid half of the usual entrance fee.[103] Similarly, table 7 shows that about thirty percent of sixteenth-century mercer women paid reduced fees. This suggests these women either came from guild families or had reduced fees due to economic hardship.[104]

The underlying reasons for the lower fees remain ambiguous. Access to the mercers' guild was not determined by the inheritance of a father's title or workshop; instead, citizenship and the payment of guild fees were the only formal requirements for women seeking entry.[105] Although, in theory, women needed to obtain *femme sole* status before joining, Van Aert argues that they often acquired this status only after becoming members.[106] Reputation and financial means were the typical barriers to guild entry.[107] Danielle van den Heuvel has shown that the high costs

---

[103] De Munck, *Guilds, Labour and the Urban Body Politic*, 190.

[104] The analysis in this chapter is based on the assumption that most new members paying half the entrance fee came from guild families rather than getting a reduction because of their financial status. The fault margin might be similar for both sexes, and the argument aligns with earlier findings.

[105] Van Aert, 'Tot 'leven of overleven'?', 64–5.

[106] *Ibidem*, 73.

[107] Stabel, 'Workplace Cultures', 98; See: Van den Heuvel, 'Guilds, Gender Policies and Economic Opportunities', 127–9; Van den Heuvel, 'Partners in Marriage and Business?', 221.

of entrance fees and citizenship registration in the retail sector acted as invisible barriers for many women in the northern Low Countries. While guilds formally permitted female membership, the financial burden often prevented women from practicing their trade within official structures.[108] After all, these corporations were not charitable institutions. This situation raises the possibility that many women listed in Antwerp's guild records paying half the entrance fee between 1516 and 1555 were in fact 'guild daughters.'

The importance of a guild background for women entering the Antwerp mercers' guild differed depending on the occupation they would join within the guild. In some fields of the mercers' guild, women from guild families seem to have had an advantage. As table 8 (p. 114) shows, only eighteen percent of the men among the shopkeepers came from a guild family, while thirty-five percent of the female shopkeepers entered by parentage. The grocers show a similar difference; forty percent of women entered for half the entrance fee compared to twenty-three percent of men. The capital necessary to establish a business may have been higher for these market-based trades than for itinerant trades, such as that of the oil workers, and women in these sectors likely required more parental support for entry than men or women in other trades. As scholars have previously stated, (single) women likely faced greater difficulty than their male counterparts in accumulating the capital needed to establish a shop.[109] The data in table 8 indicate that daughters of shopkeepers and grocers held an advantage over women who established businesses independently in these occupations. In occupations requiring less starting capital, such an advantage likely held less significance.

---

[108] Van den Heuvel, 'Guilds, Gender Policies and Economic Opportunities', 127–9; Van den Heuvel, 'Partners in Marriage and Business?', 221.

[109] Honeyman & Goodman, 'Women's Work, Gender Conflict, and Labour Markets', 610; Montenach, 'Trades in Lyon', 20; Vicente, 'Images and Realities of Work', 127.

Table 8. Number and percentage of new female and male members, by occupation and fee category, in the Antwerp mercers' guild (1516–1555).[110]

Occupation	Women #	Women %	Men #	Men %
Shopkeeper	89	38	1018	28
Full entrance fee	50	56	738	72
Half entrance fee	31	35	186	18
Unknown	8	9	94	9
Oil worker	60	25	583	16
Full entrance fee	48	80	461	79
Half entrance fee	7	12	87	15
Unknown	5	8	35	6
Unknown	32	14	503	14
Full entrance fee	16	50	175	35
Half entrance fee	7	22	93	18
Unknown	9	28	235	47
Grocer	20	8	137	4
Full entrance fee	11	55	100	73
Half entrance fee	8	40	32	23
Unknown	1	5	5	4
Tinsmith	/	/	114	3
Full entrance fee	/	/	72	63
Half entrance fee	/	/	36	32
Unknown	/	/	6	5
Confectioner	/	/	105	3
Full entrance fee	/	/	77	73
Half entrance fee	/	/	19	18
Unknown	/	/	9	9
Cheese seller	14	6	100	3
Full entrance fee	9	64	76	76
Half entrance fee	5	36	15	15
Unknown	/	/	9	9
Other	21	9	1040	29
Total	236	100	3600	100

Source: SAA, FA#22; SAA, 860#7761.

[110] The category 'other' in the two tables contains all occupations performed by less than three percent of the men and women entering the guild.

Approximately two thirds of the women who entered the Antwerp mercers' guild were not direct relatives of existing guild members. On other lists, such as that of the Mechelen gardeners, nearly all women paid only half the entrance fee or less, suggesting a clear advantage for those from guild families.[111] Given that the Antwerp gardeners' guild barred single women from joining unless they were daughters of guild members, this pattern is unsurprising. While each town's guild regulations differed, they often shared similar features and may have drawn inspiration from one another.[112] It is possible that, as in Antwerp, the Mechelen gardeners' guild did not accept unmarried women unless they had familial ties to the guild.

While the percentage of female guild entrants on all records was relatively small, they constituted a diverse group. Half of the new female Antwerp mercers and nearly all the female Mechelen gardeners are identified with diminutive first names (Lynken, Mariken, Claarken, etc.). This designation may indicate that they were younger, never-married women. Retail trade may have been an ideal option for them between adulthood and marriage, due to its low entry costs and flexible time allocation.[113]

While studies indicate that women were significantly involved, and even predominant, in mercery-related trades outside of guild structures, their membership within the Mechelen and Antwerp guilds appears to have been limited.[114] However, the guild entrance lists, which record a small number of women, do not fully represent women's participation in these trades. Ariadne Schmidt and Elise van Nederveen Meerkerk estimate that approximately seventy-five percent of male guild entrants were married, with 'at least half of them' being assisted by their wives, suggesting a larger female workforce operating within the guild without

---

[111] SAM, Hoveniers-, fruiteniers- en mandenmakersambacht 16; SAM, Hoveniers-, fruiteniers- en mandenmakersambacht 17.

[112] In 1429, the Antwerp butchers' guild even sent letters to the butchers' guilds of Leuven, Brussels, and Ghent, seeking advice on a conflict between the guild and a master's son-in-law. Bisschops, 'Oudt Register, Mette Berderen, 1336–1439 (Vervolg)', 28, 104–5. Similarly, a Mechelen bakers' guild ordinance referenced practices from the Brussels bakers' guild when regulating trade practices. SAM, Bakkers 2, 27 December 1476. Transcription by Paul Behets, *Rollen en aanvullende reglementen van de Mechelse ambachten. Deel I*, 31–3.

[113] See also: Simonton, 'Widows and Wenches', 110–1; Van den Heuvel, 'Guilds, Gender Policies and Economic Opportunities for Women'.

[114] Montenach, 'Trades in Lyon', 17–8; Wiesner, 'Paltry Peddlers or Essential Merchants?', 4; Hafter, *Women at Work in Preindustrial France*, 13; Pilorget, 'Circulations Féminines et Encadrement de l'espace Urbain', 16–24.

formal registration.¹¹⁵ Furthermore, the Antwerp and Mechelen guilds faced competition from both male and female informal traders. This retail competition was not always illicit; the sale of certain goods was organized outside the guild framework. For instance, as discussed in chapter 1, ordinances concerning poultry trade refer to *voercoperen* oft *voercoperessen* (male and female sellers), not necessarily formally involved with the Brabantine guilds.¹¹⁶

3. Operating Informally: Main Street or Margins?

Informal competition, both within and outside guild structures, significantly shaped women's labor dynamics in Brabantine towns and influenced labor opportunities for Biscayan women in specific occupations. As outlined in this book's introduction, informal work encompasses activities conducted outside institutions with formal organizational legal capacities, representing a crucial, though often invisible, aspect of urban economies. From an institutional standpoint, informal operation carried inherent risks. Informal traders navigated the normative frameworks established by urban authorities—town councils and guilds—without direct institutional affiliation. The informal market was ubiquitous in the urban economies of both regions, often overlapping with institutionalized work. Such overlaps could result in complementary relationships or lead to conflicts and restrictions. Despite the inherent risks and complications, all actors in the studied occupations engaged in informal work to varying degrees.

Women's participation in informal trade circuits in Brabant and Biscay aligns with broader patterns observed across premodern urban Europe, where women played a significant role in informal economies. Bart Lambert, for instance, found that 28.3 percent of individuals of Flemish origin prosecuted for irregular trade in fifteenth-century Sluis were women.¹¹⁷ However, his findings show the need to distinguish between 'informal' and 'irregular' or 'illicit' trade. As defined here, informal work refers to activities conducted outside institutions with formal legal organizational capacities, but this definition does not inherently render

---

[115] Schmidt and van Nederveen Meerkerk, 'Reconsidering the 'First male-Breadwinner Economy'', 75.

[116] SAA, GA#4253, 25 August 1481.

[117] Lambert, 'Merchants on the Margins', 238.

them unlawful or punishable. While irregular or illicit trade directly contravened established legal ordinances, informal trade often existed in a grey area, operating beyond institutional oversight or organization without necessarily violating regulations. Many urban (and rural) residents engaged in such practices, and not all informal activities were documented in written sources precisely because they were not always penalized.

Urban authorities often tolerated informal trade, as it was both impractical and economically unwise to suppress all unauthorized commercial activities. Even when trade explicitly violated regulations, town governments prioritized controlling only the most centralized and lucrative sectors. Small-scale informal activities frequently went unrecorded, as they were crucial for the distribution of goods to people in the lower strata of the towns.[118] Informal trade, as Susanne Schöts has argued, ensured the distribution of goods that formal traders could not sell, making it particularly vital for lower-income urban residents.[119] This dynamic underscores the flexibility of urban economies in Brabant and Biscay, where economic necessity often took precedence over strict regulatory enforcement. The principal distinction between the two regions concerns the nature of competition between formal and informal traders; in Biscay, unlike Brabant, informal saleswomen did not directly compete with formal guild members.

Informal markets were influenced by the rules, norms, and barriers imposed by established socioeconomic institutions, as well as by spatial organization. This influence was particularly evident in Brabant, where formal trade, organized through guilds, was not only regulated institutionally but also physically separated from informal trade. The structure of the meat trade in Leuven and the fish trade in Mechelen illustrate this dynamic. In Leuven, the butchers' guild operated as a predominantly masculine institution, with household members permitted only limited participation. As a result, the Leuven meat hall emerged as a distinctly gendered economic space, reinforcing the boundary between formal and informal markets.[120] While informal trade could not easily penetrate this exclusive domain without circumventing regulations—thus veering into

---

[118] Stabel, 'From the Market to the Shop', 102; Jeggle, 'Blurred Rules', 77 and 88–9; Vicente, 'Images and Realities of Work', 133; Montenach, 'Formal and Informal Economy in an Urban Context', 104.

[119] Schöts, 'Female Traders and Practices of Illicit Exchange', 136.

[120] Shennan Hutton has studied the gendered spatial divisions of Ghent's fifteenth-century market halls. Adding the surrounding areas to this analysis reveals the more complex realities of the premodern urban socioeconomic organization. See: Hutton, 'Women, Men, and Markets'.

Figure 6. View of the sixteenth-century Mechelen Meat Hall with its adjacent informal market stalls. Drawing by JB. De Noter, eighteenth century.
Source: Regionale Beeldbank, Verzameling Schoeffer, Sch. 328. "het vleeshuys en oude visch-merkt 1520". Image number: SME001001674. https://www.regionalebeeldbank.be/beeldbank/1113766.

irregular or illicit activity—it was nonetheless tolerated and even relied upon in adjacent spaces. Informal trade flourished just outside the meat hall, with *pensvrouwen* (tripe sellers) and dealers of animal byproducts doing business outside the core activities of the butchers' guild. Structures built to support these trades further illustrate the nuanced boundary between formal and informal markets (a parallel situation existed in Mechelen, as shown in figure 6).[121]

A similar spatial division between formal and informal trade characterized the Mechelen fish trade. The fish market (see figure 7), located adjacent to the old meat hall until the early sixteenth century, served as a site for formal fish transactions. Mechelen's visible informal fish trade, conducted by, among others, female herring sellers, occurred in the streets surrounding the fish market. These informal traders often maintained connections with members of the more exclusive guilds. Neither the guilds nor the informal market operated in isolation; rather, they functioned in a complementary relationship, as evidenced by their physical proximity within the urban Brabantine meat and fish trade.

---

[121] Vandeweerdt, "Van den Vleeschouweren oft Pensvrouwen". A similar significance of structures supporting the informal market is evident in a 1510 source concerning the fishmonger women of Bilbao.

Figure 7. Drawing of the formal section of the medieval fish market on IJzerenleen Street in Mechelen.
Source: Regionale Beeldbank, Verzameling Schoeffer, Sch. 456. "Gezigt der oude vischmerkt in 1500". Image number: SME001001545. https://www.regionalebeeldbank.be/beeldbank/1117173.

*

Who participated in informal trade? The boundaries between formal and informal work were often blurred in premodern towns. Rather, they were two sides of the same coin, practiced by the same actors and contributing to shaping the same labor fields.[122] Participants in informal trade included a diverse group of individuals: local citizens, residents from the surrounding hinterlands, and interregional traders. They engaged in informal activities either as their primary occupation or as a supplementary one, operating both within and outside the constraints of urban regulations.

In Bilbao, as discussed in the previous chapter, informal sellers were the primary distributors of daily commodities. These sellers primarily competed among themselves and with urban residents who purchased products directly from wholesalers. The twenty-one saleswomen listed in the 1470 taxation records as bread, fish, fruit, or retail commodity sellers were part of this group. Their tax amounts suggest they belonged to the lower social strata of Bilbao. Further information about Bilbao's informal workers is provided by ordinances for fishmongers selling in

---

[122] Buchner & Hoffmann-Rehnitz, 'Introduction', 12–21.

the square and at the Portal de Zamudio, in addition to court cases against tradeswomen (discussed in subsequent chapters). While all operated within the informal economy, their positions within it varied significantly. For instance, *cojedoras*—brokers in Bilbao's grain trade—were often perceived as unnecessary intermediaries, and their activities frequently bordered on, or overlapped with, what the town council considered illicit work. Conversely, the nineteen fishmongers with fixed positions at the main square, who rotated market tables, and the four candlemakers who received licenses after exams in 1546 and 1547, represented the more established end of the informal spectrum.

The absence of formal institutions organizing and executing tasks similar to those of itinerant traders made Bilbao's informal market indispensable to both urban residents and visitors. However, precisely because of this lack of formal competition, the Biscayan case study necessitates a careful distinction between informal and irregular work. In Bilbao, informal traders were still bound by a set of regulations that, as discussed in chapter 3, could impose restrictions on women's work similar to those enforced by guilds in Brabantine towns. Nevertheless, Bilbao's informal market was integral to daily life, offering opportunities for women.

In Brabant, the informal market is most visible through its direct competition with the influential craft guilds. Informal traders could be guild members infringing the rules, operating on the margins, or the corporations' informal competitors. In Antwerp and Mechelen, the primary challenge to guild authority did not originate from within the guilds themselves. Premodern towns boasted vibrant informal markets that operated alongside formalized trade. Excluding women from guild membership did not effectively address the issue of women's significant roles in "networks that directly competed with the guilds," as Anne Montenach also observed for early modern Lyon.[123]

The Brabantine guilds, often backed by town councils, sought to limit both competition from the informal market and the participation of women within it. This dynamic is particularly evident in Mechelen's fish trade, where the fishmongers' guild controlled various segments of the industry, aiming to monopolize the lucrative wholesale market and the sale of imported sea fish. As noted earlier, a group of itinerant women traders known as *harincvrouwen* sold herring, directly competing with

[123] Montenach, 'Trades in Lyon', 28.

guild members engaged in the same trade.¹²⁴ Despite this competition, the guild could not entirely exclude informal traders from the market. Further complicating matters, some of these herring sellers were wives of guild members, providing an additional incentive for the guild to tolerate their presence.

A similar situation unfolded in Antwerp, where the *uitdraagsters* operated alongside the old clothes sellers' guild. While these women did not hold prestigious positions within the trade, they could not be entirely banned either. Overall, in Brabantine towns, the guild-based organization of work created complex interactions between formal and informal trade—a dynamic not visible in Biscay. While guilds sought to maintain control over key sectors, informal traders continued to provide alternative channels of commerce.

*

Having established the omnipresence of the informal economy in both Brabant and Biscay, we now turn to the types of work conducted informally and the motivations of informal traders. Based on sources from these two regions, three observations emerge. First, informal work could occur by breaking the rules of a formal context. However, the absence of formal institutions in Bilbao means that we cannot detect this type of informal work in the Biscayan case study. Second, even in the informal economy, rules had to be followed. However, in both regions, the informal market becomes visible only through infringements of these rules. Third, the livelihoods of men and women in Brabant and Biscay depended on the informal market. Necessity provided ample ground for the informal economy and could lead to conflicts not only between authorities and informal traders but also among the traders themselves.

(1) In the area of trade, mostly small-scale, ordinances restricting women's opportunities were instituted by guilds and town governments. However, in an economy marked by scarcity, all town residents needed to generate income. When unable to earn a livelihood through formal institutions or perceive an opportunity to supplement their formal income, they resorted to the informal market.¹²⁵ In Brabantine towns,

---

[124] SAM, Visverkopers 14, 26 July 1454.
[125] Humphries & Sarasúa, 'Off the Record: Reconstructing Women's Labor Force Participation', 41; Janssens, *The Rise and Decline of the Male Breadwinner Family?*, 5; Howell, 'The Problem of Women's Agency', 23–4.

guild affiliation created a more distinct, yet complex, boundary between informal and irregular work. Through town council ordinances, guilds regulated occupational participation. Guild members could engage in informal activities, such as holding dual occupations or involving household members without formal guild membership. For example, in 1440, Simon Beys, formerly a tailor, joined the Antwerp old clothes sellers' guild after leaving the tailors' guild. However, the deans of the old clothes sellers accused him of continuing to practice as a tailor, which was in violation of guild privileges. As a result, Simon faced a choice between the two occupations.[126] Being a member of one guild did not prevent him from simultaneously engaging in another trade.

Brabantine sources primarily reveal attempts to expand work activities beyond formal boundaries through records of punishment—instances where work crossed into irregularity. For example, the Mechelen fishmongers' guild punished the widow Eskens and Romment Quistwater's wife for selling outside the designated market area. These activities were deemed irregular solely due to guild regulations.[127] Similarly, herring sellers, who were not guild members, operated informally because the guild defined their trade as such. Consequently, guild affiliation often blurred the lines between informal and irregular activities, as the guild itself determined the parameters of both.

The Brabantine guild-centered regulation has no parallel in Biscay. In Bilbao, illegality stemmed from violating town council regulations governing traders, with punishment contingent on apprehension, as in Brabant. However, unlike Brabant, where guilds dictated occupational boundaries, Bilbao lacked such corporations. Consequently, punishment was not levied for performing guild-defined work. Instead, the town council policed women's labor activities based on the nature of the activity itself, not on the identity of the person performing it. For example, ordinances concerning fishmongering addressed violations such as fraud, disputes, or disruptions, reflecting the council's focus on maintaining order and market integrity, rather than enforcing guild monopolies.

Women fishmongers in Bilbao were granted specific rights and activities but occasionally expanded their trade by disregarding these regulations. In the next chapter, we will encounter Mayora de Iturribalzaga.

[126] Bisschops, 'Het 2e oudt register, in 't perkament gebonden 1438–1459 (Vervolg)', 30, 390–1.
[127] SAM, Visverkopers 321, fol. 29r, 1499.

She was among the fishmongers granted a fixed market stall in the 1510 ordinance. However, from 1525 onward, she engaged in a prolonged conflict with Bilbao's town council due to her side business. Rather than limiting herself to sardines and dried fish, which offered limited profit, Mayora illicitly included fresh fish in her merchandise, despite repeated council prohibitions. Mayora and other tradeswomen chose to expand their trading activities against the town council's wishes, thereby becoming both irregular and informal actors in Bilbao's urban economy.

(2) The informal market was not just a side business for urban inhabitants. It was crucial to the income of many people. Given the nature of the written documentation, examples of non-irregular informal trade are scarce. However, it was likely more accepted in both regions than is typically acknowledged. For example, Willem de Bruyne and Kateline Dierix, the married couple who sold fish oil at Antwerp's Slijkpoort, are a perfect example of urban residents probably making a full-time living with their informal activities. Six days after the Antwerp governors gave them permission to trade at the Slijkpoort, they petitioned for permission to dock a boat to bring their merchandise to their market stand. Moreover, they rented this area from another Antwerp citizen. Even with their business being informal, the married couple was invested in it.[128]

In Mechelen, an example from the town's wool combers and carders demonstrates that informal work did not always generate conflicts with the town council and guilds. In 1450, the council issued new regulations for wool combers and carders, requiring citizens engaged in wool combing to swear an oath before town and guild officials. In accordance with these regulations, three men and two women appeared before the council to affirm their participation in the process of textile production.[129] This example highlights how formal regulations could integrate informal practices into the structured framework of guild-controlled industries in Mechelen. A similar stability characterized informal activities among urban residents in Bilbao. For instance, the council mandated that *regateras* selling oil and candles in shops maintain a stock of both products.[130] This requirement necessitated investment in commodities. Informal

---

[128] Bisschops, 'Het 2e oudt register, in 't perkament gebonden 1438–1459 (Vervolg)', 30, 41–2.
[129] SAM, Magistraat (Ordonnantiën) Serie III, nr.2, 17v, 15 June 1450.
[130] Enríquez Fernández et al., *Libro de acuerdos y decretos municipales*, fol. 98r–99r, 28 November 1509.

workers were not criminals or illicit adversaries of the urban economy. Rather, they were skilled and enterprising tradespeople.

(3) The town councils' tolerance of informal trade did not guarantee a stable income for informal vendors. In addition to dealing with municipal regulations, they also had to deal with competitors, whether formal or informal. The importance of informal activities for people's livelihoods is reflected in the mutual conflicts between traders. The nature and intensity of these disputes are particularly well documented in sources from Bilbao. The court cases of the Chancellery in Valladolid provide extensive arguments, offering valuable insights into the activities and motivations of the parties involved. One such case vividly illustrates direct competition among Bilbao's fishmongers—who, interestingly, appear united in all other sources.

In 1511, Catalina Nafarra and María Pérez de Bermeo clashed at the Bilbao fish market in a conflict probably rooted in commercial rivalry. Both women were fishmongers, but their accounts of the altercation differ significantly. According to María, she was selling fish when Catalina approached her "with a knife in her hand." After bystanders intervened and took the knife away, Catalina allegedly attacked María, striking her, pulling her hair, and publicly insulting her. María insisted that the attack was unprovoked, claiming she had merely been selling fish to her niece. Catalina, however, presented an entirely different version of events. She accused María of stealing her customers, assaulting her, and calling her a miscreant. According to Catalina, María resorted to violence when her alleged schemes failed. She further defended herself by stating that "if she had a knife in her hand, it was only because she was cutting fish for customers."[131] Catalina also claimed that the charges were a coordinated effort by María and other fishmongers to eliminate competition. The judges ultimately ruled in María's favor, concluding that "because of this lawsuit, it seems that Catalina is a riotous woman and causes much uproar and annoyance." As a result, Catalina was banished from Bilbao for six months and received a heavy fine.[132]

The conflict between Catalina Nafarra and María Pérez de Bermeo may have escalated to the Royal Chancellery due to María's connections—she was related to a clerk of Bilbao. Similar disputes between fishmongers

[131] "Lo otro porque si la dicha parte tenia algun cuchillo en la mano [...] fue por cortar su pescado para vender a los que venian por ello [...]." ARChV, Registro de ejecutorias, 273,12, 21 April 1512.

[132] "Catalina parece por este proceso ser mujer revoltosa y causadora de muchas revueltas y enojos." *Ibidem.*

or other traders may have been resolved informally or never reached the higher courts. However, it is likely that Catalina and María were not the only fishmongers engaged in conflicts over clients and accusations of unfair competition. While institutions such as guilds imposed regulations to manage both internal and external competition, informal traders lacked such protection. Without a formal structure to mediate disputes or establish collective rules, competition among them may have been even fiercer.

The fishmongers were not the only saleswomen in Bilbao who left traces of their internal struggles. Fishmongers are stereotypically portrayed as "troublemakers, constantly engaging in scolding and fighting."[133] Other court cases, such as the conflict between a group of young women involved in Bilbao's linen trade, show the same assertive economic competitors. Ibañez de Mendieta was a young woman who probably had been able to move up from fishmongering to the linen trade through family connections. While these connections might have furthered her business, she kept struggling with her colleagues, who saw the newcomer as a competitor. In 1561, Ana, Catalina, and Antonia de Escalante, three sisters, entered into an open conflict with Ibañez in an attempt to protect their business.[134]

Competition among traders was prevalent across various contexts. In Brabant, evidence reveals the strong emotions that often accompanied trade conflicts. The sentence book of the Antwerp mercers' guild records 17 cases involving women accused of gossip and verbal aggression, some directly linked to market disputes. Similarly, the sentence books of Mechelen's fishmongers document frequent market disruptions, where both men and women were punished for disorderly conduct. Unlike the detailed court records from the Chancellery, these sentence books provide only brief summaries, limiting the depth of analysis possible. While some conflicts may have been rooted in personal disputes, competition clearly played a role in many interpersonal tensions. This factor is evident in the case of Beyken Vermeulen, a fishmonger's wife, who was sentenced for spreading the rumor that Grietken Venne falsely sold *ale* (eel) as if it were high-quality *palinc* (pike eel).[135] Through ordinances, the Brabantine town councils sought to mitigate these conflicts. In Mechelen, the gardeners' guild even issued specific regulations to prevent slander among women.[136]

---

[133] Van den Heuvel, 'The Multiple Identities of Early Modern Dutch Fishwives,' 587–8.
[134] ARChV, Sala de Vizcaya, 561, 2, 3 March 1563.
[135] SAM, Visverkopers 321, 135r, 1535.
[136] SAM, Hoveniers-, fruiteniers- en mandenmakersambacht 7, 12 December 1491.

At the heart of many of these internal struggles was economic competition, as both male and female traders sought to secure their livelihoods and support their households.

*

Given its complex and interconnected nature with formal settings and the legal/illegal dichotomy, 'informal work' is crucial for understanding women's work opportunities. For women, the informal market represented an extension of the economic system in which they operated. Within the context of guilds and institutionalized work, their opportunities were constrained by patriarchal mechanisms (see chapter 3). The lives of many men and women in premodern towns were broadly shaped by these formal structures, with limited variability. The informal market did not dismantle these structures; as demonstrated in the Brabantine and Biscayan case studies, it subtly expanded the operating space for men and women. Particularly in small-scale market-oriented work, the informal market provided a framework for women to engage in economic activities that were not entirely tied to the existing institutional, often masculine, structures.

4. Conclusion

Understanding women's work activities in Brabant and Biscay requires analyzing key socioeconomic institutions that structured their labor: the household, craft guilds in Brabant, and the informal market. This chapter has demonstrated how these institutions functioned and interacted differently in each region.

In Brabant, strong ties existed between guilds and the household economy, with women's work often dependent on both. Although less visible, the informal market was undoubtedly present, used by both formal and informal workers—sometimes alongside guild activities, sometimes in defiance of guild regulations. In contrast, Biscay lacked a significant cooperative household economic unit and guild presence in small-scale trade. Despite the nuclear couple being favored by Biscayan customary law, household cooperation in occupations not organized by institutions with legal capacities, often related to interregional trade, was limited.

Instead, Biscay had a well-developed informal market, where women primarily occupied intermediary roles in small-scale commodity trade.

The varying market structures and institutional influence shaped women's work opportunities differently in each region. However, attributing these differences solely to institutional factors would be reductive. Institutional impact was intertwined with social status, market sectors, broader socioeconomic contexts, and the diverse categories of women. For instance, a married woman in the Antwerp mercers' guild faced distinct labor opportunities and restrictions compared to a fishmonger's wife in the same town. Similarly, in Bilbao, a young sardine seller could advance through connections with influential urban residents.[137] Their individual experiences were shaped by a complex interplay of factors.

Institutions functioned differently, and their impact on women's economic roles was not fixed. Nevertheless, in the patriarchal societies of Antwerp, Mechelen, and Bilbao, institutions with legal and organizational authority generally restricted women's economic activities, whether deliberately or inadvertently. As a result, women often found ways to navigate, challenge, or even leverage these institutional frameworks to secure their livelihoods. The next chapter examines how these patriarchal institutions responded when women's market activities pushed beyond established boundaries.

---

[137] This example is based on the court case between María Ibañez de Mendieta and the three de Escalante sisters. See page X. ARChV, Sala de Vizcaya, 561, 2, 3 March 1563.

CHAPTER 3

Limiting Women's Work

Catalina Nafarra, the fishmonger we encountered in the previous pages, was portrayed in the records as a riotous and disruptive woman. No such judgments were recorded for her Brabantine counterparts—such as the widows and wives of Mechelen fishmongers who violated guild bylaws—even though women appear frequently in Brabantine sentence books as well. For the urban authorities documenting these cases, one thing was clear: women's labor, like men's, required regulation. Irregular practices were targeted, even when authorities lacked the means to suppress them effectively. Yet beyond the regulation of market conduct, women's work was also shaped by distinctly gendered controls. In both Brabant and Biscay, institutions such as town councils and guilds imposed legal and structural limitations on women's economic activities. This chapter explores these constraints by way of three guiding questions: Which institutions restricted women's work? Which activities were targeted? And how—and why—were such restrictions enforced?

We will see that both economic and gendered motivations shaped how guilds and town governments regulated women's work. In Bilbao, women were rarely prosecuted for participating in informal trade per se, but rather for engaging in specific practices deemed unacceptable. With no socioeconomic institutions beyond the town council to support them, women were directly subject to the council's restrictions. Cultural norms—often implicit but deeply rooted—also steered women into particular economic roles. In some sectors, women did not simply compete with male traders tied to powerful institutions; they dominated. Still, the council's economic concerns did not preclude the use of gender as a regulatory tool. Many restrictions on small-scale women's work in Bilbao reflected the town's socioeconomic organization, yet they were also underpinned by gendered assumptions and values.

In Antwerp and Mechelen, women were penalized both for working in guild-monopolized trades and for engaging in prohibited practices. The later restrictions visible in the Brabantine sources show mechanisms similar to those in Bilbao. Economic concerns certainly influenced how women's work was regulated, but the masculine, hierarchical nature of Brabantine guilds added a further layer to the categorization of labor as legitimate or illicit. While both regions show that economic motivations played a role, the Brabantine case reveals more explicitly how gendered cultural norms were enforced through guild structures.

This chapter contributes to scholarship on the limiting effects of institutions on women's labor, particularly in the Brabantine context.[1] It also shows that the reach of guild restrictions extended further than previously assumed. A case study of the Mechelen fishmongers reveals that even the household economic unit—typically considered the anchor of women's participation in guild activities—was not immune to the guilds' regulatory efforts.[2] Still, as in Bilbao, women in Antwerp and Mechelen also faced restrictions that were not solely rooted in gendered exclusion. This initial exploration of the guild effect, which will be developed further in chapter 4, highlights the need for a more nuanced understanding of how different institutions shaped women's labor positions and interacted in organizing the urban workforce.

The chapter begins with an analysis of the Biscayan case, focusing on how the town council restricted women's work in certain sectors for economic and cultural reasons. The council's goals likely included maintaining market order, regulating economic actors, and safeguarding public revenue through excises, with gendered justifications often serving as tools to these ends. The chapter then turns to Antwerp and Mechelen, where both guilds and town governments imposed limitations on women's work. Though separate entities, the guilds held substantial influence over town governance, and their masculine character shaped both institutional policy and legal outcomes. Finally, we consider how women's economic opportunities changed over the course of the sixteenth century. While the extent and nature of these changes remain subjects of scholarly debate, the Brabantine and Biscayan sources suggest a certain decline in women's opportunities within formal institutions. I argue that this shift was driven less by broad structural transformations than by changes in the organization of specific sectors of the urban economy.

---

[1] Ogilvie, *A Bitter Living*, 326–31; Bennett, *Ale, Beer, and Brewsters in England*, 60–76.

[2] Strong cases of women's opportunities in the context of the household unit can be found in, among others: Simonton, *Gender in the European Town*, 26–52; Howell, *Women, Production, and Patriarchy*.

1. Bilbao's Council and the "Protection of the Consumer"

In 1488, the Bilbao town council promulgated an ordinance on the fish trade, citing that many people—"men, women, menservants and servant girls"—were transporting fish into town and selling individual fish ('per eye') without first having them approved by the town's official fish weighers, as required.[3] The council addressed all individuals involved in these illicit practices, not just women.[4] Rather than invoking gender as a justification, the ordinance was framed as a measure to protect the town's excise income. Bilbao's ordinances rarely relied on gendered or patriarchal rhetoric. While the council did address women in ordinances concerning trades where female labor predominated, it seldom excluded them outright. Instead, the justifications were primarily economic.

However, economic arguments were not free from gendered assumptions. Gendered ideas influenced which trades were deemed problematic and how women's work was evaluated. A few ordinances suggest that the council's decisions were shaped by an awareness of gender roles. Moreover, women's dominance in certain market sectors was itself a product of culturally embedded gender norms. Thus, the economic motivations behind restrictions on women's work must be interpreted within their broader patriarchal context. Finally, the contrast between normative regulations and actual judicial outcomes reveals the council's practical awareness of the gendered nature of labor in Bilbao. A sixteenth-century court case against a group of female fishmongers shows that gender could be explicitly invoked in court proceedings, even if it was not the principal motivation for intervention, highlighting how patriarchal institutions imposed gendered limitations in both subtle and overt ways.

Earlier studies have argued that the scrutiny of the female occupations in Bilbao originated in the council's suspicion of these women.[5] The *narratios* of several ordinances cite fraud and offenses. In an ordinance

---

[3] "[...] que ningunas nin algunas presonas, ommes nin mugeres, moços nin moças, qualesquier que sean, truxieren a esta villa para vender [...] pescados que por peso se ayan de dar, suelen ser pesados, que en tal caso non las puedan vender por ojo saluo por peso pesado [...]." Enríquez Fernández et al., *Ordenanzas municipales de Bilbao (1477–1520)*, fol. 36v–37r, 17 December 1488.

[4] Jessica Dijkman also emphasized the importance of controlling public weights in late medieval Holland—a concern that aligns closely with the Bilbao town council's efforts to regulate who managed the public scales. See: Dijkman, *Shaping Medieval Markets*.

[5] Rivera Medina, 'Cuerpos de mujer en el mundo laboral bilbaíno', 4; Iziz & Iziz, *Historia de las mujeres en Euskal Herria*, 242.

of 1509, the council stated that no one "nor any woman" could put up stalls obstructing passage through the streets.[6] This type of explicit reference to women might reflect suspicion of female traders. However, it is also possible that the council addressed women because they were crucial actors in sectors that required supervision: food trades and retail sales. Since no other Bilbao institution organized these trades, the council was left as the only body with the responsibility and legal capability to regulate them. The abundance of ordinances regulating their work might, as such, be no different from the many ordinances about guild work in the Brabantine towns. Moreover, the conclusion about suspicion might primarily reflect later views on Basque women from contemporary historians rather than what can be concluded from the sources of that era.[7] Women's participation in these occupations had been normalized. As such, the council's objective most often was simply "situating and regulating their [the women's, ed.] activities, rather than preventing them from operating businesses."[8]

Even if the regulation of small-scale trade did not stem from gendered suspicions, the council kept a close watch on women and their trading activities. The motivation for most of these ordinances is what José Ángel García de Cortázar et al. have called the protection of the consumer. Bilbao's council wanted to guarantee access to food supplies for all citizens.[9] By setting rules and organizing the town economy, the council claimed that it was contributing to the common good of the town, much like guilds and municipal authorities did elsewhere in Europe.[10] Moreover, as we will see, as elsewhere in Europe, in Bilbao, gender could be used as an argument, and women were subject to certain gendered restrictions. The

---

[6] "Otrosy, manda que se goarde la hordenança que ninguno nin ningunas personas non sean hosados de thener en las cales, fuera de los tableros, ningund enbaraço nin enpacho alguno, nin se asyenten ningunas mugeres nin otras personas en syllas fuera de los tableros, so pena de çient maravedis a cada vno por cada bez." Enríquez Fernández et al., *Libro de acuerdos y decretos municipales*, fol. 26v–27r.

[7] Different essays in the *Itsas memoria. Revista de estudios marítimos del País Vasco*, 8 (2016) point to the role of women in the Basque fish industry and the bad reputation of Basque women fishmongers from the seventeenth century onwards, when the fish industry lost its importance in some towns.

[8] Montenach & Simonton, 'Afterword', 224.

[9] García de Cortázar et al., *Vizcaya en la edad media*, 2:329.

[10] Haemers, 'Governing and Gathering about the Common Welfare of the Town'; Solórzano Telechea, 'Ideologies and Political Participation of the Commons in Urban Life'; Lecuppre-Desjardin & Van Bruaene, 'Introduction. Du Bien Commun à l'idée de Bien Commun', 1–9; Howell, 'Whose "common good"? Parisian market regulation, c. 1300–1800'.

difference is that in Bilbao, this rationale happened without excluding women from certain trades.

One sector where the council's so-called protection of the consumer is evident is the trade of candles and oil. As discussed in the previous chapter, the *regateras que venden aceite y candela* were saleswomen operating under licenses from local authorities. To open a shop, they needed permission from the sole institution in Bilbao that was authorized to grant it. Both the weights of the commodities and the prices the saleswomen could charge were predetermined.[11] Additionally, the council required that "each of them at all times have their shops stocked with candles and oil, [...] and to have both oil and candles, and not one without the other."[12] This combination of regulations reveals that even informal saleswomen in Bilbao were not free from institutional oversight, even though they were not regulated by traditional economic institutions like guilds. Crucially, however, the council did not aim to exclude women from these trades. Instead, it ensured that the *regateras* would have exclusive rights to sell oil and candles, as long as they adhered to the stipulated requirements.

Bilbao's town council appears to have employed similar economic arguments in regulating the grain trade. In 1482, the council introduced new regulations for bread sellers, citing that "the bread sellers were accustomed to coming to the market and buying many *fanegas* of grain every week [...] which they would send to others overseas." According to the council, this practice led to grain shortages in Bilbao, prompting them to again fix the quantities, method, and prices the *panaderas* had to uphold when buying grain.[13] Similarly, in the neighboring town of Guernica, the town council implemented comparable regulations, accusing bread

---

[11] See, for example: Enríquez Fernández et al., *Ordenanzas municipales de Bilbao (1477–1520)*, fol. 25r–26v, 19 September 1487.

[12] "Otrosy, se obligaron de tener cada vna todos tienpos su tyenda abasteçida de candelas e aseyte, e de dar de la suerte e en los preçios susodichos e de tener todas aseyte e candela e non el vno syn el otro [...]." Enríquez Fernández et al., *Libro de acuerdos y decretos municipales*, fol. 98r–99r, 28 November 1509.

[13] "[...] por quanto las panaderas desta villa han acostunbrado e acostumbraban de venir al mercado e de conprar cada semana muchas fanegas de trigo todos tienpos, en manera que pujava el trigo en grand cantidad; e avn, conpraban en grand cantidad para algunas presonas, las quales diz que lo enbiavan por la mar, en manera que esta villa reçibia grand dapno [...]." Enríquez Fernández et al., *Ordenanzas municipales de Bilbao (1477–1520)*, fol. 17r–17v, 11 January 1482.

sellers of purchasing excessive amounts of grain, thereby preventing other residents from buying grain for their own use.[14]

Throughout the fifteenth and sixteenth centuries, recurring regulations addressed various trades in daily commodities, prohibiting their export from Bilbao. While the council's claims of fraud and economic damage in the ordinances' *narratios* served to legitimize the regulations, the persistent use of this argument in both ordinances and court cases suggests a genuine concern. This concern was particularly focused on ensuring the availability of food stock within Bilbao. The many regulations for Bilbao's female sellers of food and other daily commodities, discussed in the previous chapters, were often the direct results of the council's prioritization of local supply.

Even with the council's regulations of women's informal work often stemming from their dominating presence in small-scale market segments, this directive originated in a deeper-seated gender division of the town's economy. It is significant that artisan occupations such as leather production, butchering, and knife making, regulated in town ordinances, show no evidence of female involvement in Bilbao. Instead, women overwhelmingly populated retail sectors, highlighting an inherently gendered division of labor that operated without a necessity for explicit institutional intervention or limitations. These sectors catered to the economic circumstances detailed in chapter 1, primarily attracting women driven by financial motivations. While the council's regulations in Bilbao may not have been solely motivated by gender biases, they were nevertheless influenced by and contributed to this fundamental gendered division of labor. While in Brabant, we will observe that institutional limitations imposed by guilds and town councils clearly delineate gendered divisions, the situation in Bilbao reveals a deeper cultural layer that influenced the limitations on women's work, operating independently of formal institutional constraints. However, the more deliberate processes of limitation were not always driven by gender in Biscay.

*

[14] Bolumburu Arizaga, Ríos Rodríguez & Del Val Valdivieso, 'La villa de Guernica en la baja edad media', 218–9.

Women's informal work in Bilbao was deeply embedded in the organization of the town economy. The council, therefore, typically intervened only when certain behaviors were deemed harmful to the town, its economy, or its residents. Because informal work became irregular only through the council's judgment, there was no clearly defined or fixed boundary around it. The council of Bilbao cited harm to the town's economy as the rationale for prohibiting specific activities. However, the council's focus on economic practices did not preclude the use of gendered arguments. Gendered reasoning could be invoked to legitimize the economic motives behind regulatory measures. In 1526, for instance, the council accused the female fishmongers of habitually purchasing all the available fish for themselves and their associates, then reselling it at extortionate prices. As a result, the council prohibited sellers of dried fish and sardines from buying fresh fish for any purpose other than personal consumption.[15] One of the fishmongers, Mayora de Iturribalzaga, contested this new ordinance. The ensuing court cases clearly show how Bilbao's female fishmongers had to contend with restrictions justified through gendered arguments, despite being allowed to trade without formal organization.

Mayora de Iturribalzaga was a citizen of Bilbao. She was a married woman, although we know nothing about her husband beyond his name. Her trade activities likely began in 1509, when the town council granted her permission to resell fish within the town.[16] As one of the informal saleswomen still acknowledged by the council, Mayora was subject to its regulations. A year later, she was involved in a petition the fishmongers presented to the town council (see chapter 4).[17] She appealed to the *Corregidor* of Biscay—a royal representative with authority over town councils—requesting the annulment of the new regulation. In February 1528, the *Corregidor* ruled in the council's favor. Mayora was found not guilty and did not have to pay additional fines, but the ordinance remained in effect. Mayora pursued her case at the royal courts in Valladolid, but without success. All courts rejected her appeal.[18]

The 1526 ordinance, stating that "no one, neither man nor woman, sellers of dried fish nor sardines nor others, can sell fresh fish imported

---

[15] AFB, Municipal, 0304/001/011, 1532.

[16] Enríquez Fernández et al., *Libro de acuerdos y decretos municipales*, 55r, 4 July 1509.

[17] Enríquez Fernández et al., *Ordenanzas municipales de Bilbao (1477–1520)*, fol. 276r–279r, 2 October 1510.

[18] AFB, Municipal, 0304/001/011.

into the town," was not the first one prohibiting these practices.[19] Already in 1515, the council promulgated an ordinance prohibiting the *mugeres pescaderas* from selling fresh fish in bulk because of their malpractices.[20] Although Mayora de Iturribalzaga denied performing the practices the town council accused her of, it is likely the council did indeed make this ordinance because too many sardine sellers committed fraud while selling fresh fish. As Ariadne Schmidt also found for the early modern northern Low Countries, the Bilbao fishmongers might have "included illegal activities among their living strategies out of necessity. The thin line that divided legal from illegal activities was often easily transgressed—deliberately or in some cases possibly unintentionally."[21] In the case of Mayora, this was the type of fish she sold, its quality, and the price she charged for it. However, the economic argumentation and protection of the consumer alone were insufficient to convince the higher judges. While the ordinances of Bilbao mostly relied on economic arguments, the court cases reveal the appearance of gendered arguments.

At court, Mayora de Iturribalzaga had to base her arguments on her good name and experience as a fishmonger, but even more so on her rights as a citizen of Bilbao. She repeatedly stated that all citizens had the right to trade freely—a privilege included in Biscayan customary law. Bilbao's town council, on the other hand, could engage directly. They attacked Mayora and her labor practices, claiming that Mayora "and her colleagues from the aforesaid occupation of selling fresh fish committed much fraud and malpractice,"[22] accusing her directly based on economic arguments. But they also attacked Mayora personally, claiming that "Mayora was an arrogant and ill-reputed woman who swindled many people, both men and women, who wanted to buy fresh fish from her."[23] The personal attack on Mayora made for strong arguments in court.

---

[19] "Hordenaron e mandaron que ningunas ni algunas presonas, varones ni mugeres, vendedores del pescado cecial ni sardinas ni de otra manera de oy dia en adelante no sean osados de tomar cargo de vender nigun pescado fresco que a esta dicha villa veniere ni lo vendan [...]." AFB, Municipal, 0304/001/011, fol. 4r.

[20] Enríquez Fernández et al., *Libro de acuerdos y decretos municipales*, 20v, 8 May 1515.

[21] Schmidt, *Prosecuting Women*, 248.

[22] "[...] la dicha Mayora de Yturribalçaga e otros sus conpaneras en el dicho oficio de vender del dicho pescado fresco abian fecho e hazian muchos fraudes e malicias [...]." AFB, Municipal, 0304/001/011, fol. 6v–7r.

[23] "Lo otro por que la dicha Mayora abia y hera mujer muy soberbia e de mal decir e tal que abia denostado a muchas personas an si onbres como mujeres muy honrados que yban por pescado fresco [...]." *Ibidem*, fol. 7r–7v.

Particularly interesting is the council's argument that "since Mayora was a woman, she did not know how to cut fish properly or like the fish cutters did it, and she cut it in a way that left it torn apart, mashed, and ruined."[24] This statement is one of the few instances where the Bilbao council argued against a specific labor activity performed by a woman purely from a gendered perspective. Most arguments against Mayora, and those found in the majority of Bilbao ordinances and court cases, were economically based. The question remains why they considered this argument valuable enough to present in court. A 1548 ordinance mandated that Bilbao's fish sellers had their commodities weighed and priced by an inspector appointed by the town council before being allowed to sell them.[25] The issue in the 1527 court case with Mayora cutting the fish might not have been about her gender per se; rather, if it were not for her gender, she would not have been able to perform this task in the capacity of a town official. In Bilbao, as in other places, political roles or roles requiring authority over a group of men and women (in this case, fishmongers and large-scale fish traders) were exclusively occupied by men. Although Mayora might have been perfectly capable of cutting fish without spoiling it, she was not permitted to do so because, as a woman, she could never receive formal permission from the council. Thus, her gender provided a convenient argument.

In the court case between Mayora de Iturribalzaga and the council of Bilbao, Mayora presented a letter from the town councils of Bermeo and Plentzia, two neighboring towns. These maritime towns provided Bilbao with fish. Fishmongers from Bermeo and Plentzia went to Bilbao in little boats called *pinazas* to sell fish, among others, to the Bilbao fishmongers for resale. The two town councils did not agree with Bilbao's new ordinance and stood up for Mayora's court case. Their reason was the extra tax that the Bermeo and Plentzia fishmongers had to pay to the official inspector in Bilbao: 20 *maravedís* per load of fish. They were not explicitly opposed to or in favor of the women fishmongers who retailed the towns' fish in Bilbao. The gendered argument of Bilbao clearly could not be generalized to an opposition against women practicing this trade. Rather,

---

[24] "Lo otro porque la dicha parte contraria como hera muger no sabia cortar el dicho pescado como se debía no como hazian los cortadores que oy dicha estan puestos e lo que cortaba e daba hera todo despedazado, machucado e perdido [...]." *Ibidem*, fol. 7r.

[25] Rodriguez Herrero, *Ordenanzas de Bilbao, siglos XV y XVI*, 1948.

it may have aligned with the council's broader objective of tightening its grip on Bilbao's fish trade and the tax revenues it generated.

As discussed, gendered arguments in Bilbao's court cases often stemmed from the town council's aim to exert greater control over the town economy and the female actors operating within it. Regulations affecting women in these sectors typically did not ban their occupations outright but focused on economic practices the council sought to curb, mainly to prevent income loss or loss of control over the market. The absence of formal organization helped maintain a clear hierarchy between the legally recognized town council and the informal fishmongers. Bilbao's patriarchal structure may have directed specific groups of women toward certain market segments, but once in place, gender-based limitations were minimal. However, gender remained a criterion through which the town council justified its actions. The conflict involving Mayora de Iturribalzaga is a well-documented example of the council's gendered biases. Clearly aware of Bilbao's gendered labor market divisions, the council selectively used gender arguments to their advantage when this suited them.

2. Brabantine Guilds and Town Councils

In the Brabantine towns, women's work was restricted not only by the guilds but also by the council itself. The council, significantly influenced and often formed by guild members, collaborated closely with the corporations in their efforts to manage informal competitors and address infringements by guild members and their families. Both institutions often shared similar attitudes towards women's work. On the one hand, we observe economic and organizational motives behind regulations and judgments, identical to those of the Bilbao council. The presence of guilds did not solely define the limitations; these restrictions also stemmed from broader economic motives. On the other hand, the council and guilds imposed restrictions on women's economic participation because guilds organized work in Antwerp and Mechelen. Depending on the labor sector, this regulation often meant that female outsiders, and sometimes even insiders, faced economic limitations imposed by the guilds.

The Brabantine municipal governments regulated economic practices, often with the participation or at the instigation of the guilds. However, in some cases, we see the influence of the councils without interference from the corporations other than their seats in the town governments. In the *Correctieboeken* of Antwerp, the town government registered a few sentences given to women for illicit trade activities. The Antwerp *Vierschaar*, a governmental tribunal common in the Low Countries' judicial system, pronounced these sentences.[26] In Antwerp's sentence registers, prosecutions for illicit trade were rare compared to the many prosecutions recorded in similar sentence books that Bart Lambert has studied for fourteenth-century Sluis, in Flanders.[27] Most men and women sentenced in the Antwerp correction books had committed other offenses, such as verbal and/or physical violence, sex offenses, or "lewd ways of life." Offenders were sent on pilgrimages—with the destinations aligned to the weight of their transgressions.

Five sentences illuminate the possible market transgressions that female urban residents might commit. Katelijne Truykens, for example, was sent on a pilgrimage to 's-Hertogenbosch in 1482 because she had encouraged other women to charge an impermissibly high price for rye bread.[28] Janne Vosselmans was sent to the same place in 1445 because she had sold rotten goods.[29] Liesbet Alaerts was sent on a pilgrimage to Mechelen because she had sold tin and lead scales pretending they were silver.[30] Jan Volcmaer and his wife had sold bad-quality bread and were sent on a pilgrimage to Cologne.[31] Finally, in 1438, six women were sent to Mechelen for selling poultry illicitly.[32] While the offenses varied, each case involved attempts to circumvent market regulations.

Some saleswomen, such as the six women who sold poultry illicitly, might have made a main income from a trade not (yet) formalized in a guild. For these trades, the council might have been the primary institution practicing control, similar to how this regulation happened in Bilbao. The problem with the *Correctieboeken* is that the abstracts of the *Vierschaar*'s sentences do not give any legitimation from the town government about the infringements or judgments. As a result, we cannot trace whether the

---

[26] The *Vierschaar* included the bailiff, the mayor, and the aldermen of the city. See: Verwerft, 'De beul in het markizaat van Antwerpen', 232.

[27] Lambert, 'Merchants on the Margins'.

[28] Melis–Taeymans, *Correctieboeck*, 263, 12 August 1482.

[29] *Ibidem*, 163, 18 June 1445.

[30] *Ibidem*, 152, 15 May 1442.

[31] *Ibidem*, 130, 7 May 1438.

[32] *Ibidem*, 125, 29 January 1438.

town government, Antwerp citizens, or the craft guilds instigated them. The sentences mostly prove that the guilds were not the only institutions controlling women's economic activities, even if their efforts were more visible in the source base.

Economic Motivations, Gendered Outcomes

In Brabant, just as in Biscay, local governments and craft guilds shared similar concerns over the effect of irregular trade on the town economy. Punishment for irregular activities by some female urban residents followed the same patterns as punishment for male residents. In 1542, the Antwerp mercers fined the widow of Jan Roelants for selling poor-quality tin.[33] In 1550, she was fined again for the same transgression.[34] The widow was not fined because she engaged in guild work informally. She was probably a guild master's widow, exercising her widow's right. However, her faulty work decreased product quality and, with it, the guild's regulations and reputation.

In the premodern period, the reputation of guilds was a significant factor influencing the trust of potential buyers in guildsmen's and guildswomen's products.[35] The penalties for urban residents who threatened this reputation are not surprising. Male members received sentences for similar offenses. The Mechelen fishmonger Gielis Vijt, for example, was sent on a pilgrimage to Valenciennes and fined two pounds of wax for the guild's chapel because he had offered bad herring for sale by switching crates of good herring with crates of rotting fish.[36] In 1523, the Antwerp mercers sentenced two grocers for selling flawed goods.[37] As Peter Collinge has also found for the eighteenth-century English mercer companies, the guilds in the Brabantine towns "took action against them [men, ed.] for the same reasons that they did against women."[38]

In addition to economic quality, guilds and local governments in the Brabantine towns also policed cultural practices. Town and guild authorities were especially vigilant about urban residents working

---

[33] SAA, GA#4212, fol. 157r, 1542.
[34] SAA, GA#4212, fol. 164r, 1550.
[35] Stabel, 'Workplace Cultures', 98.
[36] SAM, Visverkopers 321, fol. 65r, 1509.
[37] SAA, GA#4212, fol. 127r.
[38] Collinge, 'Guilds, Authority and the Individual', 291.

on Sundays. A 1433 ordinance from the Leuven blacksmiths noted that some guild members were working on Sundays, violating the Church's prescription. As a consequence, the town council of Leuven repeated the prohibition against work on Sundays.[39] The guild sentence books of the Antwerp mercers and the Mechelen fishmongers also show this concern for cultural infringements. In 1517, for example, seven women were fined because they had sold fish on Sundays during Lent.[40] In 1526, the widow of Claes Heyns had to pay three *stuivers* to the mercers' guild of Antwerp because she had worked on Sundays.[41] A few years later, 'fat Liz,' a cheese seller, shouted at the mercers' deans and jurors that they "stunk and were drunks who would use the fines for drinking" after guild authorities fined her for working on Sundays and religious holidays.[42] All of these offenders were allowed to continue selling commodities but were charged fines for the circumstances surrounding some of those sales.

Another reason the guilds punished market offenders regardless of gender was the risk of internal conflict, verbal aggression, and gossip directed at the guilds themselves. In 1436, in Antwerp, three siblings clashed with the deans of the mercers' guild. Jacob and Michiel, the two brothers, worked illicitly as tinsmiths. After repeated warnings, the dean of the guild went to their house to summon them to court. The brothers responded with threats, and their sister—Perinne, who apparently lived with them—spat in his face. The brothers were fined, and Perinne was sent on a pilgrimage to Cologne.[43] Her degrading assault on the dean was clearly taken more seriously than her brothers' (idle) threats.

For Perinne, possibly a young, unmarried woman living with her brothers, the conflict must have carried considerable weight to provoke

---

[39] "Want sommighe vanden gesellen van den smede ambachte – als maerschalcke smede, mesmakers, potghieters, plattijnmakers, sadelmakers ende meer anderen die int selve ambacht zijn – op sondage vigilic dage ende andere geboden heylige dage ontidichlijck gaen sitten wercken ende huer ambacht doen ende oick op huere vinsteren voer huere doren hen werck voortdoen ende voortsetten gelijck oft werckdach waere, gode noch 't gebot van der heyliger Kerken niet aenzien. [...] Daerom is overdragen in der stadtrade met vollen gevolghe dat van nu voertaen man noch wijff van den voirscreven ambachte des meer doen en selen in gheenre wijse." SAL, 4648, fol. 12v–13r, 6 December 1433.

[40] SAM, Visverkopers 321, fol. 85v, 1517.

[41] SAA, GA#4212, fol. 131r, 1526.

[42] "[...] seggende dat wij sloecklars waren ende dat wij den wijn darop dronken ontfangen vor de bruecken [...]." SAA, GA#4212, fol. 142r.

[43] Bisschops, 'Oudt register, mette berderen', 98–9.

such a dramatic reaction. This response is unsurprising, as the conflict revolved around the family's market activities. Similarly, in 1403, Alijt, the servant of the fishmonger Jan van Brussel, was sent on a pilgrimage to Cologne by the Antwerp tribunal. She had "often spread bad words about" her master, "because of which he [had, ed.] jeopardized his life and lost much of his property as a result." Alijt was also banned from Antwerp for two years. The tribunal clearly considered her actions serious and aimed to ensure the behavior would not be repeated.[44] Why Alijt slandered her employer remains unknown, but guilds took verbal slander seriously: loss of prestige could damage both individuals and corporations. Measures taken in response were not tied to gender.[45]

The sentence book of the Antwerp mercers' guild records 51 cases involving the prosecution of offenses by women or by men and women between 1499 and 1539.[46] These prosecutions reflect a regulatory approach like that of the Bilbao town council: women traders, though actively participating in economic life, operated within institutional frameworks shaped by cultural norms and systemic imbalances. The limitations they faced were driven by socioeconomic concerns rather than by an explicit desire to exclude them on the basis of gender alone. Women's appearances in the mercers' sentence books are unsurprising. Laura Van Aert's extensive study of women in this guild highlights their strong position between 1548 and 1748.[47] Her findings, consistent with research from Denmark, France, and Germany, show that the mercers' guild was exceptionally inclusive, admitting both male and female members.[48] The Antwerp mercers' sentence book further illustrates women's presence in the guild. Importantly, none of the recorded sentences appear to have

---

[44] "Item, Alyt, Jans maerte vors., ommedat sy hem diewile quade boetscapen aenbracht heeft daer hi syn lyf omme in avontueren heeft gheset ende syns goeds vele daeromme ghequyst […]." Van den Branden, 'Clementijnboeck 1288–1414', 404–5.

[45] Notwithstanding, there are types of offenses for which guilds and urban governments punished women, as well as those for which we only or mostly see male offenders. Table 9 (p. X) provides an overview of offenses committed by Mechelen fishmongers. It shows that physical violence was exclusively a male offense, while verbal violence was committed by both men and women. Behavioral offenses were closely tied to separate behavioral norms based on gender. About gendered offenses, see: Kamp, *Crime, Gender and Social Control*, 59–85.

[46] SAA, GA#4212; SAA, GA#4276.

[47] Van Aert, 'Tot 'leven of overleven'? Winkelhouden in crisistijd.'

[48] Gold, 'On the Streets and in the Markets'; Jacobsen, 'Women's Work and Women's Role'; Montenach, 'Trades in Lyon'; Schöts, 'Female Traders and Practices of Illicit Exchange'; Wiesner, 'Paltry Peddlers or Essential Merchants?'.

been issued with the goal of excluding women traders. Of the 51 women prosecuted, 17 were sentenced for verbal violence and 12 for fraudulent practices.[49] These rulings stand in stark contrast to the sentences in the Mechelen fishmongers' guild, discussed further below.

*

Most Brabantine ordinances regulating women's work—often in the context of guild activities—do not explicitly exclude women. Implicit gendering through the mere existence of guild structures was probably the norm, as will be discussed in the next section. A notable exception to explicitly prohibited positions for women is found in the old clothes sellers' guilds, where they were barred from serving as *schatters* ('estimators'). In 1436, and again in 1550, the town council of Antwerp promulgated an ordinance that prohibited female guild members from this role.[50] Estimators were responsible for calculating the value of used goods offered for sale by citizens or other town residents, earning slightly more than one percent of the estimated price per valuation.[51] While women could be members of the old clothes sellers guild, the town government clearly delineated gendered roles within it, explicitly excluding women from the estimator position.

Several explanations can be offered for why women were excluded from the estimator position. The Antwerp ordinance reveals that estimators, chosen from craft members, were required to work in pairs to value goods.[52] Rather than reflecting doubts about individual women's abilities, the broader context of patriarchal societies may have contributed to their exclusion from the role of estimator.[53] Town councils and guilds might have viewed women's economic activities as potentially risky, influenced by concerns about misconduct and fraud.[54] Societal distrust of women in public functions may have extended to the old clothes sellers' guild, leading to their exclusion from the estimator role.

---

[49] SAA, GA#4212; SAA, GA#4276.

[50] Geudens, *Dit raect het oude cleercoopers ambacht*, 6; SAA, GA#4273, fol. 7v–13v, 19 January 1550

[51] Geudens, 18–21.

[52] Geudens, *Dit raect het oude cleercoopers ambacht*, 6.

[53] Indeed, as Ariadne Schmidt found for seventeenth-century Leiden, the position of estimator was a typically female position in Leiden, where the work of secondhand dealers was not organized in a guild. Schmidt, *Overleven na de dood*, 136–8.

[54] Wiesner, 'Gender and the Worlds of Work', 212–4; Broomhall, 'Women, Work, and Power', 204–5; Montenach, 'Trades in Lyon', 23; Vicente, 'Images and Realities of Work', 129–30.

A similar concern about regulating women's behavior is evident in the Mechelen town council's ordinance for gardeners, fruit sellers, and basket makers, which prohibited "the women from the foresaid guild" from using "ugly and slandering words against one another."[55] The guild and town government's decision to address this specific behavior among female guild members suggests a perception that women's verbal conflicts were particularly problematic. Men may not have committed such offenses as openly, or the consequences of women doing so were perceived as more severe in a society where their actions could damage not only the reputation of the victim but also that of the male head of the female culprits' household.

The exclusion of women from positions like estimator might, furthermore, reflect broader gendered dynamics within guilds and society. As discussed in Chapter 4, while some guilds admitted female members, positions of authority were predominantly reserved for men. The role of estimator in Antwerp's secondhand trade involved determining the prices at which people could sell their goods, a function that inherently involved authority. Authority, defined as "the publicly recognized right to give direction and expect compliance,"[56] was often considered a male domain, especially in the public sphere. Consequently, women's judgments may not have been granted the same legitimacy in the public eye. Their activities in such a role may have been perceived as less authoritative or easier to contest than men's.

In contrast to Antwerp, the Mechelen old clothes sellers' guild did not explicitly prohibit women from serving as estimators. However, as Danielle van den Heuvel argued regarding retailers' guilds in the early modern northern Low Countries, the absence of explicit gender restrictions does not necessarily imply gender neutrality in practice.[57] It is possible that in the Mechelen guild, an explicit rule excluding women from the estimator position was deemed unnecessary because the exclusion was a generally accepted norm. The town government's ordinance stipulated that guild members could only become estimators after three years of membership but added that "if he is the son of a free old clothes seller [he can make

---

[55] "Item, dat de vrouwen van den voerscreven ambachte die deen tegen dander zelen kynen ende malcanderen lelijke ende schofftelijke woerden van hoeren ende andere geven [...]." SAM, Hoveniers-, fruiteniers- en mandenmakersambacht 7, 12 December 1491.

[56] Ormrod, *Women and Parliament*, 12–3.

[57] Van den Heuvel, 'Guilds, Gender Policies and Economic Opportunities for Women', 129–30.

estimates, ed.] after a year and a half."[58] This emphasis on male lineage suggests a preference for male guild members in this role, potentially excluding masters' daughters.

The prohibition of women acting as estimators in Brabant, similar to Bilbao's ban on women controlling the public weights, reveals a broader pattern of restricting women's roles in evaluating and managing economic value in these societies. The preceding pages have analyzed the institutional constraints on women's labor in Antwerp, Mechelen, and Bilbao. We have seen that despite regional differences, the causes and motivations behind these limitations were often strikingly similar. Cultural norms in these premodern European societies consistently restricted women's economic roles. Urban authorities—whether the town council of Bilbao or the town councils and guilds of Antwerp and Mechelen—played an active role in reinforcing those norms. While similar mechanisms were at work in both regions, the constraints on women's labor were exactly the same. In Brabant, an added layer of restrictions stemmed from the organization of work within the craft guilds themselves.

The 'Guild Effect'

The exclusion of women from certain positions in Brabant closely parallels the findings from Biscay. In both regions, authorities invoked gendered arguments to justify regulatory measures that ultimately served economic interests. However, the exclusion of women from both formal guild positions and informal economic activities appears more deeply rooted in the Brabantine context. In what follows, the economic, cultural, and gendered factors of this 'guild effect'—the exclusionary impact of work organized in craft guilds—will be analyzed. I will argue that the interplay of these factors helps explain the more pronounced exclusion of women from the formal and informal labor landscape in Brabant. The gendered factor especially deserves special attention, as it highlights how guild structures, depending on local contexts, not only restricted independent female traders but also placed limits on women's activities within the household economic unit.

*

[58] "[...] zoe verre hij vrij oudecleercoopers zoen es den tijt van anderhalff jaer." SAM, Oudkleerkopersambacht 1, fol. 1r–29v, 16 December 1577.

The Brabantine sources clearly demonstrate the guilds' determination to preserve their exclusive character. Informal competitors—whether inside or outside the guild—were seen as a threat to members' income and became the target of regulatory actions. Both men and women were punished for violating guild monopolies. In 1471, for example, the drapers' guild of Antwerp charged Jan van der Rijt and Jacob Hagen with circumventing guild rules. Jacob, a cloth merchant, had arranged for Jan, a cloth manufacturer, to produce cloth using tools supplied by Jacob. The guild intervened, asserting that only guild members were allowed to own such tools.[59]

Similar sentences against breaking the guild monopoly can be found in other Brabantine towns. In Leuven in 1504, three women were prosecuted by the fishmongers' guild for selling saltwater fish. The women, who lived in houses bordering the town's fish market, claimed that their location entitled them to sell fish. The fishmongers countered that only guild members had the right to sell saltwater fish. The aldermen sided with the guild, forbidding the women from selling fish from their homes, as they were not members of the corporation.[60]

These types of conflicts were directly tied to the guilds' efforts to assert economic and political control over urban labor markets. Activities such as women selling saltwater fish or merchant-manufacturer collaborations were rendered 'irregular' only because powerful guilds had claimed these areas of work. The three factors constituting the guild effect—economic, cultural, and gendered—interacted closely in such cases. The prosecution of the three women in Leuven illustrates this interplay particularly well. Since the fishmongers' guild did not admit female members, the women were automatically excluded, not only because of the guild's pursuit of monopoly control, but also due to its gendered framework.

Even when the guilds' pursuit of monopoly did not lead to gendered exclusion or a complete prohibition of outsider participation, they still added another layer of control over the urban labor market. This restriction is particularly evident in the regulation of female wage workers. As discussed in chapter 1, women engaged in artisanal trades outside the household most frequently appear in the sources as wage laborers. Guilds took a pragmatic approach to this informal workforce: they sought to limit wage workers' presence while also accommodating external help where

---

[59] Génard, 'Register van den dachvaerden' 20, 227–30.
[60] SAL, 4659, fol. 10v–11v, 18 December 1504.

necessary. In Mechelen, the hatters' guild had ordinances promulgated by the town council, which were designed to protect both guild masters and the wage workers they employed. Similarly, in Leuven, the weavers' guild petitioned the town council to protect the work of female spinners. Given the spinners' indispensable role in cloth production, it is unsurprising that guild members supported their inclusion by relaying their complaints to the authorities.[61] Though female wage workers were not full members of the guilds, they were permitted to perform specific tasks from which the corporations themselves benefited.

*

As noted in this book's introduction, the Brabantine guilds were deeply embedded in every aspect of their members' lives—not only economic, but also military, cultural, religious, and political. This extensive control is particularly visible in the sentence books of the Mechelen fishmongers. Between 1492 and 1561, they issued 65 sentences against members who failed to comply with cultural obligations (see table 9, p. X). In 1495, for example, Jan van Exele, Jan de Gortere, and Gabriel Nootens were punished for skipping the Our Lady procession.[62] These punishments fall into the same category as the Antwerp council's sentence of the fishmonger Jan Bernaert and his servant for "living in sin."[63] Guilds regulated nearly every aspect of their members' lives, not always with gender as the primary concern.

Women were not targeted by these cultural rules. However, the military and political dimensions of guild life imposed additional barriers to their participation. Even if women obtained membership, they were barred from political engagement. This limitation extended to widows inheriting their husbands' positions, thus preventing full membership. The military role of guilds reinforced this exclusion. A telling example is the 1489 dispute between Liesbeth Coolputs and the Mechelen shopkeepers. In 1489, the shopkeepers argued that Liesbeth had to repay the entrance fee after her marriage to Roemond Roobosch. Moreover, the mercers' deans and jurors demanded that Roemond fulfill the

---

[61] See: Vandeweerdt, 'Women, Town Councils, and the Organisation of Work', 71.
[62] SAM, Visverkopers 321, fol. 14v, 1495.
[63] Melis–Taeymans, *Correctieboeck*, fol. 3r, 11 February 1415.
60v, 17 August 1437.

guard duties of a guild member in his wife's name. The guild cited its privileges, which stated that a woman in the craft guild had to renew her membership when she married by paying the entrance fee again. Moreover, a widow enjoying the widow's right would also have to pay the fee again if she remarried and her husband wanted to practice the craft. Although her husband argued that "his wife, when she was still her own woman [read: was unmarried and thus legally independent, ed.], had bought and received the craft," the aldermen of Mechelen decided that Liesbeth's husband would have to perform his wife's guard duties and pay the entrance fee once more.[64] Despite technically holding membership, Liesbeth could never fully participate in guild life. Her exclusion from its military functions revealed how institutions reinforced masculinity, even when women met the formal criteria for inclusion.[65]

*

Up to this point, the influence of guilds on who could participate in guild-regulated work—and which practices were recognized as part of guild activity—did not always operate through explicitly gendered mechanisms. Rather, it followed the same patriarchal reasoning as we can find in the Biscayan case study. Nevertheless, the inherently masculine character of the guilds should not be overlooked. The records from the Brabantine towns reveal a shared understanding between urban governments and craft guilds: these institutions were designed to be male-dominated, and this masculinity was consciously upheld. This idea can be traced back to show how urban authorities and guilds used it as a legitimate rationale for restricting women's labor participation in both formal and informal contexts.

An internal dispute within the glove and purse makers' guild of Antwerp in 1474 illustrates this dynamic. Contrary to guild custom, one group of masters had hired women and apprentices to stuff and knit gloves and purses. These masters defended their practice by arguing that women were suited for this work, stating that they "[...] did not do anything other than knitting gloves or purses and stuffing them, which

---

[64] "[...] dat deselve sijn wijf tanderen tijden hairsselfs wijf zijnde tselve hair ambacht gecocht ende gecregen hadde ende de pennignen dairaf betaelt [...]." *Ibidem*.

[65] Hafter, *Women at Work in Preindustrial France*, 166; Hutton, 'Women, Men, and Markets', 414.

is women's work and should be done by women."[66] However, a second group of masters countered this argument, asserting that:

> [...] no one can have more than two apprentices, and neither should the aforesaid work be done by the foresaid women, because the aforesaid work is a craft of men, who have to work and be burdened with the craft, and that with the work of the foresaid women, the good men of the craft guild would be deprived of the work [...].[67]

Moreover, they claimed that previous regulations had explicitly prohibited women from participating in the guild's work.[68]

Although women's labor was central to the conflict, women themselves were excluded from participating in the dispute or the subsequent regulation. The underlying cause of the conflict was the guilds' continual desire to limit competition for guild masters. The masters protested that two groups that challenged their patriarchal structure—female wage workers and apprentices—were becoming too involved in the guild's work.[69] In a masculine institution such as the Antwerp glove and purse maker guild, labor was expected to be performed by male hands—with one notable exception: female household members of glove and purse makers were still allowed to perform this 'women's work.'

Unsurprisingly, in 1474, the aldermen of Antwerp upheld the guild's masculine character by prohibiting the employment of women working for wages. While cultural factors had long shaped the exclusion of women from guild structures, the immediate impetus for banning female labor was the guild's desire to protect its exclusivity and limit competition from

---

[66] "[...] noch anders en doen dan dat zy deselve hantschoene oft tesschen naeyen ende stofferen, dwelke vrouwenwerc is ende vrouwen betaemt te doene [...]."Génard, 'Register van den dachvaerden', 400–1.

[67] "[...] nyement sculdich en is te houdene meer leercnapen dan twee, ende dat ooc de voers. hantieringe den voers. vrouwen nyet en betaemt noch en behoort te doene, want de voers. liantieringe een ambacht is van mannen, die metten ambachte moeten scoten, loten ende te laste staen, ende dat bider hantieringen vanden voers. vrouwen de voers. neringe den goeden mannen vanden selven ambachte soude moegen ontrocken worden [...]." Ibidem.

[68] The purse and glove makers of the neighboring Brabantine city of Leuven filed a similar ban on female work in 1403. The regulation to which the Antwerp craft members referred could possibly have been promulgated in the same period, since craft regulations were often similar in the Brabantine cities. SAL, 1523, fol. 207r–210v, 22 August 1403.

[69] De Munck, Guilds, Labour and the Urban Body Politic, 180–210.

an informal workforce. The voluntary turn of some guild masters toward the (cheaper) female labor force was not enough to override the guild's institutional commitment to upholding its patriarchal character. That masculine identity had to be preserved, even against the wishes of part of the guild community itself.

The same dynamic that led the glove and purse makers to exclude female wageworkers, using a strongly gendered rhetoric in the 1474 dispute, can be found in an ordinance from the Antwerp gardeners' guild in 1492. A group of male guild members appeared before the town government, complaining that many single women had joined the guild. The result was unwelcome competition for the guilds' younger journeymen. Moreover, according to the guild members, the admission of these women violated an earlier privilege, stating that no single woman could join the guild. The example of the Antwerp gardeners shows that even when they were admitted to a guild, women might not have had all the opportunities given to men, despite what earlier studies have found.[70] The single women who joined the Antwerp gardeners' guild were serious competitors for younger male craft members. If these women had worked informally as gardeners before entering the guild, they would have had previous experience.

Maybe the Antwerp gardeners guild allowed single women to enter the guild to avoid losing the fees from their income, just as guilds elsewhere included informal traders.[71] As Hafter has found for early modern Lyon, economic pressure or necessity might have superseded the importance of earlier regulations.[72] Nevertheless, once the guild saw the consequences of its policy for young male members, the leadership redoubled the guild's exclusive, masculine character.[73]

The Antwerp aldermen must have agreed with the members of the gardeners' guild, as they renewed the regulation. However, they added an exception for gardeners' daughters whose parents were deceased.[74] This proviso underscores the importance of separating the guild effect not only based on the categories of women but also on the specific work fields and local contexts. As observed, the Antwerp mercers did not appear to have

[70] As also found by Peter Stabel. See: Stabel, 'Women at the Market', 270.
[71] Crowston, 'Women, Gender, and Guilds', 30.; Dumont, 'Women and Guilds in Bologna'.
[72] Hafter, *Women at Work in Preindustrial France*, 291–2.
[73] Howell, 'The Problem of Women's Agency', 30–1.
[74] SAA, GA#4001, fol. 64v, 30 July 1492.

restricted women once they were integrated into the guild. The gardeners and glove and purse makers did so, and similarly, the Mechelen fishmongers also imposed restrictions, as we will discuss in the next section.

The masculine identity of the guild appears to have been a sufficient reason to exclude women. This awareness of the gendered character of guilds is evident not only in the limitations imposed on women's work but also in the regulation of guild organization more generally. For instance, an ordinance of the Mechelen glove makers regarding the guild's poor box states that, within a married couple, only the man was required to contribute—"since he is the breadwinner."[75] The use of gendered language reveals a conscious strategy: urban authorities legitimized the operation of institutional practices like the guild poor box through patriarchal and masculine values. Even though wives were a recognized and often (though not always, see next section) essential workforce within the guilds, the guilds' organizational framework favored male members.

*

While the gardeners and the glove and purse makers of Antwerp found it relatively easy to convince the town council of the need for exclusionary regulations, both groups made exceptions for the household members of guild masters. During this period, guilds and their household workshops were central to the urban economies of the southern Low Countries. As Bert De Munck has noted, at least during the fifteenth and sixteenth centuries, "corporative and patriarchal values and practices" often overlapped.[76] However, the Brabantine case study reveals that women's labor was not consistently recognized or valued, even within the household economic unit. The following pages analyze the circumstances under which the fishmongers' guild in Mechelen resisted the otherwise ubiquitous model of household cooperation, thereby adding another dimension to the analysis of the guild effect.

---

[75] "[...] als man ende wijf levende bijeen huyshoudende dat die man sal alle weke heffen die busse ende die vrouwe niet want hij dat broot winnende es [...]." SAM, Handschoenmakers-, tesmakers-, riem(be)slagers-, witledermakers- en schedemakersambacht 554bis, fol. 6v–7r. Although this ordinance does not have an exact date, I suspect it to be from around 1550, judging by the records surrounding it in the register. The explicit reference to the man as breadwinner is a particularly significant counterpoint to the argument of earlier studies that the idea of the male breadwinner model emerged in a later century.

[76] De Munck, *Guilds, Labour and the Urban Body Politic*, 181.

152 CHAPTER 3

Table 9. Overview of registered sentences by type of offense and gender of the accused, based on the Mechelen fishmongers' guild's sentence books (1492–1561).

Offense type	Gender of the accused party				
	Men	Women	Men and women	Unknown	Total
Irregular work	296	33	35	2	366
Verbal violence	347	14	1	/	362
Physical violence	171	/	/	1	172
Craft insubordination	131	3	1	/	135
Cultural/religious offense	64	/	/	1	65
Debt conflict	33	4	/	/	37
Gossip/false accusations	10	1	1	/	12
Theft	5	1	/	/	6
Damage	6	/	/	/	6
Unknown	95	5	2	/	102
Total	1158	61	40	4	1263

Source: SAM, Visverkopers 321; SAM Visverkopers 322.

The most revealing insights into spousal cooperation and guild restrictions emerge from the sentence books of the Mechelen fishmongers. These registers document the wide range of offenses for which guild members and their household members were prosecuted (see table 9).[77] Nearly one third of the recorded sentences concerned urban residents working in violation of guild regulations. Of these, five percent were issued to women, and another four percent to couples or groups of men and women. Irregular work was the most common offense for which women were punished, and this category also showed the highest proportion of female offenders. While these numbers do not necessarily mean that women engaged in illicit work more frequently than men, they do indicate that the guild paid particular attention to women's irregular economic activities—or that women's work was more readily classified as illicit. Moreover, these

---

[77] Between 1492 and 1561, there are 1,084 sentences in the two guild sentence books. The higher number of offense types in table 9 results from the existence of 179 sentences with a double offense type-tag. A 1520 sentence, for instance, falls under both the 'verbal violence' and 'irregular work' categories. Anthonis van Exele was sent to Valenciennes because he had said that Jan Waelpot was a cheater and a snitch. Furthermore, he worked as a fishmonger after the guild jurors prohibited this activity. SAM, Visverkopers 321, fol. 93v, 1520.

types of offenses were likely seen as ones that an offender might risk committing, in the hope of going unnoticed. Overall, the infringements recorded in the fishmongers' sentence book reflect the guild's efforts to exert control over trade within its jurisdiction.

Spousal cooperation was not always welcomed by the Mechelen fishmongers' guild. Nearly half of the judgments involving women concerned the labor of female members of fishmongers' households. It was common for craft members to be sentenced to a pilgrimage because their wives had sold fish. The exact circumstances that triggered such punishments remain unclear. In principle, fishmongers' wives in Mechelen were often exempt from regulations excluding non-guild members. For example, in 1454, they were granted permission to sell herring, and in 1508, they were exempted from a prohibition on selling *stokvis* and dried fish.[78] Research on other towns in the Low Countries has also highlighted the essential role of fishmongers' wives in premodern fish markets.[79] Nevertheless, their permitted activities had clear limits. In 1493, the wives of Claes Quayvoer, Rutten Ruts, and Anthonis van Exele were all sentenced to a pilgrimage to Mons for selling fish at their husbands' market stalls.[80] They were not alone—similar sentences appear frequently in the following years.

In 1497, the wives of Claes Quayvoer and Anthonis van Exele were once again sent on a pilgrimage to Mons because they "stood at their husbands' stall and sold fish."[81] They were accompanied by Gheertruyde van den Broeke, the wife of the fishmonger Wouter Ruts. In 1479, and again in 1512, Wouter was sent to Mons for allowing his wife to sell fish. In spite of these sentences, Gheertruyde was an active participant in the fishmongers' guild. Between 1493 and 1518, she and her husband were frequently punished by the guild's jurors and aldermen. In 1508, she was sentenced to a pilgrimage to Mons and fined a pound's worth of candles. The fishmonger

---

[78] SAM, Visverkopers 14, 26 July 1454; SAM, Visverkopers 23, 16 October 1508.

[79] Harmsen & Hubers, "En zij verkocht de vis ...", 31–3; Van den Heuvel, 'Partners in Marriage and Business?', 225–7; Van den Heuvel, 'The Multiple Identities of Early Modern Dutch Fishwives', 590–1; Verstrepen, 'Het sociaal-economisch beleid van de stad Antwerpen', 78.

[80] "Claes Quaeyvoer wijf eenen wech te Berghen omdat sij aen huers mans banck visch vercochte. Betaelt 4 stuivers. Rutten Ruts wijf oick eenen wech te Berghen om tselve van Claes wijf. Betaelt 4 stuivers. Antheunis Exele wijf oick eenen wech te Berghen omdat sij aen huers mans banck ghestaen en visch vercocht. Betaelt 4 stuivers." SAM, Visverkopers 321, fol. 4v–5r, 1493.

[81] "Item, Claes Quayvoers wijf eenen wech te Berghen Henegouwe omdat sij de snijlinck loeft ende vercoopt op de merct ende bij hueren man steet meest den tijt neven de banck." SAM, Visverkopers 321, fol. 20v, 1497.

Anthonis Venne had demanded the money which she owed him for the herring she had sold. She had answered: "I do not have to give you any money because you are a dishonest man."[82] Clearly, Gheertruyde van den Broeke was no stranger to the fish trade in Mechelen. She was involved in a social network of fishmongers—sufficiently so to receive credit from another guild member.[83] Nevertheless, she and her husband were prosecuted several times because of her trade activities. The sentence books do not clarify the circumstances that made the work of Gheertruyde problematic for the guild.

Based on the historical records of the Mechelen fishmongers, I see two possible reasons for these restrictions on the work of craftsmen's wives within the household economic unit. First, the usual lenience towards guild members' spouses might not have applied in certain circumstances. The type of spousal cooperation practiced by the Mechelen fishmongers suggests two possibilities. As Van den Heuvel found, in Leiden, spousal cooperation in the fish trade could involve husband and wife performing identical tasks. Either this type of partnership was not commonly practiced in sixteenth-century Mechelen, or the fishmongers' guild actively discouraged such forms of cooperation.[84] Together with the butchers, the fishmongers of the southern Low Countries were organized into some of the most exclusive guilds, limiting membership to the sons of fishmongers—or, in Mechelen, also to the sons of fishmongers' daughters.[85] In 1518, the town council of Leuven ordered that butchers' wives could only manage a market booth in the meat hall when their husbands were out of town or ill.[86] I argue that the Mechelen fishmongers' guild endorsed a similar model of restricted spousal cooperation. Throughout the sixteenth century, as the fish trade in Mechelen evolved, the nature of spousal cooperation changed as well. In response, married couples encountered increasing resistance from guild authorities.

The fishmongers of Mechelen operated on different scales. Some of them merely sold fish brought to the town's fish auctions so that it could

---

[82] SAM, Visverkopers 321, fol. 56r, 1508.

[83] Ogilvie, 'How Does Social Capital Affect Women?'.

[84] Van den Heuvel, 'Partners in Marriage and Business?', 225.

[85] SAM, Visverkopers 14, 26 July 1454; SAM, Visverkopers 23, 16 October 1508; De Munck, *Guilds, Labour and the Urban Body Politic*, 194; Prak, 'Corporatism and Social Models', 286.

[86] SAL, 4748, 20 October 1566.

be resold by other guild members.⁸⁷ Others were involved in fishing and might have left their wives behind to run their stalls for long periods of time. Wouter Ruts, for example, was probably the second type of fishmonger. He was punished twice for fraudulent practices involving fish sold from his own boat.⁸⁸ It is not surprising that his wife was an active participant in the town's fish trade and managed to get credit from other fishmongers. The leaders of the fishmongers' guild in Mechelen might have encouraged similar partnerships in which husband and wife complemented each other's work.

While complementary spousal cooperation was accepted, the guild might have tried to obstruct husbands and wives from teaming up in the fish market to do identical tasks. The scale of Mechelen's fish trade might have changed, changing the activities of the participants in the trade with it. Whereas production (in this case, fishing) and sales had before been conducted by households, the increasing importance of auctions and external supply transformed the traditional gendered division of work. Wives could no longer sell commodities supplied only by their husbands. Van den Heuvel has described a similar change in the early modern Dutch food trade.⁸⁹ This shift had a great impact on the wives of the Brabantine guild members, whose work had traditionally been "encapsulated in the patriarchal household that had become the dominant economic unit of production."⁹⁰ If supplies and commodities came from outside the household economic unit, wives' involvement in trade might no longer have been obvious, making them little more than outsiders involved only informally in the guild.⁹¹

The guilds were not lenient when it came to competition from outsiders. If the fish trade in Mechelen changed and became more commercialized, fishmongers' wives—whose work had fit within the older framework of spousal cooperation—were now taking on the same tasks as their husbands. In 1541, for example, the wife of the fishmonger Jerome van den Stocke was sent on a pilgrimage to Mons because "she sold [fish] and was

---

[87] Members of the fishmongers' guild had a monopoly on the trade in saltwater fish. Schoeffer, *Historische aanteekeningen rakende de kerken, de kloosters, de ambachten en andere stichten der stad Mechelen.*

[88] SAM, Visverkopers 321, fol. 54r, 1508; SAM, Visverkopers 321, fol. 22r, 1497.

[89] Van den Heuvel, 'Partners in Marriage and Business?', 226.

[90] Schmidt, Devos & Blondé, 'Introduction. Single and the City', 6.

[91] Crowston, 'Women, Gender, and Guilds', 23; Howell, 'The Problem of Women's Agency', 30–1.

not in the craft guild."[92] The guild seemed to be trying to limit spousal cooperation when the two spouses worked too closely together, thereby competing unfairly with unmarried and younger members. As discussed above, a tension existed between the guild's leniency toward spousal cooperation and its drive for exclusivity. The jurors of the Mechelen fishmongers' guild likely worked alongside their own spouses, which may have contributed to the guild's ambivalent stance in decision-making.[93]

As we will discuss in the next section, the fishmongers' guild of Mechelen limited the possibilities of women working within the framework of the household economy throughout the sixteenth century. However, evidence also reveals an inconsistent attitude towards the participation of wives in the guild. Whereas spousal cooperation at the same stall at the fish market was discouraged and penalized in some cases, fishmongers' wives still had opportunities in others. Women like Gheertruyde van den Broeke seem to have been active participants in the fish trade when their husbands were out of town or absent from the market. Craftsmen's wives were still allowed to sell certain fish types and operate as *harincvrouwen* on the margins of the guild. The guild did not terminate the role of fishmongers' spouses in their quest for exclusivity. Nevertheless, the sentence books and subsequent ordinances show that the corporations could contest even established household cooperation.

Not all judgments concerning fishmongers' wives in the Mechelen guild's sentence book stemmed from structural concerns about women's labor. A second, more circumstantial reason for punishing wives' market activities can be found in the guild's privileges. In 1448, the Mechelen fishmongers stipulated that a wife could not take over her husband's stall if he was being disciplined and temporarily banned from the guild.[94] Typically, guild members were prohibited from working until they had complied with their punishment—usually a pilgrimage, a fine, or a temporary ban. For example, in 1497, Marten Papegaey was banned from practicing his trade for offending another craftsman; neither he nor his wife was

---

[92] "Item Jerome van den Stoc wijf omdat sij vercocht en niet int ambacht en es [...]." SAM, Visverkopers 321, fol. 155v, 1541.

[93] Martha Howell draws a similar conclusion in her *Women, Production, and Patriarchy*, stating that exactly the mechanisms organizing small-commodity production—among others guilds—weaponized society against the omnipresent family production unit. See: Howell, *Women, Production, and Patriarchy*, 180.

[94] SAM, Visverkopers 11, 27 January 1448.

allowed to work until Marten paid his fine and publicly sought forgiveness.[95] Some punishments were more severe: in 1537, Romment Merten was expelled from the trade for two years for selling rotten herring.[96] Additional penalties were imposed on those who attempted to work while still under penalty. Occasionally, these punishments also extended to women. In 1524, for instance, Simon van den Stene and his wife were both banned from the trade, as they had continued working after Simon was sent on a pilgrimage to Valenciennes.[97]

Some condemnations of fishmongers for allowing their wives to sell fish may have stemmed from earlier punishments or temporary bans. Between 1493 and 1517, for instance, either Wouter Ruts or Gheertruyde van den Broeke was sentenced to a total of sixteen pilgrimages—four of them explicitly because Gheertruyde sold fish at Wouter's market stall. It is possible that some of these verdicts were linked to previous sentences. However, several of the judgments against Gheertruyde do not correspond to earlier condemnations, and their formulaic language differs from the standard phrasing used to punish craftsmen who violated bans. When Jan van Exele was penalized, for example, the record stated that "he practiced his craft while this was prohibited." In contrast, the verdicts against Wouter Ruts consistently use the phrasing "she sold next to her husband at the market stall."[98] One judgment even states that Wouter's wife was condemned because "she did not leave her craft."[99] Notably, this sentence appears on the same folio as an order sending her on a pilgrimage to Mons for insulting Anthonis Venne. This verdict suggests that Gheertruyde van den Broeke was not being punished merely for her husband's infractions, but for her own actions—underscoring her active role in the trade.

Women navigated a landscape of shifting constraints. The labor of guild members' wives was generally tolerated, so long as it conformed to household-based expectations. Yet when it fell outside that norm, it could be challenged just like any other informal outsider's trade. The variation in guilds' gendered policies cautions against generalizing the guild effect for all occupations. Still, the institutional presence and authority of

[95] SAM, Visverkopers 321, fol. 21r, 1497.
[96] SAM, Visverkopers 321, fol. 139v, 1537.
[97] SAM, Visverkopers 321, fol. 103r, 1524.
[98] SAM, Visverkopers 321, fol. 20v, 1497.
[99] "Wouter Ruts wijf eenen wech te Camerake van ongehoorsamheyden om dat sij haer ambacht niet en heeft gelaten ende onser liever vrouwen twee pont was." SAM, Visverkoepers 321, fol. 56r, 1508.

Brabantine guilds introduced limitations on women's work in small-scale trade that had no parallel in Biscay.

3. Growing Restrictions?

One prominent debate in the scholarship on women's economic history concerns how institutional mechanisms influenced changes in women's economic opportunities over time. The 'decline thesis' and the 'guild debate' are among the most frequently discussed theories regarding women's labor in premodern Europe. Since the emergence of women's history and gender studies, scholars have debated the extent to which women's economic opportunities changed during the late medieval and early modern periods. They have shown that women's access to work varied according to social class and economic status and was shaped by a range of intersecting factors. At the core of this debate is the question of whether women's economic opportunities—particularly their access to independent and high-status work—declined over the course of the late Middle Ages and early modern period.[100]

In my research, the extensive body of literature on the decline thesis has proven especially valuable for understanding the mechanisms that shaped women's labor positions. The chronological scope of this study and the fragmented nature of the sources complicate efforts to trace long-term developments for women active in small-scale trade in Antwerp, Mechelen, and Bilbao. Nevertheless, certain trends indicating change can be discerned in both the Brabant and Biscay regions.

In Biscay, the town council of Bilbao increasingly sought to exert control over the informal economy. These efforts resulted in restrictions on women's activities, particularly in areas such as brokering, quality and quantity control, and price setting. The council appears to have succeeded in centralizing the daily commodity market in Bilbao, even without the framework of formal guild organization. In Brabant, the serial sources do not suggest a clear trend of declining opportunities for women. Consistent with earlier studies, the urban markets in Brabant remained relatively

---

[100] Clare Crowston gives a good, though slightly outdated, overview of the decline thesis in: Crowston, 'Women, Gender, and Guilds'. Anna Bellavitis offered alternative theories aside from a critical analysis of the decline thesis: Bellavitis, 'The 'Decline Thesis' and the Guilds: An 'Accordion Movement'?'.

accessible to women, although they continued to face limitations from institutions such as the guilds. Nevertheless, as seen in the Mechelen fish trade, some traditionally domestic occupations seem to show a trend toward further marginalizing women within the guilds.

*

Guild membership and entrance lists offer some evidence for tracing changes in the formal integration of women into corporate structures over time. For the Antwerp mercers' guild, I calculated the moving average of new members from 1516 to 1555 by sex and in five-year intervals, along with the percentage of women entering the guild. As shown in figure 8, these data provide insight into the limited changes in the opportunities women had to formally join the Antwerp mercers' guild.

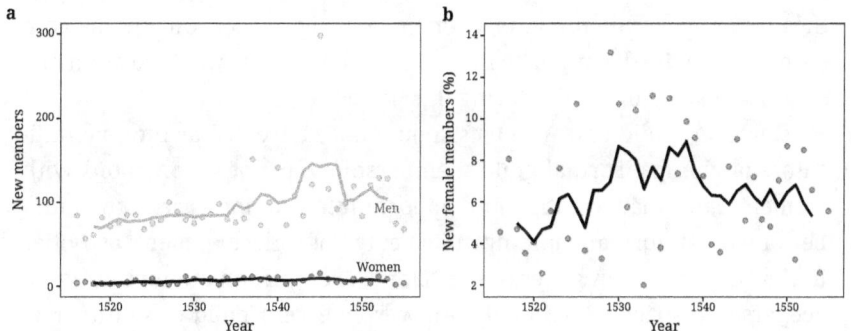

Figure 8. Five-year moving averages showing (a) the total number of new members per sex and (b) the proportion of new female members in the mercers' guild of Antwerp (1516–1555).[101]
Source: SAA, FA#22; SAA, 860#7761.

The percentage of women admitted to the Antwerp mercers' guild remained consistently low throughout the period. Unlike the dramatic fluctuations in the number of new male entrants, the proportion of women fluctuated only slightly around a low baseline.[102] Although women never

---

[101] The lines on both figures represent the five-year moving average for the entering members. The dots are the separate values for men and women entering in each year on which the calculation is based.

[102] See also in: Schmidt, 'Women and Guilds', 178–80.

made up the majority of new entrants, the data do not indicate a steady decline in their access to guild membership during the first half of the sixteenth century. In fact, the entrance lists show modest increases in the percentage of new female members over time. According to earlier studies, by the eighteenth century, women made up as much as twenty percent of the membership in the Antwerp and Mechelen mercers' guilds.[103] Additional case studies show similar increases in female membership in other guilds throughout the seventeenth and eighteenth centuries.[104]

Although the number of women entering the Antwerp mercers' guild did not decline between 1515 and 1555, the annual percentage varied significantly. As figure 8(b) illustrates, some years saw a peak of up to twelve or even fifteen percent, while others dropped to nearly zero. Similar patterns emerge in the membership lists of other guilds: in the Mechelen gardeners' and shopkeepers' guilds, for instance, the percentage of female entrants reached up to twenty-five percent in certain years.[105] Despite these short-term fluctuations, women working in their own name consistently remained a minority in the guilds, and there is no indication of a significant structural shift during this period.

However, guild entrance lists should not be treated as the sole indicators of change. Formal guild membership was not synonymous with women's labor participation and opportunities. An increase in the number of women formally joining guilds may not reflect women's activities in the corporation in general. In 1614, for example, an attempt by shopkeepers to restrict entry into the Antwerp mercers' guild was ultimately unsuccessful. The guild authorities argued that open membership was vital, particularly because "many orphans and widows who could do nothing else" relied on shopkeeping for income.[106] Rather than exclude these women, the guild preferred to include them, as an alternative to their dependence on one of the town's poor relief institutions.[107] As Van Aert has pointed out, this inclusive stance contributed to the declining

---

[103] Van Aert, 'Tot 'Leven of overleven'?'; De Smet, 'Bijdrage tot de sociale geschiedenis van het Mechelse ambachtelijke milieu'.

[104] Bellavitis, *Women's Work and Rights*, 49.

[105] These lists are too limited, however, to provide a valuable quantitative analysis.

[106] Van Aert, 'Tot 'leven of overleven'? Winkelhouden in crisistijd', 187.

[107] Merry Wiesner found this motive as well for early modern Germany. See: Wiesner, 'Gender and the Worlds of Work', 223.

status of shopkeeping, making it a low-status occupation in which many women were concentrated.[108]

Studies of more prestigious guilds, by contrast, often show a decline in women's participation over time.[109] This decrease confirms the need to differentiate between guilds based on status and function when analyzing women's roles. In the Brabantine context, such differentiation is crucial for understanding the uneven landscape of women's economic opportunities. This complexity is also reflected in the normative ordinances of the Mechelen fishmongers and the Antwerp old clothes sellers, where subtle changes can be detected. Throughout the period from 1450 to 1550, guild ordinances were predominantly masculine in tone. Decisions concerning the work of craft members were typically framed in masculine language, and official attention to women's roles remained limited. However, from the mid-sixteenth century onward, specific shifts in local context sometimes led to more explicit constraints on women's work.

As discussed in the previous section, the Mechelen fishmongers seem to have gone through such a change that resulted in increased scrutiny of their members' wives. The persecutions of wives undertaking their husbands' work, registered in the guilds' sentence books, slowly sank in to become a new normative framework. While the circumstances that produced each decision might have been rather arbitrary, collectively, they define the movement towards an increasingly masculine corporation.

It appears that the discontent of the guild was gradually absorbed into official policy over the course of the sixteenth century. By the late fifteenth century, penalties were levied only when wives were too visibly involved in their husbands' trade. By the mid-sixteenth century, though, new informal practices had emerged that implicitly prohibited such cooperation. In 1555, Aert van Quaeribbe was penalized for breaking the oath that his wife "will not be selling at the market stall" alongside him.[110] Throughout the first half of the sixteenth century, guild members seemed to have recognized the guild's limitation on spousal cooperation. By the end of the century, these unwritten norms had been codified: a 1584 ordinance

---

[108] Van Aert, 'Tot 'leven of overleven'? Winkelhouden in crisistijd', 187; Gold, 'On the Streets and in the Markets', 36; Van den Heuvel, 'Selling in the Shadows', 144.

[109] Coomans, 'Policing Female Food Vendors', 102–3; Stabel, 'Workplace Cultures', 97; Honeyman & Goodman, 'Women's Work, Gender Conflict, and Labour Markets', 613.

[110] "[...] zoude mijn wijf niet alzoe wel in de banck vercoepen als ick [...]." SAM, Visverkopers 322, fol. 13r, 1555.

from the Mechelen town government explicitly prohibited fishmongers' wives from selling fish at the market or engaging others to do so on their behalf. The ordinance stipulated that only the husband or another free fishmonger could sell at the market, signaling a decisive institutional shift.[111] This formal exclusion not only redefined women's roles but also indicated that fishmongers themselves may have lost control over their supply chains, leaving their wives reduced to informal competitors in the resale of saltwater fish.

A similar trajectory is visible in the case of the Leuven butchers. In 1566, the guild requested an ordinance barring butchers' widows from selling meat in the Meat Hall, arguing that the widows were depriving younger craft members of opportunities. Although the town council of Leuven approved the ordinance, they clearly knew they were contradicting older customs. That same year, they made immediate exceptions for two butchers' widows. Just four years later, a revised ordinance allowed widows to manage their late husbands' stalls again, albeit with restrictions on the types of meat they could sell. By 1655, the ordinance was fully annulled.[112]

Even though these changes in women's work opportunities in Brabant might have merely been fluctuations, shifts in guilds' production and commercialization processes did impact women's access to work. The context varied by guild, but the result was a similar pattern of exclusion. The Brabantine case studies suggest that the decline in women's economic opportunities is most visible in occupations that were vulnerable to shifting urban contexts. With the decline of Leuven and Mechelen as commercial hubs and decreasing population numbers, their more traditional occupations likely suffered. The economic decline of cities like Leuven and Mechelen and their shrinking populations had a tangible impact on traditional, often domestic, occupations. In this light, the findings on the Leuven butchers and Mechelen fishmongers echo the conclusions of scholars such as Olwen Hufton, Merry Wiesner, and Sheilagh Ogilvie. As guilds' economic prospects waned, their members responded by doubling

---

[111] "Item, dat van nu voirtaen gheenen vischcoopers vrouwen met visch op de merct in de bancken mogen voortstaen, noch dien lonen oft vercoopen noch te doen loven oft vercoopen bij yemanden anders directelijc oft indirectelijc in eeniger manieren. Maer zullen de mans schuldich wesen hunzelfs visch in persoone te vercoopen oft bij yemanden anders vrij vischcooper wesende doen vercoopen [...]." SAM, Visverkopers 30, 16 June 1584.

[112] Vandeweerdt, "Van den vleeschouweren oft pensvrouwen", 27–8; Meulemans, 'Leuvense ambachten: de beenhouwers', 296–7.

down on exclusivity—thus reinforcing the masculine character of the corporations.[113]

In contrast, the Antwerp mercers—associated with more modern forms of commerce—benefited from Antwerp's commercial boom. They did not face the same pressures to restrict access, and no additional limitations on women's membership appear to have been introduced. Without claiming to prove the 'decline thesis', it is notable that the occupations most impacted by change were often those rooted in domestic and traditionally feminine spheres. The comparison with Bilbao further illustrates what might have happened in Brabant, had guilds not intervened to regulate these trades. In the Biscayan towns, typically female occupations largely remained in female hands, although we see patterns of centralization and exclusion imposed from above by town councils rather than guilds.

*

While sixteenth-century evidence from both Biscay and Brabant does not point to a straightforward, linear decline in women's economic opportunities, it does reveal a gradual trend toward increasing restrictions in specific trades. In Bilbao, regulations and court cases from this period indicate the town council's efforts to assert greater control over the urban economy. This centralization resulted in heightened scrutiny of women's involvement, particularly in the trade of imported bulk goods. While the roles of female retailers were largely preserved, women who acted as intermediaries in interregional trading networks appear to have faced diminishing opportunities.

The increasing constraints on women's economic roles are especially visible in Bilbao's grain trade. The council excluded most women from tasks such as grain weighing and price setting. Although women remained active in certain parts of the trade—they even predominated in some informal branches such as the *cojeduría*—overall control was firmly in masculine hands. A 1509 ordinance explicitly defined grain weighing as a masculine responsibility. As early as 1500, the council had already prohibited *roderas*—women who transported grain to the mills—from handling

---

[113] Hufton, *The Prospect Before Her*, 93; Wiesner, 'Gender and the Worlds of Work'; Wiesner, 'Guilds, Male Bonding and Women's Work'; Ogilvie, *The European Guilds*; Ogilvie, *A Bitter Living*.

the weights, arguing that this function opened the door to fraud.[114] Even if such regulations were motivated by economic concerns, the result could still be the increasing limitation of women's work opportunities.

The town council had been addressing the *cojedoras*' brokerage activities in the grain trade regularly since the fifteenth century.[115] However, the regulation of their work intensified during the early sixteenth century, as the council increasingly blamed these women brokers for fraud and market distortion. In 1508, it claimed the city was suffering because *cojedoras*, "who were kin of the *mulateros*," were inflating grain prices by purchasing stock from merchants without there being a need for their services.[116] By 1524, the situation was, in the council's view, out of control. It banned the *cojeduría* altogether, targeting the "eight or nine women brokers who receive money from the grain [imported into Bilbao, ed.]."[117] As discussed in the following chapter, this ordinance sparked a protracted conflict, as women continued to pursue brokerage despite the official ban. These ordinances and the ensuing disputes illustrate the council's growing determination to eliminate women's positions in brokerage.

The court case between the Bilbao council and Mayora de Iturribalzaga further highlights changes in the council's attitude towards the women traders. Mayora contested the 1526 ordinance before the council and higher judges, but the council's efforts to limit women's involvement in the sale of fresh fish had begun earlier. In 1515, the council issued its first ordinance targeting female fishmongers, which prohibited them from selling fresh fish in bulk, but not from selling pre-cut fresh fish as was the case in the 1526 ordinance.[118] Whether the 1515 ordinance was actually enforced is unclear. Mayora argued that the previous *Corregidor* of Biscay had declared it invalid and had annulled it. If true, this account suggests that the council's efforts to restrict the *pescaderas*' trade in 1515 were unsuccessful, but that they tried to do so, nevertheless.

---

[114] Enríquez Fernández et al., *Ordenanzas municipales de Bilbao (1477–1520)*, fol. 281r–282r, 20 March 1500.

[115] Castrillo Casado, *Las mujeres vascas durante la baja edad media*, 281.

[116] "[…] en el trigo pasa(roto) burleria en el conprar del que hera que las amas(roto) de la dicha villa que heran parientes de los mula(roto), por faser abançar en el presçio, avnque non tenia nesçesidad de conprar, por alçar en el preçio e por ayudarles, ponian en los preçios mui altos, porque las otras mugeres e moças al mesmo preçio lo conprasen, lo qual hera en grand dapno de la dicha villa […]." Enríquez Fernández et al., *Ordenanzas municipales de Bilbao (1477–1520)*, fol. 127r, 8 November 1508.

[117] ARChV, Sala de Vizcaya, 3467,5, 27 June 1536.

[118] Enríquez Fernández et al., *Libro de acuerdos y decretos municipales*, 20v, 8 May 1515.

In 1532, Mayora and three other women were fined for selling fresh fish.[119] Despite the 1526 ordinance, the practice continued, prompting the council to reinforce its regulations repeatedly. Over time, however, women's involvement in the sale of whole fresh fish appears to have diminished. In 1548, the council went further and prohibited the sale of fresh fish in Bilbao's main square. This injunction added a spatial dimension to the restrictions, as the main square had traditionally been a key site of female commercial activity, particularly in the fish trade.[120] The final ruling by the *Chancillería* in the conflict between Mayora and the council did not bring about an immediate transformation in fishmongers' practices, but it marked a further step in a long-term trend toward limiting women's trade activities.

Throughout the sixteenth century, the Bilbao town council increasingly sought to restrict women's roles in traditionally 'feminine' trades, particularly their intermediary positions as brokers. More often than not, however, these efforts appear driven less by gender ideology than by a desire to establish a stable source of tax revenue from goods imported into and sold within the city. In the ordinance that led to the court case between Mayora de Iturribalzaga and the council, the authorities stated that no one could sell fresh fish "except for Fortuño de Gueldo, who has been appointed to sell the fresh fish [by weight, ed.]."[121] It is implausible that one man alone was responsible for all fresh fish sales. More likely, the council inserted an official intermediary into a distribution process that had previously been managed informally by (female) fishmongers. This new intermediary acted as the council's representative, ensuring proper collection of excise duties. While women may have continued to participate in the trade, they likely lost a degree of independence due to the insertion of this council-appointed figure into the local market structure.

Like the fishmongers, the *cojedoras* also functioned as intermediaries in trades that connected Bilbao to surrounding towns and regions. Over the course of the sixteenth century, the council appears to have tightened its grip on precisely those market sectors that involved the movement of bulk goods and required oversight through import taxation. Women

---

[119] AFB, Municipal, 0304/001/011.
[120] Rodriguez Herrero, *Ordenanzas de Bilbao*, 42.
[121] "Salvo que vaya el tal pescado fresco que por peso se obiere de vender a poder de Fortuno de Gueldo, aceclador que para ello nonbraron e pusieron por vendedor del dicho pescado fresco [...]." AFB, Municipal, 0304/001/011, 4r.

active in these sectors came under increased scrutiny, and in some cases, their participation was curtailed altogether as the council took a firmer stance on brokerage. Unlike the Brabantine towns, where the decline meant that an already existing craft guild took over the organization of these tasks, Bilbao underwent a process of centralization that placed brokerage directly in the hands of the town council's own male representatives, rather than leaving it with the women who had previously held these roles.

By the latter half of the sixteenth century, references to women in Bilbao's fish trade ordinances had markedly declined. The 1548 ordinances continued to regulate the fish trade but largely abandoned the earlier explicit focus on female fishmongers. Instead, the language of regulation shifted toward more gender-neutral—or ambiguously gendered—terms, such as 'anyone', 'no one' (which in Spanish can imply "no man"), or masculine nouns like 'citizen', 'inhabitant', or 'retailer.' Particularly notable is the use of *regatones*, the masculine form of the word used to designate small-scale resellers. Earlier ordinances had referred explicitly to the *regateras* of Bilbao.[122] This shift raises the question of how reflective the council's language was of actual practice and the gender of those involved in the trade. Despite the changing terminology, women's involvement in the fish trade did not entirely disappear. The 1548 ordinance still mentioned women in the context of retail and sardine sales, suggesting that the council's restrictions may have focused mainly on activities that generated excise revenue.

Evidence from later periods shows the persistence of women in the northern Atlantic Iberian fish trade.[123] Even today, female fishmongers are commemorated in several towns and coastal villages across northern Spain (see figure 9). However, the conditions under which they worked—and the scale or independence of their activities—likely changed over time. Other trades, such as the bread trade and small-scale retail, remained clearly associated with women in the Bilbao ordinances of 1548 and 1593.

---

[122] See, for example: de Mañaricua, *Las Ordenanzas de Bilbao de 1593*, 88–9; Rodriguez Herrero, *Ordenanzas de Bilbao*, 45.

[123] See: *Itsas memoria. Revista de estudios marítimos del País Vasco*, 8 (2016).

LIMITING WOMEN'S WORK 167

Figure 9. Statue by Joaquín Lucarini in homage to the Bizkaian sardineras, *Santurtzi (1963).*
Source: Wikimedia. Picture by Ghirlandaio70.[124]

---

[124] https://es.m.wikipedia.org/wiki/Archivo:La_Sardinera.JPG

4. Conclusion

The Antwerp old clothes sellers explicitly prohibited women from becoming estimators, much like the Bilbao town council barred women from weighing grain brought into the town. In both regions, women operated under constraints rooted in premodern patriarchal culture. Despite significant institutional and organizational differences between the Biscayan and Brabantine case studies, some of the underlying mechanisms that restricted women's economic opportunities were strikingly similar. Most notably, the authorities' desire for economic control frequently translated into constraints on women's labor, demonstrating that guilds should not be regarded as the sole or even the primary source of these limitations. Even so, in Brabant, the presence of corporate institutions added an additional layer of exclusion not evident in Biscay.

In both contexts, the urban authorities' efforts to assert control over the economy resulted in regulations that restricted women's participation. In the small-scale trades of Bilbao, although the organization of work afforded some flexibility to women, certain tasks remained explicitly reserved for men. The council exerted close control over the town's saleswomen and did not hesitate to ban specific female-dominated activities. Even though the Bilbao council held a near-monopoly on regulating economic practices, it still needed to legitimize its ordinances—at times by invoking gendered reasoning. Comparable motivations are evident in the sources from Brabantine town governments, often reinforced or instigated by guild interventions.

Two primary mechanisms can be identified behind the regulatory actions that limited women's economic opportunities in both regions:

(1) First, concerns about fraud and economic malpractice frequently prompted new regulations and the prosecution of offenders. The repeated invocation of such concerns in both court cases and ordinances suggests that safeguarding economic integrity was a key driver for authorities. In the informal economies of urban premodern Europe, town governments sought to impose order and prevent malpractice that could lead to financial losses, both for private actors and public revenue. Both men's and women's trades in Brabant and Biscay were subjected to scrutiny for this reason. However, this general regulatory impulse does not fully explain the distinctly gendered patterns of exclusion.

(2) The second mechanism behind the limitations on women's economic opportunities is gender-based exclusion. In both Brabant and Biscay, gendered restrictions were often applied without the need for further justification. As Bailey, Colwell, and Hotchin argue in their edited volume on women and work in premodern Europe, economic history approaches often marginalize the cultural dimensions of work, despite the fact that labor and economic life were deeply intertwined with the reproduction of social hierarchies and values.[125] In these premodern urban societies, patriarchal norms embedded in legal, institutional, and social frameworks contributed to the systematic restriction of women's labor opportunities. Thus, even within very different systems of labor organization, women in both Brabant and Biscay encountered similar cultural and structural barriers. The prohibition on female brokers in Bilbao from touching the weights and the ban on wage-earning women in Antwerp's purse and glove making trades exemplify how gendered norms were used to justify exclusion across distinct local contexts.

Cultural values shaped the boundaries of women's work in both regions, regardless of which institutions held authority over its organization. This insight lends further support to Sheilagh Ogilvie's concept of "institutional enforcement," though I extend the notion of 'institutions' beyond guilds to encompass all bodies with legislative capacities. In the conclusion of *The European Guilds*, Ogilvie argues that while the exclusion of certain groups from formal urban economies reflected prevailing cultural norms, "economic discrimination was facilitated, and sometimes entirely fabricated, by rules and enforcement mechanisms imposed by institutions such as guilds."[126] In both Brabant and Biscay, male-dominated institutions with regulatory authority restricted women's economic activities. However, while Ogilvie and other scholars have concentrated on case studies where guilds or other powerful socioeconomic institutions structured significant parts of the urban economy, the addition of the Biscayan case allows us to isolate the guild effect more clearly. By comparing Biscay with Brabant, it becomes evident that guilds imposed an additional layer of restrictions— limitations that may not have existed without their influence. In this light, the guild effect emerges as a crucial differentiating factor between the two regions in terms of constraints on women's work.

---

[125] Bailey, Colwell & Hotchin, 'Approaching Women and Work in Premodern Europe', 9.
[126] Ogilvie, *The European Guilds. An Economic Analysis*, 575.

As earlier studies have shown, urban residents' survival strategies did not always align with the guilds' programs of exclusivity and masculinity, leading the guilds to seek ordinances protecting their limited membership.[127] Guilds created an exclusive labor framework and prosecuted those who violated it. In 1983, Grethe Jacobsen noted that the stricter work structure with closed guilds in Denmark during the late Middle Ages led to an increase in offenses related to irregular trade.[128] A particularly telling example is the case of the Mechelen fishmongers. The guild's sentence book reveals how the corporation vigilantly defended its privileges and monopolies, thereby narrowing the space for women's work even within the guild's household economic model. However, the 'guild effect' was not uniform; it depended on local circumstances and the specific nature of the labor involved, once again showing the need for a more nuanced and context-sensitive analysis of this mechanism.

In contrast, no equivalent of the 'guild effect' appears in the Biscayan case study. The absence of formalized labor organization in Biscay gave rise to a more informal market economy, which allowed women to dominate certain trades. This informality shaped both regulation and labor practices in Bilbao and left space for women active in the town's small-scale trades. Yet it also meant that women lacked institutional protections when the town council began curtailing their opportunities. In the next chapter, we will approach the 'guild effect' from another angle. While in both regions, institutions that restricted women's labor were guided by economic motivations and cultural values, their impact on individual women's experiences—and women's ability to resist or adapt—could be strikingly different.

---

[127] Gold, 'On the Streets and in the Markets', 37; Honeyman & Goodman, 'Women's Work, Gender Conflict, and Labour Markets', 611; Howell, 'The Problem of Women's Agency'; Montenach & Simonton, 'Introduction', 4–5.

[128] Jacobsen, 'Women's Work and Women's Role', 11. Anne Montenach has noted a similar mechanism in early modern France. See: Montenach, 'Trades in Lyon in the Late Seventeenth and Early Eighteenth Centuries'.

CHAPTER 4

Wielding the Framework

On 11 January 1497, the town council of Bilbao established the prices that the *regateras* could charge for candles and oil. The council promulgated this ordinance "with the consent of the retail women, calling them before the council."[1] In Bilbao, only the town council held the authority to issue work regulations since neither the retail women as a group nor any other institution had the power to do so. Nonetheless, the saleswomen provided their consent before the council published its decision. Also, without consent, the Bilbao saleswomen had strategies to deal with the council's regulations.

Throughout this book, we have explored women's economic activities, yet the women in question have predominantly remained objects rather than subjects of these activities. The guilds, household economy, town councils, and socioeconomic (cultural) mechanisms primarily drove their roles. However, one piece of the puzzle remains missing: the ways in which these women were active agents within the mechanisms that shaped their labor opportunities. Not only did they engage in a wide range of economic activities with remarkable ingenuity, but they also managed to stretch the framework imposed by guilds and town councils. In this chapter, we will examine the mechanisms and strategies that groups of women or individual women employed to sustain and enhance their economic opportunities.

In Brabant, the influence of guilds on economic organization often overshadowed the initiatives taken by women. In a few instances, we see clear strategies employed by groups of women. More often than not, individual women demonstrated their resourcefulness by utilizing a varied set of tools to argue their cases. They skillfully wielded available tools—such as court arguments, recalling earlier privileges, and leveraging group affiliations—to achieve their objectives. In Biscay, the

---

[1] "[…] los sobredichos sennores del regimiento, con acuerdo de las regateras de candela e azeite llamandoles al conçejo, ordenaron e mandaron e mandaron que diesen las candelas e azeite al presente fasta que sea sebo e para que sea su voluntad a los preçios siguientes […]." Enríquez Fernández et al., *Ordenanzas municipales de Bilbao (1477–1520)*, fol. 83r–83v, 11 January 1497.

informal nature of trades involving daily commodities increased the visibility of women sellers in the town ordinance while also revealing the strategies and cooperation among these groups of women regarding their economic activities. The absence of formal competitors allowed these women to cooperate informally and confront the council as a group. However, Bilbao's lack of formal economic institutions did not necessarily confer a greater advantage to these women, given the absence of a firmly established framework they could rely on. Instead, I argue that the Bilbao saleswomen were more dependent on the goodwill of the council and their personal networks.

Demonstrating how Biscayan and Brabantine women navigated the framework of their labor opportunities involves two key aspects. First, we will examine women's direct and indirect influence on the regulation of their work. The differing positions of authority and attempts to influence municipal authorities reveal a notable imbalance between the Brabantine and Biscayan case studies. The absence of guilds and the presence of a strong household economy in Bilbao gave women the incentive to exert influence more visibly and effectively compared to their counterparts in Mechelen and Antwerp. The second part shows the other side of this lack of institutionalization. Based on court cases and sentences, we will see that the lack of group affiliation and privileges left the Bilbao saleswomen with few effective defense strategies, while some Brabantine women could rely on their affiliation with patriarchal guilds or household units. However, in both regions, judicial case dossiers show the women traders as savvy economic actors, adept at navigating the legal landscape.

1. Influencing Regulation

This section examines the influence that women in Bilbao, Antwerp, and Mechelen exerted over the regulation of their work. In many premodern European regions, masculine middling groups and associations, such as craft guilds, held significant sway over local governments. In some cases, this influence was formalized through direct representation; in others, it remained more informal.[2] By contrast, the ways in which women influenced local governance have received considerably less scholarly

---

[2] See several chapters from: Haemers & Eersels, *Words and Deeds*.

attention. This section explores how women in the three towns occasionally shaped local policy and secured positions of authority connected to their work. Furthermore, I will discuss the formal offices held by women in these towns that were tied to their occupational activities.

As highlighted by Mary Erler and Maryanne Kowaleski in their influential 1988 publication, *Women and Power in the Middle Ages*, a crucial distinction exists between 'influence' and 'authority.' The contributors to their edited volume explore women's empowerment, broadening the concept of 'power' to include 'informal influence,' defined as "the ability to act effectively, to influence people or decisions, and to achieve goals."[3] For the purposes of this study, I propose extending this definition to include the influence on institutions. Since the publication of Erler and Kowaleski's volume, scholars have further demonstrated how, depending on their marital status and position within the community, some women were able to shape their labor opportunities.[4] As we will see, this informal influence also enabled women in Brabant and Biscay to effect changes—albeit occasionally—in the regulations governing their economic activities.

'Authority,' by contrast, can be defined as "the publicly recognized right to give direction and expect compliance."[5] In urban contexts, women rarely held such formal authority, which in these patriarchal societies was typically reserved for men and masculine institutions.[6] Nevertheless, some notable exceptions existed. In Brabant, for instance, widows acting as substitutes for their deceased husbands could hold positions of authority that were otherwise inaccessible to women. I argue that this possibility was closely tied to the prevalence of the household economy in Brabantine towns. In Biscay, meanwhile, women occasionally assumed low-level positions of authority due to their occupational standing—a direct result of their dominant presence in specific labor sectors.

---

[3] Erler and Kowaleski, *Women and Power in the Middle Ages*, 2–10.

[4] See, among others: Bailey, Colwell & Hotchin, 'Approaching Women and Work'; Ling et al., 'Marriage and Work'; Schmidt, 'Contested Authority'.

[5] Ormrod, *Women and Parliament in Later Medieval England*, 12–3.

[6] Erler & Kowaleski, *Women and Power in the Middle Ages*, 2.

Wielding Authority

In patriarchal premodern urban societies, women were generally denied access to government and positions of authority. The Brabantine towns were no exception to this phenomenon. In Antwerp and Mechelen, women were excluded from participating in guild politics, even if they held guild membership. In late medieval Biscay, citizens from rural areas and small-scale towns could participate in the towns' plenary meetings, which gave citizenship a political dimension. As heads of households, widows often participated in these rural *asambleas*.[7] However, there is no evidence to suggest that women in Bilbao participated in these assemblies. As the fifteenth century progressed, the local government of Bilbao became increasingly exclusive, paving the way for an oligarchy dominated by urban aristocratic and merchant families.[8] As such, this section starts from the assumption that formal political authority was in the hands of men in both regions.

While sustained formal political participation by women in Brabant and Biscay was limited, a few women nonetheless attained positions typically inaccessible to their gender. In the Brabantine towns, widows formed a notable exception: they were permitted to join guilds that were otherwise formally closed to women, owing to their right to continue their deceased husbands' businesses. This right afforded them a degree of economic and, at times, institutional participation that was not available to other women.[9] For instance, in an ordinance from Leuven, the barbers' guild excluded all women except for masters' widows, who were permitted to continue practicing the craft—provided they remained unmarried.[10] Typically, this right did not extend to positions of authority within the guild. However, norms and practices did not always align. In some cases, widows not only assumed control of the household workshop but also took on roles of authority within the guild organization itself.

---

[7] Castrillo Casado, 'Las mujeres del común y la sociedad política'; Del Val Valdivieso, 'Los espacios del trabajo femenino', 69–70.

[8] Castrillo Casado, 'Las mujeres del común y la sociedad política', 502–3; Ignacio Salazar, 'Gobierno local en el Bilbao bajomedieval', 183–97.

[9] Studies on the widow's right in the premodern Low Countries include, among others: Burm & De Munck, 'Het broodje gebakken?'; Howell, *Commerce before Capitalism*, 100–1; Schmidt, *Overleven na de dood*, Wyffels, 'Women and Work in Early Modern Printing Houses'; Wyffels, 'De drukkersvrouwen van Sint Lucas'.

[10] SAL, 1523, fol. 129v, 14 February 1439.

As discussed in chapter 3, women were barred from serving as estimators in the old clothes sellers' guild of Antwerp—a position that conferred authority and carried political weight within the guild. This role remained inaccessible to women, even those who had obtained guild membership. Nevertheless, in 1410, a woman named Zoete Volbrechts appeared on the Antwerp aldermen's list of 'sworn estimators.'[11] She may have been the widow of an old clothes seller. In the aldermen's registers, one entry refers to a Zoete van den Scrieke, widow of Claus Volbrechts, while three later records mention a Zoete Volbrechts.[12] If these documents refer to the same individual, Zoete remained a widow from at least 1410 to 1426, during which time she was active in trading annuities and moneylending. No further records directly link her to the old clothes sellers' guild. It is possible that Claus Volbrechts had only recently died in 1410, and that Zoete was permitted to assume the role of estimator as a temporary exception to guild policy. Alternatively, she may have appealed directly to the aldermen to bypass guild restrictions. As guild labor was typically organized around the cooperation of the nuclear couple, a widow's right to continue her husband's functions often served as a practical necessity for maintaining the household's livelihood after the husband's death.[13] Given that the appointment of a female estimator was highly unconventional, the position might have been assigned to her only in the absence of other adult male successors.

The same mechanism might have been at play with the widow of Daneel de Coninck, whom we encountered in chapter 2. Her name appears on the list of deans in the account book from 1566 of the Mechelen glove makers' guild.[14] While we may never know the exact nature of her duties, it is clear that she bore some responsibility for the guild's accounts that year. In the context of Brabant's household-based economy, such exceptions were not unheard of: some widows temporarily assumed roles traditionally reserved for men.[15] Such positions were inaccessible to never-married women in Brabant—a finding that aligns with research on early modern Swedish society, where marriage often functioned as a crucial stepping stone to

---

[11] Van den Branden, 'Clementijnboek 1288–1414 (Vervolg)', 64.

[12] SAA, SR#5, fol. 234v, 1415; SAA, SR#12, fol. 335v, 1426, SAA, SR#12, fol. 391r, 1426.

[13] Bennett, 'Public Power and Authority in the Medieval English Countryside', 23–6.

[14] SAM, Handschoenmakers-, tesmakers-, riem(be)slagers-, witledermakers- en schedemakersambacht 557, fol. 50v.

[15] Schmidt, 'Contested Authority'.

women's authority.[16] In the cases of Mechelen and Antwerp, 'authority' might be too strong a word, given the limited information about their actual work tasks. Nonetheless, these widows encountered a significantly more extensive framework of opportunities than other women.

An important sidenote to women's limited authority in their economic activities is that, once more, they were probably not banned from this because of a lack of skill or perceived skill. When it came to skill, some women easily gained authority over some men. This development is especially visible in trade guilds. As Jeremy Goldberg has argued, within the domestic economic unit, gender was less important than seniority.[17] In 1454, the town council of Leuven ruled that Andries de Meyer, the husband of the mercer Machteld van Wynge, could enter the town's mercers' guild provided that his wife trained him. Machteld probably was not a newcomer to the mercers' trade since the surname 'van Wynge' appeared in other documents of the mercers of Leuven. Her family's established position in the guild might have influenced the guild's decision.[18] Married women were recognized as valid contributors to a household economic unit. Machteld, raised in a mercers' family, was entrusted with oversight of her husband's training, much like a few female members of the Antwerp mercers' guild responsible for apprentices.[19] However, in the case of Machteld and Andries, it is possible that Andries assumed authority over Machteld's activities within the guild once he had gained sufficient experience.

In Bilbao, women's positions of authority and power did not necessarily stem from their position in the household. Instead, women's occupations could provide a foundation for their influence over the market and its policies. Sánchez de Salcedo was one of the women who fulfilled an official position of leadership in Bilbao. She appears twice in historical documents from 1509. First, on 16 February 1509, four women *cojedoras* were called before the council to pledge oaths that they would practice the occupation in accordance with the council's demands. They had to "hand over well and loyally to the excise collector the [grain] excises." Sánchez de Salcedo was to act as overseer for these women *cojedoras*.[20] Probably, Sánchez had

---

[16] Ling, et al., 'Marriage and Work', 91–9.
[17] Schmidt, Devos, and Blondé, 'Introduction. Single and the City', 7.
[18] SAL, 4648, fol. 397r–397v, 22 November 1454.
[19] For example, the widow Reyners became involved in a dispute with another mercer, who accused her of stealing his apprentice. SAA, GA#4212, fol. 45v, 14 August 1534.
[20] Enríquez Fernández et al., *Libro de acuerdos y decretos municipales*, fol. 18r, 9 February 1509.

been formally appointed by the council to ensure the good conduct of the other brokers. The overseers of the grain weights stood guard over the weights and decided who could weigh their own merchandise. Although Sánchez might not have had a high position, she exercised influence over one of Bilbao's most crucial trade items. One week after the brokers swore their oaths, Sánchez was called before the council, who instructed her that "since she guarded the weights, she could give no weights to the *mulateros*," who brought grain into the town on mules.[21]

In 1509, Mari Saes de Balmaseda assumed a position similar to that of Sánchez de Salcedo. The town council of Bilbao needed a "trustworthy person of good conscience who would exercise well and loyally" the position of bread weigher. In 1515, this "good, trustworthy person of good conscience" was Mari Saes de Balmaseda. She swore ("sy, juro e amen") before the council that she would conduct the job honestly. In return, she would receive a fixed salary.[22] Neither Sánchez nor Mari was identified by family relationship or marital status. Instead, they acquired positions because of their occupations and reputations. The town council of Bilbao did not bypass appointing these women to positions of authority because the council considered that these women had sufficient expertise.

We should remember that Sánchez de Salcedo and Mari Saes de Balmaseda ranked quite low in the hierarchy of authority in Bilbao and had no direct say over policies. They could exercise authority over other women *cojedoras* and bread sellers, as well as over the *mulateros* with whom the female brokers closely cooperated. Zoete Volbrechts, the estimator of the Antwerp old clothes sellers, had authority over formal guild members. While Zoete's authority over secondhand dealers probably originated in her position in the institutionalized household economy, female authority in Bilbao stemmed from the prominent role of women in certain branches of the labor market. The Bilbao women held positions of authority because the council had decided to award those positions to them. There were few mechanisms to safeguard these positions for Bilbao's tradeswomen, though. The role entrusted to Sánchez in 1509 by the town council did not protect her work as a broker. Two decades later, when the Bilbao council prosecuted the women brokers, she was one of the brokers arguing for the continuation of the occupation.[23]

[21] *Ibidem*, fol. 20v, 16 February 1509.
[22] *Ibidem*, fol. 57v–58r, 23 November 1515.
[23] The details of this conflict will be discussed in the next chapter.

Direct Influence

While holding positions of direct authority was largely unattainable for women, formal office was not the sole avenue for influencing trade practices. Particularly in Bilbao, women's direct influence on council policies is evident through petitions. Petitions were "one of the most frequently used collective means of the citizens' repertoire to influence urban politics."[24] They were policy proposals presented by an individual or community. In the Low Countries, "the petition was the instrument par excellence through which burghers could exercise influence on the urban legislation."[25] This practice was not unique to the Low Countries; middling groups in regions like Castile also utilized petitions to appeal to local governments.[26]

Craft guilds were the most visible collectives that used petitions. Because their economic and political strength gave them the power to pressure local governments, they frequently requested new ordinances or changes in existing regulations by means of these oral or written requests.[27] Although less common, communities of working women in both Biscay and Brabant also engaged in petitioning. These actions, as observed by Mark Ormrod in late medieval England, reflected a sense of belonging to broader social or institutional orders and a perceived right to supplicate collectively.[28] While lacking the same level of political pressure as guilds, these instances demonstrate women's agency in attempting to shape local governance.

In the fifteenth and sixteenth centuries, Bilbao was governed by an oligarchy; the same aristocratic and merchant families rotated through the town's government posts.[29] Socioeconomic institutions were not represented on the town council, though a few merchant associations did gain importance at the end of the fifteenth century.[30] Nevertheless, the governors had to consider and manage their citizens' complaints. In 1488,

---

[24] Haemers, 'Ad Petitionem Burgensium', 378.

[25] Schmidt, 'Contested Authority', 215. See also: Haemers, 'Governing and Gathering about the Common Welfare of the Town', 160.

[26] Solórzano Telechea, 'The Politics of the Urban Commons'.

[27] Eersels, 'The Craft Guilds are the City', 230–2.

[28] Ormrod, *Women and Parliament*, 64.

[29] Salazar, 'Gobierno local en el Bilbao bajomedieval'.

[30] García Fernández, 'Las cofradías de oficios en el País Vasco', 31; Solórzano Telechea, 'The Politics of the Urban Commons', 189–90.

citizens complained about Bilbao's retail women (*regateras*) and the times and locations of their trade activities. As a result, the council promulgated an ordinance specifying the hours and locations where women were allowed to trade.[31] The council of Bilbao also had to consider requests from the town's occupational groups. On 29 January 1509, for example, the butchers of Bilbao complained that the price they were allowed to charge for bacon was too low and successfully convinced the council to increase it.[32] Petitions in Bilbao were often presented orally, directly to the council members, which is not surprising considering the size of the town.

The council of Bilbao had to consider requests from the town's (female) occupational groups. In the ordinances' *narratios*, evidence of oral petitions by groups of saleswomen responsible for retail sales and distribution of food supplies in Bilbao occasionally appears. On 18 September 1510, the council banned the fishmongers from Bilbao's market square on the grounds that the smell of their fish was a blight on the marketplace. The fishmongers were instructed to open shops on the surrounding streets.[33] Two weeks later, on 2 October, nineteen female fishmongers submitted a petition to the council and the *Corregidor* of Biscay—among them were Mayora de Iturribalzaga, Catalina Nafarra, and María Pérez de Bermeo, all of whom we have encountered in previous chapters. They argued that since foreign merchants came to the market square specifically to buy fish, the fishmongers would lose income if these merchants could no longer find them. Furthermore, they argued, the smell of fish would be even worse in the town's narrow streets. The *Corregidor* sided with the fishmongers, obliging the council to revise the previous ordinance and set up a wooden shed in the market square in which the fishmongers could sell fish.[34]

The 1510 petition was not an isolated instance of Bilbao's fishmongers directly influencing ordinances. In 1509, Mari Pérez de Durango, a fishmonger at the Portal de Zamudio, petitioned the council, alleging that fishmongers in the main square were monopolizing the town's fish supply. Her plea resulted in a council order mandating that the square fishmongers allocate "one-third of the fish to be sold at the Portal de

---

[31] Enríquez Fernández et al., *Ordenanzas municipales de Bilbao (1477–1520)*, fol. 35r–35v, 24 September 1488.

[32] Enríquez Fernández et al., *Libro de acuerdos y decretos municipales*, fol. 13r, 29 January 1509.

[33] Enríquez Fernández et al., *Ordenanzas municipales de Bilbao (1477–1520)*, fol. 273v–274r, 18 September 1510.

[34] *Ibidem*, fol. 276r–279r, 2 October 1510.

Zamudio in the nets that are there so that it will be divided better among the citizens of this town."[35] Mari Pérez de Durango framed her request as benefiting all Bilbao citizens. It is plausible that she acted as a representative for other fishmongers who had their trade at the Portal de Zamudio. Members of (occupational) groups needed to consult and cooperate before they submitted requests and petitions to the town council.[36] Despite their exclusion from formal authority, the Bilbao fishmongers demonstrated an understanding of their leverage as essential town provisioners. It is possible that trading in their own names had required these women to develop political awareness and learn how to act on it.[37]

In Brabant, female petitioners and women's direct influence on regulation were less common than in Biscay. Petitions for changes to town regulations were typically submitted by recognized associations. In Brabantine towns, guilds stood out as the most influential of these associations in shaping local government regulations related to labor.[38] While there is little evidence of individual petitions in the Brabantine towns, this scarcity appears to reflect a structural limitation: the dominance of the guilds restricted women's opportunities to voice concerns or make requests directly to local authorities. This dynamic is illustrated by the 1474 ordinance of the Antwerp glove and purse makers. As discussed earlier, some guild masters objected to women participating in the guild. In response, the guild formally excluded women wageworkers. However, authorities permitted the female members of guild masters' households to continue their work for the guild.[39] Although this exemption may have resulted from complaints by both guild masters and their wives, the ordinance itself did not acknowledge the wives' voices, highlighting the indirect and often invisible nature of women's influence within Brabantine guild structures.

---

[35] "[...] caso que las regateras de la plaça tengan tomado todo el pescado, que le den la terçia parte para que sea vendida en el dicho Portal de Çamudio en los redes que ende estan, porque sea meyor repartido por los vesinos de la dicha villa [...]." Enríquez Fernández et al., *Libro de acuerdos y decretos municipales*, fol. 49r–49v, 13 June 1509.

[36] Haemers, 'Ad Petitionem Burgensium', 380–6.

[37] A similar case can be found in Mark Ormrod's analysis of women arguing in the courts of late medieval England. Ormrod, *Women and Parliament*, 64; Erler & Kowaleski, *Gendering the Master Narrative*, 4.

[38] Eersels, 'Requested and Consented by the Good Crafts', 91–112.

[39] Génard, 'Register van den dachvaerden', 400–1.

As most petitions concerning work regulations in Brabantine towns came from the guilds, it is not surprising that the only female petitioners emerged from one of the few recognized female occupational groups that did not belong to a guild. In 1478, the *uitdraagsters* of Leuven submitted a petition to the town council in response to a measure imposed by the old clothes sellers' guild. The guild, they claimed, "wanted to oblige them to pay twenty guilders, which they thought was a great novelty and against all they had done and been accustomed to before then." According to the *uitdraagsters*, the guild was attempting to control and restrict their work opportunities. In response, the women appealed to the Leuven council, asking it to intervene.[40]

The council ultimately did not confirm their request, suggesting that the *uitdraagsters* might indeed have lost some of their independence to the guild. As Bernard Capp has observed about women's petitions in early modern England, "such petitions reflect nonetheless a first step towards consciously political activity."[41] The mere act of organizing as a group may have fostered a sense of collective identity among the *uitdraagsters*, similar to that observed among female vendors in Bilbao. Their frequent contact with the old clothes sellers' guild may also have led them to adopt certain guild-like strategies. Still, their shared identity and tactics were not enough to sway the Leuven council, as the *uitdraagsters* lacked the "clearly established and recognized legal rights" held by the guild.[42]

Consent, Bargaining, and Leverage

In Bilbao, women's efforts to influence town regulations appear to have been more consistent than those of their counterparts in Brabant. While tradeswomen in Biscay often used official complaints and petitions to voice their concerns, they also influenced the town council's decision-making more indirectly. As discussed in chapter 1, Bilbao's retail women were generally not wealthy; some may have belonged to the lowest social

---

[40] "Item, heden zijn comen voer den raide van der stad zeker vrouwe personen uutdragerssen den raide van der stad te kynnen gevende hoe dat de geswoirene van den ouden cleercopers ambachte hen wouden bedwingen te moeten verborghen tot der sommen toe van twintich rijnschgulden, dwelc hen dochte zijnde een grote nieuwicheit ende tegen tghene des men in dien tot noch toe hadde gedaen ende gehanteert [...]." SAL, 1524, fol. 9r, 15 July 1478.

[41] Capp, *When Gossips Meet*, 306.

[42] This situation was also found by Susan Broomhall in her study of informal linen resellers in early modern Rouen. Broomhall, 'Women, Work, and Power in the Female Guilds of Rouen', 206.

classes. Although they were permitted to work independently, regardless of marital status, this autonomy may have stemmed more from necessity than choice. As Laurence Fontaine has noted, economic hardship might have driven them into these visible roles, yet that same necessity also "opened up areas of freedom to them."[43] Historical records suggest that the council of Bilbao had to take these women's perspectives into account when regulating their work.

The most subtle form of influence visible in the ordinances of Bilbao was the consent of female occupational groups to the council's new regulations. Their accord can be found in the ordinances of three occupations: fishmongers, bakers, and retailers. On 3 July 1512, the town council of Bilbao promulgated a new ordinance for the town's bread bakers and bread sellers. This ordinance announced decisions on bread prices, women's salaries, and work arrangements. The ordinance had been made in agreement with the bread bakers.[44] The consideration given by the town council of Bilbao to the bakers regarding the regulation of their work has already been established by María Isabel del Val Valdivieso, who showed that the bakers of Bilbao actively participated in setting the town's grain prices.[45] Bread was a staple in the urban diet, and since women were primarily responsible for baking, they held significant leverage over the council. Even though the oligarchic town council retained the authority to punish women for any misconduct, it could not impose regulations on their work without their agreement.

The fishmongers and retailers of Bilbao exercised a similar kind of influence. As distributors of essential goods throughout the town, they held enough leverage to compel the council to include them in regulatory decisions. In 1497, and again in 1509, the *regateras de candela e azeite* appeared before the council to give their consent to newly set prices for candles and oil.[46] A similar situation occurred in 1515, when the council decreed that sellers of fresh fish must begin selling cut fish by weight rather than by piece, as had previously been the practice.[47] The saleswomen had not

---

[43] Fontaine, 'Makeshift, Women and Capability', 57.

[44] Enríquez Fernández et al., *Ordenanzas municipales de Bilbao (1477–1520)*, fol. 139v–141r, 3 July 1512.

[45] Del Val Valdivieso, 'El trabajo de las mujeres', 70.

[46] Enríquez Fernández et al., *Ordenanzas municipales de Bilbao (1477–1520)*, fol. 83r–83v, 11 January 1497; Enríquez Fernández et al., *Libro de acuerdos y decretos municipales*, fol. 98r–99r, 28 February 1509.

[47] Enríquez Fernández et al., *Ordenanzas municipales de Bilbao (1477–1520)*, fol. 156v, 18 May 1515.

requested this regulation, nor was their involvement in the decision-making process guaranteed. Nonetheless, the council required their consent to enact the ordinance, showing that these women, by operating collectively, had succeeded in asserting a degree of influence.[48]

The council could penalize women who did not follow the ordinances, as they had accepted them by giving their consent upon promulgation. Still, granting consent seems to have been part of a larger political strategy of the female traders. On 21 February 1509, eleven *regateras* appeared before the council to hear a new ordinance. They swore that "they each will supply their stores with candles and oil" and comply with "the foresaid prices and conditions." The council noted explicitly that the women had consented to the new prices and work conditions (mainly about the weight of the candles).[49] Yet, upon giving their consent, the retailers had also received certain privileges from the council.

> And the said council promised them to protect and fulfill the aforementioned, and to guarantee the prohibition that no one else sell oil or candles in retail, except the aforementioned licensed parties [that is, the *regateras*, ed.].[50]

By accepting the new ordinance, the retail women had established a monopoly over the sale of candles and oil in Bilbao. Their consent to the ordinance was the result of a give-and-take process, much like the procedures that accompanied petitions from male guilds. Once women were recognized as an occupational group—even without formal institutionalization—they could claim rights comparable to those of male associations. However, the question remains to what extent their gender shaped the local government's responses to their demands.

---

[48] Martha Howell and Daryll Hafter found a similar political sense for groups of women workers elsewhere in premodern Europe. See: Howell, 'Achieving the Guild Effect without Guilds', 123; Hafter, *Women at Work in Preindustrial France*, 154.

[49] "[...] luego las sobredichas regateras se obligaron por sus personas e vienes, cada vno por sy, de tener e vasteçer cada vno su tyenda e de dar abasto de candelas e aseyte desde oy dia fasta el dia de Todos Santos [...]. Para todo lo sobredicho las sobredichas regateras, cada vna sobre sy e por sy, para basteçer cada vno su tyenda e dar abastadamente en los preçios e condyçiones susodichos durante el sobredicho termino, se obligaron, so las penas susodichas consentyendo en todo lo susodicho." Enríquez Fernández et al., *Libro de acuerdos y decretos municipales*, fol. 21r–21v; 21 February 1509.

[50] "E el dicho conçejo les prometyo de les guardar e cunplir lo susodicho e de debedar e plegonar que otro ninguno non benda aseyte nin candela por menudo, saluo los sobredichos obligados." *Ibidem*, fol. 21r–21v, 21 February 1509.

The group of *regateras* in Bilbao consented to ordinances about their work. They could claim the trade for themselves as the council recognized them as a legitimate group of traders. A clear arrangement between the council and the saleswomen—respecting regulations versus guaranteeing the women's monopolies—can also be seen in a 1509 ordinance concerning the *pescaderas*. The council needed to regulate the fish trade, as they complained that many of the fishmongers selling dried fish "do not give good fish and sell the fish for higher and lower prices" than those set by the council. It seems that the town council of Bilbao could not simply force new regulations on the fishmongers. The council had to promise the group of women to limit competition from foreign merchants and other fishmongers who had not sold dried fish before and now wanted to distribute fish in Bilbao.[51] Because of their important role in provisioning Bilbao, the town council had to take the female fishmongers into consideration when regulating their work.

In the Brabantine towns, there are no recorded instances of women exerting indirect influence on local governments comparable to those observed in Bilbao. This absence may reflect yet another case in which women's voices were overshadowed by the dominant voices of male guild members or household heads. Nevertheless, the absence of visible influence in the written sources does not mean that women remained silent on matters of urban or guild politics. In 1508, for example, the Mechelen fishmongers' guild admitted a sixteen-year-old boy as a master. The wife of Rombout Venne—whom we encountered in chapter 2 as an active participant in her husband's trade—openly expressed her discontent, declaring that "now the guild has come into the hands of children." The guild did not tolerate such public dissent, and in response, Rombout Venne's wife was ordered to undertake a pilgrimage to Halle.[52]

As Jelle Haemers and Chanelle Delameillieure have shown, Brabantine urban governments routinely confronted women's subversive "discussions about how a city should be governed."[53] The Mechelen fishmongers'

---

[51] "[...] que por quanto las regateras que benden en la dicha villa el pescado seçial remojado por menudo non dan a las veses buen pescado e suele muchas veses tomar el dicho pescado muchas alçadas e baxadas en el preçio a las veses, e despues de puesto por el regymiento vn preçio [...] E el dicho conçejo les prometyo que otra regatera ninguna en el sobredicho tienpo non bendera en la dicha villa pescado remojado synon las sobredichas obligadas [...]." *Ibidem*, fol. 87r–87v, 14 November 1509.

[52] "[...] soe seyde sij, "nu es d'ambacht toet de kinderhanden comen"." SAM, Visverkopers 321, fol. 54r, 8 May 1508.

[53] Haemers & Delameillieure, 'Women and Contentious Speech'; Haemers, 'Verraders, muitmakers en boeven!'.

sentence books and the *Correctieboeken* of the Antwerp aldermen contain examples of women voicing criticism, either in relation to their involvement in their husbands' trades or in their own names.[54]

Although in Brabant women could be prosecuted for their political opinions, and both guild and urban authorities took their expressions of discontent seriously, it remains uncertain how women's words influenced their own labor opportunities. Indirect forms of influence may have existed, but they are difficult to trace. Individual complaints or informal petitions from craft guild members—especially those that may have preceded official guild petitions or regulations—rarely appear in normative sources. Moreover, formal petitions were typically submitted after meetings of guild members.[55] It is possible that women's grievances reached guild authorities indirectly, perhaps through their husbands in some households. However, there is no evidence of such dynamics in the surviving written sources of Antwerp and Mechelen.

2. Going to Court

Let us revisit two examples from chapter 3. First, Mayora de Iturribalzaga was ordered to stop selling fresh fish following a lengthy court case against the town council. Second, the Mechelen fishmongers punished Gheertruyde van den Broeke, the wife of fishmonger Wouter Ruts, for slandering a guild member acting in an official capacity. These cases illustrate the kinds of consequences women in both Brabant and Biscay could face as a result of their market activities. Women in neither region were passive subjects simply following the rules imposed by patriarchal institutions. On the contrary, they navigated, used, and at times stretched the institutional frameworks available to them in attempts to avoid the consequences of their (sometimes transgressive) actions. The active voice of Brabantine and Biscayan saleswomen is the focus of this section. We will examine the arguments they made in judicial cases related to their market

---

[54] In Antwerp, for example, in 1437, Katelijne van Bierbeek was sent on a pilgrimage to Aachen, in Germany, after she had spoken negatively about the town and its craft guilds. Melis-Taeymans, *Correctieboeck*, 60v, 17 August 1437. In Leuven, we can also find examples of women disagreeing with the craft guild governors and their policies. The fishmonger Machtilde Poerloeck, for example, scolded a guild official after he disapproved of her merchandise. ARB, 12654, fol. 344v, 1422–1423.

[55] Haemers, 'Ad Petitionem Burgensium', 380–6.

activities. These arguments are not necessarily different in Brabant and Biscay. However, the outcomes of the cases—and the moments and ways in which women used these arguments—reveal a clear difference, shaped by the distinct organization of women's labor in the two regions.

Biscayan Tradeswomen in Court

One of the challenges with the Biscayan source material is the lack of documentation on women's minor offenses. Since minor transgressions and their adjudication were typically not recorded, there is little surviving evidence from the lower courts, such as those of the town councils. Only when fines or sentences were contested and brought before the higher courts of the duchy or kingdom did written records become available.

The sparse documentation of a few court cases involving irregular work nevertheless provides a detailed picture of how these cases progressed—from the lower judicial venues available to Bilbao's residents to the final judgments issued by the highest courts in the kingdom of Castile. These cases include extensive arguments, both from the women involved in market activities and from the town council, which sought to curtail what it saw as economic infringements. Traditionally, Bilbao's urban residents were expected to appeal first to the *Corregidor* of Biscay—as we saw in the fishmongers' petition of 1510. After that, they could bring their case to the *Sala de Vizcaya* at the Royal Chancellery in Valladolid, and, finally, appeal to the president of the Chancellery.[56] Only those cases that reached this level have been preserved.

The court reports generated from these conflicts are both extensive and complex. Three of them offer insights into women's positions on the urban labor market. Since the case of Mayora de Iturribalzaga has already been discussed, I will now turn to the court cases of the town council of Bilbao against the *cojedoras* and against the hosts of the *plumeras*. In the final part of this section, we will discuss their motivations, arguments, and the outcomes of the cases in more detail.

*

---

[56] Emperador Ortega, 'El archivo de la Real Chancilleria de Valladolid y la Sala de Vizcaya'.

The case against the hosts of the linen buyers (or *plumeras*) started in 1517, when a group of seven female linen sellers appeared before the town council to complain about their hosts. The *plumeras* were women living in the county of Biscay and surrounding areas who traveled to Bilbao to buy linen cloth. They would use the linen to make padded products, such as mattresses and pillows, and sell these, possibly in Bilbao or nearby areas.[57] They came to Bilbao for multiple days and lodged with citizens of the Biscayan hub. In 1488, the women linen sellers in Bilbao complained about the hosts extorting them by charging for facilitating transactions between the linen sellers and linen buyers.[58] Reacting to those (written) complaints, the council of Bilbao promulgated an ordinance in 1488 that prohibited hosts from charging more than half a *maravedí* per *vara* of linen for brokering. The council had to remind the hosts about the regulation through new ordinances in 1499 and 1515.[59] Despite these regulations, the linen sellers summoned four hosts before the council in 1517 and accused them of extortion. According to the sellers, the hosts asked for money in return for bringing linen sellers to the buyers' shops. If they did not pay the hosts, the hosts threatened to go to other sellers who would pay them. The council fined the hosts two hundred *maravedís* and repeated the prohibition on brokerage.

After being fined, three hosts appealed to the higher court of the *Sala de Vizcaya* in the Royal Chancellery in Valladolid. The hosts claimed that they had the right to "show the tradeswomen the shops, houses, and booths where the linen sellers in Bilbao were," charging one *maravedí* for this as they had done "as long as it could be remembered."[60] Their arguments had little impact on the prohibition against charging money for brokerage. The higher court claimed that:

> *Doña* María López de Angulo and her associates are not to demand or collect *blancas* for the *varas* of linen purchased by the tradeswomen linen buyers in the aforementioned town, but rather, they are to permit the aforementioned

---

[57] Castrillo Casado, *Las mujeres vascas*, 292.

[58] Enríquez Fernández et al., *Ordenanzas municipales de Bilbao (1477–1520)*, fol. 33r–33v, 11 July 1488.

[59] *Ibidem*, fol. 98r–100r, 28 June 1499; Enríquez Fernández et al., *Libro de acuerdos y decretos municipales*, fol. 59r, 10 December 1515.

[60] "[...] a las mercaderas les mostrar las lonjas e casas e tiendas de las vendederas de lienços de la dicha villa como ficieron desde del dicho tienpo ynmemorial [...]." ARChV, Registro de Ejecutorias, Caja 359, 65, 1523.

foreign tradeswomen to freely go and purchase from any shop or stall of any seller.[61]

Nevertheless, the higher court agreed to the women's appeal of the fine and ordered the town council of Bilbao to return the goods it had confiscated as collateral.[62] Both the council and the women protested against this decision: the council because they did not want to return the goods, and the women because they wanted permission to charge for their role as intermediaries between linen buyers and sellers. Neither side's protests were effective, and the president of the Royal Chancellery confirmed the decision of the higher court and closed the court case on 30 January 1523.[63]

Twenty-four years later, on 21 January 1547, there were more complaints about the hosts of the *plumeras*, as some of them had continued to charge money for brokerage. The mayor of Bilbao interrogated seven hosts (two married couples, one man, and two women) and fined them 500 *maravedís*. The hosts again appealed to Valladolid, claiming that they had to charge for brokerage to recoup the costs of lodging and feeding the *plumeras*. The judges in Valladolid turned a deaf ear to their complaints and, on 27 May 1549, decided that the fine given by Bilbao's mayor had been appropriate.[64] The 1549 sentence was not the end of the struggles between the linen traders' hosts and the Bilbao town council. More than four decades later, in the 1592 ordinance, the council still needed to address the hosts, repeating complaints against their brokerage. Once again, the council had to put the practice under strict fines.[65]

*

For the town council of Bilbao, brokerage by intermediaries was a recurring problem in other sectors besides the linen trade. In the second court

---

[61] "[…] con este aditamiento que debo mandar y mando que a la dicha dona Mari Lopez de Angulo e sus consortes no demanden ni lleven las blancas por razon de las varas de lienços que las dichas mercaderas plumeras conpraren en la dicha villa signo que dexen a las dichas mercaderas forasteras quisieren puedan libremente yr a conprar a qualesquier tiendas e lonjas de qualesquier mercaderes ansi de la dicha villa como burgaleses y estrangeros como quisieren." AFB, Municipal, 0031/002/010, fol. 10v.

[62] AFB, Municipal, 0031/002/010, fol. 10r–10v.
[63] *Ibidem*, fol. 13r–14r.
[64] *Ibidem*, fol. 16r–23r.
[65] de Mañaricua, *Las ordenanzas de Bilbao de 1593*, 96–7.

case, the council was essentially contesting the same irregular activities, this time by the *cojedoras*. The *cojedoras*, as we have seen in the previous chapters, were female brokers who guarded grain brought in by merchants on mules and handled the payments of buyers. On 7 October 1524, after already having tried to limit their activities for almost twenty years, the town council of Bilbao published an ordinance prohibiting the occupation altogether. The council claimed that the women brokers committed fraud and deception and were increasing grain prices for their own profit.[66] The local government called four *cojedoras* to appear before them and listen to the ordinance being read aloud so that they could spread the word about the new regulation. A fine of 5000 *maravedís* was set for those breaking the new rules.[67]

Rather than simply accepting the new ordinance, in 1525, the *cojedoras* appeared before the higher court of Biscay at the Royal Chancellery of Valladolid to argue for its annulment. The first of their main arguments was that the town council and the *Corregidor* of Biscay had no authority to enact this ordinance, as it infringed upon the county's privileges. They argued that, as citizens of Biscay, they had the right to earn a living and trade freely, without interference from the town council. Because the ordinance contradicted this privilege, it was considered invalid. Next, the *cojedoras* stressed that the council's claims of fraud and extortion were lies; they conducted trade fairly and honestly, and the grain merchants chose, on their own initiative, to work with *cojedoras*.[68] Finally, the women pointed to others in the town, such as the hosts of the *plumeras*, who had been permitted to earn a living through brokerage.[69] Although the conflict between the town council and the hosts had already been formally resolved by that point, and the hosts were officially forbidden from engaging in brokerage, it is clear that the activity continued—openly, not just in secret. The apparent persistence of this practice suggests that

---

[66] "[...] dexan los dichos trigos en el mercado a su cargo de las dichas cogedoras e ellas azen lo que quieren e dan a los que ellas querieren dexando a otros que lo abian e querían comprar e vender mas caro de lo que el mulatero abia de vender [...]." ARChV, Sala de Vizcaya, Caja 3467, 5, fol. 6r.

[67] In 1524, a wage worker earned thirty-eight *maravedís* for a day's work. The income of the *cojedoras*, who—as we will discuss in a later section—probably belonged to lower classes, was likely less than this amount. The fine of 5,000 *maravedís* for practicing *cojeduría* was thus an enormous amount.

[68] ARChV, Sala de Vizcaya, caja 3467, 5, fol. 3r.

[69] "[...] e abia otras mugeres e personas que tenían cargo de ospedar a las plumeras e de les comprar e vender lienços e otras cosas por salarios que les daban e asy mismo corredores e huéspedes que tenían semejantes oficios [...]." ARChV, Sala de Vizcaya, caja 3467, 5, fol. 3r–3v.

the prohibition may not have been fully accepted by the broader population. Indeed, the *cojedoras* invoked the hosts' brokerage activities as a precedent to legitimize their own roles as intermediaries.

Both sides made extensive arguments and counterarguments. On 9 December 1525, the *Corregidor* ordered that the women could not practice their occupation while the court case was being adjudicated, and if they did so, the town government could imprison them. This decision evoked a new flurry of arguments from both parties. When several of the women were imprisoned, their attorney demanded compensation for the damages they had suffered as a result of their imprisonment. Furthermore, he argued that the grain merchants required intermediaries, and that the council, well aware of this need, sought to eliminate the brokers only to replace them with its own representatives.[70] On 3 November 1526, the higher court of Biscay decided in favor of the council. Although brokering was prohibited, the arguments of both parties had made an impact. The fine for women disobeying the regulations was lowered to 600 *maravedís*. Furthermore, the higher court determined that if the council required intermediaries in the grain trade in the future, it had to allow the same group of women to do so.[71]

A few months later, in May 1527, the president of the Chancellery confirmed the sentence of the higher court and closed the case, but it was opened again in 1531. Many of the women involved in the first court case, as well as a few new ones, had again begun to work as brokers, with permission of the council, or so they claimed. They were interrogated and fined.[72] In 1535, the council summoned several *cojedoras* to appear before the *Corregidor* of Biscay for practicing the occupation. They were all found guilty, once again. It is unclear whether all the women engaged in brokerage consistently paid the fines imposed on them. However, it is evident that court cases against them had little short-term impact.

The last information we have about the occupation of the *cojedoras* comes from 1536, when the higher court and president of the Chancellery in Valladolid permitted a woman, Marina de Bedia, a former broker, to collect rents on grain from the merchants—a task closely related to her former occupation. The later ordinances do not mention the *cojedoras* again. Nevertheless, the struggle against intermediaries attempting to

[70] ARChV, Sala de Vizcaya, caja 3467, 5, fol. 9r.
[71] ARChV, Sala de Vizcaya, caja 3467, 5, fol. 9v–10v.
[72] In the next section, I will discuss their arguments in more depth.

profit from merchants bringing goods into Bilbao persisted. The 1548 and 1592 ordinances reflect the town council's repeated efforts to prohibit brokerage and to prevent inhabitants from meddling with the weighing and price setting of imported goods.

*

The two court cases from Bilbao, along with the case against Mayora de Iturribalzaga and the other sardine sellers, shed light on the irregular economic activities women undertook to support themselves and their families. These cases also clearly illustrate how the town council responded to such activities. Initially, the council showed a degree of leniency—up to a point. The *cojedoras* claimed that the council had permitted them to practice their trade, even though it was formally prohibited by the council's own ordinances. Similarly, as Mayora de Iturribalzaga argued in her defense, *sardineras* had sold fresh fish for many years before the council acted by issuing a new ordinance.[73]

The council's first step was to issue normative ordinances. These allowed officials to fine women found guilty of irregular trading practices—although there certainly was a disconnect between the council's official norms and the day-to-day practices. Ordinances had to be repeated frequently, as it proved difficult to eliminate women's informal trade. Finally, when women refused to comply with new regulations—as happened in all three court cases—the council did not shy away from following up with the extensive litigation.

The women in court wielded the same economic reasons in their court cases, albeit with little success. They tried to prove the necessity and normality of their market-oriented work, defended their good reputations and rights as citizens of Bilbao, and attacked the intentions of the town council. Finally, they tried to show that their work was part of older customs. Few of these arguments would prove to be effective, however. As their work was informally organized, there was little evidence for them to introduce, while the council could fall back on its legal and judicial power and authority.

---

[73] "[...] porque la dicha su parte abia mucho tiempo que tenia el dicho oficio de bender los dichos pescados frescos [...]." AFB, Municipal 0304/001/011, fol. 12v–13r.

In their conflict with the Bilbao council, the *cojedoras* argued that they were "honest citizens of Bilbao, who paid and contributed to the needs and tax levies, and who had the option and liberty to gain a living as they saw fit."[74] This type of argument was not unique; it also appears in the court cases involving the hosts and the *sardineras*. With it, the women sought to counter the council's accusations of "fraud and malpractice that the counterparties continuously committed" by defending the legitimacy of their work.[75] At the same time, the *cojedoras* directly challenged the council's motivations, claiming that the ordinance had been issued "out of animosity and bad will, based on faulty and deceitful information, and without legitimate cause." They further asserted that they "did not make a living from the *mulateros* in the way the council claimed," and that the council "said it acted for the common good and good government of the town, when in reality this was the complete contrary."[76] Through these arguments, the women sought to justify not only their own practices but also to discredit the council's intentions and undermine its authority.

Another way the saleswomen could challenge the council of Bilbao was by demonstrating the necessity of their work. This argument proved effective in court. In all three court cases, the saleswomen repeatedly claimed the essential role of their work in Bilbao's daily commerce. The *cojedoras* testified to their longstanding relationships with the *mulateros* and traders of Bilbao, arguing that the number of women working as brokers was evidence of the need for this position.[77] Although this argument was insufficient to win the cases outright, it influenced the judges' decision. The judges ruled that the council would have to allow the women to continue their work rather than appointing other residents as brokers

---

[74] "[...] dixo que syendo las dichas sus partes personas de honrra hijasdalgo notorias llanas e abonadas de buen vivir, vezinas e moradoras de la dicha villa que suelen pagar e contribuir como tales en los pedidos e derramas e otras cosas necesarias della e teniendo como tenia facultad e libertad [...] para ganar e buscar su vida como quien quiéralo [...]." ARChV, Sala de Vizcaya, Caja 3467, 5, fol. 2v.

[75] "[...] e sobre ynformacion a vida de los fraudes e males que las dichas partes contrarias azian continuamente [...]." *Ibidem*, fol. 4r.

[76] "[...] los oficiales del dicho concejo [...] que a la sazon hera movidos por henemystad e mala voluntad e con informaciones siniestras e no verdaderas e por causas no legitimas ni suficientes a manera de estatuto e hordenança mandaron e defendieron a las dichas sus partes su grandes penas que no tuviesen el dicho cargo no ganasen su vida con los dichos mulateros en la forma que dicho es, deziendo edando color que aquello hera lo que convenia al bien publico e ala buena gobernación de la dicha villa siendo como en la realidad de la verdad hera todo lo contrario." *Ibidem*, fol. 2v-3r.

[77] *Ibidem*, fol. 4v-5r.

if the need arose. This decision indicates that the court judges carefully considered the arguments and motivations of both parties. While they supported the council's regulations against brokerage, their actions were not specifically targeted at Bilbao's tradeswomen.

In all court cases, the women referred to their commercial positions as habits of *tiempo inmemorial* and the many other women trading in Bilbao. Mari Saes de Uribe, for example, claimed in her witness statement that she started her activities as a broker in the grain trade after having seen many different women practice it, even after the first court case that resulted in the prohibition of the occupation.[78] She was not the only woman to make this claim. The *cojedoras* collectively referenced the hosts of the *plumeras* practicing brokerage as part of their defense.[79] Their collective arguments reveal a strong awareness of their economic activities as part of an occupational group. The lenient attitude of the council in the decades preceding the court cases reinforced this view. The judges of the Chancellery reduced the *cojedoras*' fines because "it was the first time and it seemed that [Bilbao's, ed.] government had been tolerant."[80] Although the Biscayan women did not win their case, they demonstrated an acute awareness of their membership in an (informal) occupational group, along with the rights and arguments associated with it.

Though the arguments used in court by Bilbao saleswomen had limited effect, their existence demonstrates that these cases were not predetermined losses. However, the imbalance between the council, which had recognized legal authority, and the informal tradeswomen placed the women in an unfavorable position. The town council had the authority to question customs and adapt or change existing practices.[81] The women traders, on the other hand, did not. Notwithstanding, they tried countering the council's accusations by claiming the invalidity of the

---

[78] "[...]que como beyia que andaban muchas cojedoras yendo tanvien ella fue al regimiento e pidió licencia para que cojiese como las otras [...]." ARChV, Sala de Vizcaya, Caja 3467, 5, fol. 17r–17v, 4 May 1531.

[79] "[...] e abia otras mugeres e personas que tenían cargo de ospedar a las plumeras e de les comprar e vender lienços e otras cosas por salarios que les daban e asy mismo corredores e huéspedes que tenían semejantes oficios [...]." ARChV, Sala de Vizcaya, Caja 3467, 5, fol. 3r–3v.

[80] "Pero atento que es la primera bes a paresce que habido alguna tolerancia por los del dicho regimiento [...]." ARChV, Sala de Vizcaya, Caja 3467, 5, 27 June 1536.

[81] Cuenca, 'Bad Customs, Civic Ordinances, and 'Customary Time''.

new ordinances, as was the case with the *sardineras* and *cojedoras*, and by showing the longstanding custom of their work activities.[82]

Risk-Taking and Forum Shopping

As Ariadne Schmidt stated in her study of women in court cases in the early modern northern Low Countries, legal action was mostly pursued to "restore the normal situation."[83] By suing the town council in the court cases examined above, the Bilbao saleswomen must have hoped that they would be able to continue their economic activities. Nevertheless, in all cases—the council's obstruction of activities by the hosts of the linen buyers, the brokers, and Mayora de Iturribalzaga's case—the women litigants did not win sizable victories. The *cojedoras* were forced out of their occupation after the judges in Valladolid confirmed the ordinance of Bilbao's council, even if the brokerage likely continued in practice. The intermediary trade activities of the hosts of the *plumeras* were limited, and all could be fined heavily if they violated the limitations. Mayora de Iturribalzaga was fined, and her plea that she and the other *sardineras* be allowed to sell fresh fish was denied. And yet, groups of women did initiate all three cases.

In Bilbao, saleswomen sued the town government in an attempt to change local regulations. For late medieval England, Tom Johnson has stated that litigation and court cases were the urban commons' way to access town politics.[84] Although, according to Johnson, English women did not have this option, the groups of Bilbao saleswomen might have known that the higher courts offered them the best chance of influencing the town council's regulations, even if the women were ultimately unsuccessful. Nevertheless, the women were taking a large risk by launching litigation. Court cases that reached the court of appeals were costly affairs, and as was also the case in late medieval Marseille, many urban residents might have opted to pay a fine rather than go through the expensive and time-consuming application process.[85] Bilbao's saleswomen drove their cases to the highest juridical institutions, thereby risking high fines and

---

[82] Mayora, for example, argued repeatedly that the council's ordinance was not valid and not made in the interest of the town residents.

[83] Schmidt, *Prosecuting Women*, 50.

[84] Johnson, *Law in Common*.

[85] Smail, *The Consumption of Justice*, 83.

litigation costs. For a conflict to get to the *Sala de Vizcaya*, a substantial amount of money was required. The Chancellery required that the plaintiffs be able to pay the costs of the court case if their suit was lost. Moreover, in theory, only cases involving more than approximately 5,000 *maravedís* could be adjudicated by the higher court of Biscay, which decided cases appealed to the *Sala de Vizcaya*.[86]

Litigation by saleswomen that reached the higher courts likely began as oral petitions to Bilbao's council, such as the one from the fishmongers in 1510. The lack of response from the town council may have prompted the women to escalate their cases to the next institution: the *Corregidor* of Biscay, as Mayora de Iturribalzaga did. After appealing to the council, she next approached the *Corregidor* with the request to abolish the ordinance prohibiting the sardine sellers from selling fresh fish. Her first step in this process, taken between 1519 and 1521, reveals an earlier phase of the court case that is not reflected in the surviving town ordinances. As discussed in chapter 3, Mayora stated that a previous *Corregidor*, Diego Ramírez de Villaescusa, had annulled the 1515 ordinance, though no original record of this decision has been preserved.[87] However, when the council renewed its 'invalid' ordinance in 1525, the new *Corregidor* sided with the council, prompting Mayora to escalate her case to the Chancellery. It remains unclear whether she had anticipated this turn of events when first approaching the *Corregidor*—or whether such foresight might have influenced her initial litigation strategy.

We do not know how many cases initiated by the Bilbao saleswomen resulted in a victory at the level of the *Corregidor*. As the case of Mayora shows, retracted or revised ordinances were not necessarily documented as such in existing normative records. The available cases show groups of saleswomen litigating against the council only in the highest courts of the kingdom of Castile. Like Mayora, the *cojedoras* and the hosts of the *plumeras* were prepared to bring their cases before the Chancellery. When the initial phase of litigation did not end in their favor, they persisted and appealed to the highest courts. Several factors help explain why the Bilbao saleswomen were willing to take this initiative.

---

[86] Martín Rodríguez, 'Figura histórico-jurídica del Juez Mayor de Vizcaya', 648.
[87] "[...] declaro e mando que todos los que quisiesen bender pescado fresco e sardinas e otras cosas lo pudiesen hazer libremente e fueron los del dicho regimiento condenados en costas por aver fecho bedamiento [...]." AFB, Municipal 0304/001/011, fol. 3r.

One reason might have been that, as Merry Wiesner noted in her study of female peddlers in early modern Germany, the demands of running a business pushed women to develop into "forceful personalities." "Verbal dexterity, independence, and initiative" were all characteristics women needed to keep their businesses afloat, even though these features were "generally regarded as negative in women."[88] Taking legal action was one way for the *cojedoras* and the hosts of the *plumeras* to protect their businesses. However, it is a large leap from 'verbal dexterity' to litigating cases in interregional courts. Their business personalities might have motivated their independent work, but did not necessarily give them the resources or knowledge to take conflicts to the Chancellery.

A second consideration is that by utilizing precedents and other strategies discussed in the next sections, the individual advantage that women could gain outweighed the risks of going to court. Daniel Smail found that most applications to the courts of appeal in Marseilles resulted in reduced fines.[89] Bilbao's saleswomen might have known that the chance they would gain small advantages was significant if they appealed. Even though Bilbao's saleswomen failed to change the town council's ordinances, the Chancellery judges awarded them some concessions. While the hosts of the linen buyers were forced to abandon their role as brokers, the town council of Bilbao had initially fined three hosts—Elvira de Guemes, *doña María Lopez de Angulo*, and María Lopez de Laycama—200 *maravedís* and had taken the women's jewels, pots, and pans to pay the fine. Although the Chancellery judges agreed with the council's prohibition of brokerage, the judges did order Bilbao's town government to return the goods to the women.[90] A few years later, the Chancellery judges made a similar decision for the *cojedoras*. Their occupation would still be prohibited, but the town council's fines for them were substantially reduced.[91] On a group level, the *cojedoras* and linen buyers' hosts did not gain any advantage by taking their petition against the town council's ordinances to the higher courts. Individually, though, they did avoid large financial losses.[92]

[88] Wiesner, 'Having Her Own Smoke', 207.
[89] Smail, *The Consumption of Justice*, 85.
[90] AFB, Municipal, 0031/002/010, fol. 10r–10v.
[91] ARChV, Sala de Vizcaya, Caja 3467, 5.
[92] Jeannette Kamp and Ariadne Schmidt found a similar pattern in cases of illegitimate pregnancy in early modern Germany. Women reported themselves to criminal courts, because this would increase their chances of getting financial compensation and/or paternity recognition. See: Kamp & Schmidt, 'Getting Justice', 683–4.

It is important to remember that the council of Bilbao struggled to eliminate women's occupations entirely. The repeated reopening of court cases suggests that the women never fully ceased working as brokers. In fact, the Bilbao saleswomen may have strategically used litigation as a tool to gain individual advantages. At the same time, they may have known that they could continue trading illicitly—albeit at the risk of facing another court case. As Sanne Muurling has argued for early modern Bologna, it is possible that these women initiated legal proceedings "as part of a negotiation process," while leaving open the possibility of reaching an informal settlement with the town council.[93]

Tracing the motivations of the Bilbao saleswomen to pursue litigation is challenging due to the lack of detailed information about their individual financial and social statuses and their economic activities following the conflicts. The court cases, while illuminating, do not provide a comprehensive picture of the personal stakes and broader circumstances these women faced. Nonetheless, these cases reveal a group of dedicated workers willing to challenge the council of Bilbao. The outcomes suggest that the omnipresence of women traders in Bilbao's streets did not necessarily grant them a higher or more stable position. Rather, the absence of formal organization made it more difficult for them to defend their cases effectively.

*

A key difference between the Brabantine and Biscayan cases against female irregular traders lies in the timing of the litigation. In Bilbao, women brought court cases immediately after the council introduced new regulations, while in the Brabantine towns, most legal disputes emerged long after such regulations had been issued. The Brabantine cases, then, appear to have aimed less at collective regulatory change and more at securing individual advantages or exemptions. Although the surviving Brabantine conflict settlements related to urban labor are too limited to answer all our questions, they do offer valuable insight into the judicial strategies employed by defendants in select cases.

In the Brabantine towns, as women's work often took place on the margins of the guilds, it was not always clear which institutions were

---

[93] Muurling, *Everyday Crime, Criminal Justice and Gender*, 100.

responsible for controlling labor activities. Men and women could use this ambiguity to their advantage by contesting a guild's judgment in another municipal court. Since craft guilds were still subordinate to the town councils, this strategy could prove viable.[94] In 1547, Janneke de Waelinne successfully deployed this method to challenge a sentence by the Antwerp old clothes sellers' guild. The guild had fined Janneke six Carolus guilders for informal practices, and the dean confiscated some goods from Janneke as payment of the fine. Nevertheless, rejecting the guild's judgment, she argued before the aldermen of Antwerp that "she did not come to the market with the intention of auctioning or selling her goods, but she was only there to accompany her master."[95] Janneke might have been selling secondhand goods to supplement her wages as a servant. The aldermen decided against the guild's sentence and ordered the corporation to return Janneke's property.[96] Previous studies have pointed out that women could affect their opportunities by submitting their cases to local governments despite guild opposition, just as Janneke de Waelinne did in Antwerp.[97] By appealing her case to an alternate institution, Janneke turned the guild's complaints against her "into bargaining power," a successful way to exercise agency within the existing framework.[98]

'Forum shopping' between judicial authorities seems to have been a common tactic among the Brabantine urban residents. Guild members and outsiders alike tried to appeal to the sentences that guilds promulgated against offenders of their strict regulations. In 1502, the deans and jurors of the Antwerp mercers' guild called Joos Suermont before them to be sentenced for his transgressions. In their inspection of the market, guild authorities had confiscated a barrel of green ginger from Joos. Although the record does not make clear what was wrong with the ginger, Joos was summoned to appear before guild authorities. Refusing to do so, he instead sent his wife, who pleaded for restitution of the barrel. The

---

[94] González Athenas, 'Legal Regulation in Eighteenth-Century Cologne', 158; Montenach, 'Working at the Margins', 197-8.

[95] "[...] Want zij alhier op de merct aldair de voirscreven Hubrecht haer huer goet afgenomen hadde nyet gecommen en ware met intentien van huer goet te veylen oft vercoopen, mair hadde alleenlijck hueren meestere aldair passerende aengesproken [...]." SAA, GA#4274, fol. 13v-14r, 21 June 1547.

[96] "[...] ende selen daenleggeren schuldich zijn hair huer goet te restituerene." *Ibidem*.

[97] Montenach, 'Working at the Margins', 197-8; Vicente, 'Images and Realities of Work', 135; Harmsen & Hubers, "En zij verkocht de vis …", 31-3.

[98] Muurling, *Everyday Crime, Criminal Justice and Gender*, 106-7.

mercers' deans and jurors agreed and did not punish Joos but warned him not to repeat his transgressive behavior.[99] Two weeks later, one of the guild jurors followed Joos' wife as she was taking two barrels of green ginger home. When he tried to inspect the barrels, she shouted: "You traitor, are you here again to betray me as you did once at the market?"[100] Joos was again ordered to appear before the guild as he was held responsible for his wife's actions. Again refusing, he instead presented a defense to the town government of Antwerp. The mayor and aldermen of Antwerp heeded the guild's arguments against Joos and his wife, and they were fined six *rijders* unless Joos appealed the sentence within eight days.

A few days later, three friends—also members of the mercers' guild—appeared before the urban government and pleaded that Joos should be judged by the guild rather than town authorities. Possibly, the fine of six *rijders*—an amount equal to a carpenter's wages for thirty-six days of labor[101]—was higher than Joos had expected to receive from the town government, which agreed to the request of Joos' colleagues. The guild's deans and jurors decided that Joos must go on a pilgrimage to Halle, south of Brussels, and pay for four pounds of wax to be used in the guild chapel. Joos accepted this sentence and appeared before the deans and jurors of the guild on 14 November 1502, asking for forgiveness for the "injurious words that he and his wife had spoken to the deans and jurors."[102]

Why the Antwerp aldermen heeded Joos Suermont's and Janneke de Waelinne's pleas remains unclear. The aldermen might have absolved Janneke's debt to the guild because they regarded her as a poor woman. In her study of the silk trade in early modern Barcelona, Marta Vicente found that "the city regarded women's work as necessary to the city's economy and the survival of women and their families, while the guilds

---

[99] The guild's jurors and deans referenced 'discovering' Joos' transgressions, which might mean he was involved in faulty trade.

[100] "[...] soe heeft deselve Jan de Coninck hair gevolgt tot Joosens Huyse ende begeert te ziene hetgeen dat dairinne was, dwleck de huysvrouwe van Joos voirscreven nyet en heeft willen gehingen, mair heeft denselven Janne de Coninck overladen met quade ende felle wordden seggende, "ghij verrader, zijde hier weer om mij te verraden gelijck gij mij eens van den merct gedaen hebt"." SAA, GA#4212, fol. 122v, 1502.

[101] Jacks & Arroya-Abad, 'Belgium 1366–1603', *Global Prices and Income database*, last revised on 4 May 2005. https://gpih.ucdavis.edu/Datafilelist.htm.

[102] "[...] den xiiiien dach in novembris ende bidden den dekens ende gezwoirne vergiffenisse van den injurien ende wordden die hij ende zijn huysvrouwe den dekens ende gezwoirne misseet ende gedaen hadden." SAA, GA#4212, fol. 123r–123v, 14 November 1502.

considered it a threat to their interests."[103] Secondhand trade was vital to the urban economy in Antwerp and other premodern European towns. The limited funds available to some urban residents made it a significant avenue for acquiring their basic provisions.[104] What the guilds considered an infringement of their privileges, the town council might have perceived as a necessary irregularity.

As we will see, in Bilbao, women routinely used what could be called the 'poverty argument' to receive lighter sentences. Joos and his wife, on the other hand, seem to have wielded a clear strategy to jump between different judicial authorities in Antwerp. Although the couple did end up paying a fine for substandard trade practices and verbal assault, the record of the conflict offers a prime example of how urban residents used different courts and institutions to their advantage. While forum shopping did not always safeguard them from prosecution, they could choose among courts to secure the most advantageous outcome if they were caught violating regulations. Joos and his wife might have preferred a fine from the town government over a potential (temporary) banishment from the mercers' guild. When the outcome from that court was not the one for which he had hoped, he might have called upon his colleagues to obtain a transfer of venue so that he could defend himself before guild authorities. While the Antwerp *Correctieboeken* demonstrates that the aldermen punished irregular traders, the cases of Janneke and Joos reveal the same institution as one that citizens could use, or at least try to use, to their own advantage.[105]

Although citizens could use different authorities to their advantage, guilds sometimes tried to prevent appeals to the town government. Guild leaders also went to court on their own initiative to ask urban authorities to penalize irregular traders, thus preventing traders from circumventing guild judgments. Margriet Michielssen, for example, was charged by the Antwerp old clothes sellers' guild before the aldermen for buying goods at auction in order to resell them, although she was not a guild member. When she defended herself, the guild's willingness to leave the judgment up to the aldermen might have convinced these city leaders that the

---

[103] Vicente, 'Images and Realities of Work', 135.

[104] Kelsey Staples, 'The Significance of the Secondhand Trade', 297–309; Deceulaer, 'Second-Hand Dealers in the Early Modern Low Countries', 13–42.

[105] Sanne Muurling has shown a similar result for early modern Bologna. See: Muurling, *Everyday Crime, Criminal Justice and Gender*, 81–107.

guild's charges were valid. In addition to confirming the fine that the guild had suggested, the aldermen stated that the guild had been right to constrain Margriet's irregular activities.[106] The masculine guilds used the same strategies as individual urban residents did. Forum shopping among institutions could work to the guilds' advantage as well as against them.

The 'Poverty Argument'

Many urban residents turned to irregular trade activities in search of income. For some, it may have been their only means of earning enough to make ends meet. While financial hardship was not the sole reason for engaging in irregular trade, poverty often served as a compelling argument in court. Local governments were inclined to allow residents to work irregularly if this was an alternative to dependence on local charitable institutions, often funded by the same governments. In such cases, the town councils often allowed transgressions and irregular trade even if it violated their regulations.[107] Both urban residents and institutions in Brabant and Biscay invoked the 'poverty argument' in court cases related to irregular work. In Brabant, this argument was used by individual economic actors, as well as by guilds and other recognized associations. In Biscay, women similarly presented the argument before both the town council and higher courts. In both regions, the poverty argument served as a strategy for women to gain individual advantages, helping them navigate and sometimes bypass the structural limitations imposed by institutional authorities.

The limited evidence of Brabantine merchant women using the poverty argument likely reflects the scarcity of sources, as most records of irregular trade come from guild and other urban sentence books, which typically only documented final verdicts rather than the litigants' arguments. The Biscayan records provide detailed accounts of court proceedings, revealing women citing poverty as a legal justification for violating town regulations. One exception in the Brabantine sources is a conflict between a butcher's widow and the Leuven butchers' guild. In 1566, after the guild petitioned to prohibit butchers' widows from exercising their widows' rights, Margriet Schrijvers, a widow with

---

[106] SAA, GA#4276, fol. 135v–136v, 7 February 1532.

[107] Wiesner, 'Gender and the Worlds of Work', 223; Jeggle, 'Blurred Rules', 88–9; Van den Heuvel, 'Selling in the Shadows', 144.

several children and significant debts, appealed for an exemption.[108] She presented herself as "a poor widow, responsible for nine or ten children, with many debts contracted by her late husband."[109] Alongside two other widows, Margriet was granted the exemption and allowed to continue working in her late husband's trade. The town council of Leuven had little to gain by denying her the right to work, especially since she owed the town money that she could not pay if she lost her livelihood and had to rely on charity. This case, consistent with previous studies, demonstrates how the poverty argument served as a powerful tool for individuals seeking personal advantage in court.[110] Although widows in the Leuven butchers' guild were still prohibited from working, Margriet's argument for special consideration secured her an exemption.

In Biscayan court cases involving irregular trade, women also deployed the poverty argument. Two linen sellers, Joana and Milia, won an exception from Bilbao's ordinance ordering all linen sellers to have shops in the center of town. They asked, "as a method of charity," for the council to give them more time to sell linen outside of the town center.[111] The town council, "seeing their necessity", granted them exceptional permission to do so for approximately two months.[112] Once again, a personalized argument based on their financial situation proved effective in the local court. Rather than forcing Joana and Milia to become dependent on begging or locally funded charities, Bilbao's town council permitted them to continue making a living, even though they violated regulations.[113] Instead of rigidly adhering to the letter of the regulation, the council assessed cases of irregularity on an individual basis.

---

[108] SAL, 4652, fol. 204r–205v, 31 May 1570.

[109] "[...] dese arme weduwe, belast met neghen oft thien kinderen, ende bovendyen met vele schulden bij wijlen haeren man soo aende stadt als andre gemaeckt [...]." SAL, 4748, 6 September 1567.

[110] Smail, *The Consumption of Justice*, 85; Ling et al., 'Marriage and Work', 85.

[111] "Este dicho dia, por quanto por el conçejo fue e esta mandado a las dos lençeras que estan en la plaça que quitasen sus tablas e non los toviesen ende synon dentro en la villa sy queryan tener tyenda de conprar e vender, so çierta pena, e agora avian pedydo por su petyçion por via de limosna alguna largase para algunos dias." Enríquez Fernández et al., *Libro de acuerdos y decretos municipales*, fol. 19r, 12 February 1509.

[112] "Este dicho dia, respondyendo el conçejo a la petyçion de las dos lençeras que estan en la plaça, visto al presente su neçesydad que tyenen e vsando con ellas con pyedad, el conçejo les da liçençia doy fasta el dia de Pascoa de Resurreçion primero que viene que tengan en la dicha plaça sus tablas de liençe [...]." Enríquez Fernández et al., fol. 19v, 12 February 1509.

[113] Similar cases can be found in: Ling et al., 'Marriage and Work', 85; Wiesner, 'Gender and the Worlds of Work', 223.

In Castile's higher courts, women also used the poverty argument to defend their livelihoods. Several *cojedoras* of Bilbao referred to their economic status when questioned about their irregular activities. In 1531, Toda de Larrea testified that she resumed the prohibited occupation after a hiatus of several years due to a complete lack of alternative income.[114] Her colleague, Marina de Gardea, admitted knowing the occupation was forbidden, but explained that her husband's abandonment and subsequent "great necessity" compelled her to work.[115] Two more brokers, Ochanda de Zamudio and Elvira de Exarazu, also employed comparable justifications. Ultimately, all these women, with the exception of Toda de Larrea (who had previously led the *cojedoras* in the 1525 court case), received reduced fines. While the Valladolid judges did not explicitly acknowledge the women's claims of poverty as the reason for the reduced fines, the circumstances surrounding their return to the now-prohibited occupation might have influenced the judges' decision to lower the fines.

It seems that the need for an income, even from irregular work, was a powerful, advantageous legal argument in court.[116] Recognized economic institutions in Brabantine towns and irregular traders could put forward the poverty argument. Guilds often cited economic need when pleading to town councils for new regulations. In 1492, the Antwerp gardeners complained about the presence of single women in the guild. They claimed that "the number of women would multiply so that they would hurt not only the guild members but also the whole town, as the guild could not work anymore, and they would all drown."[117] Similarly, in the 1545 conflict between the Mechelen fishmongers' guild and citizens selling herring without guild membership, the fishmongers argued that the guild was vital to the town's prosperity. They contended that if the town allowed

---

[114] ARChV, Sala de Vizcaya, Caja 3467, 5, 27 June 1536.

[115] "[...] e estaba casada e se le fue su marido e aqy por la mucha necesidad se fue a la plaça a cojer trigo [...]." ARChV, Sala de Vizcaya, Caja 3467, 5, 27 June 1536.

[116] Dora Dumont argued for a similar use of the 'poverty argument' in guilds' persecution of women informal textile traders in eighteenth-century Bologna. Dumont, 'Women and Guilds in Bologna', 16–7.

[117] "Dat se soe souden vermenichfuldigen in sulcker vuegen dat zij niet alleene de goede kneepen van den selven ambachte dit in allen lasten van der stad moedt gelden ende contribueren werken niet brecken ende zij liede niet met allen verdrinken en souden, maer oic mede de gemeyne porteren ende ingesetene belasten ende beswaeren." SAA, GA#4001, fol. 64v, 30 July 1492.

citizens to continue their informal trade, the guild would suffer, and, by extension, the entire town would suffer because of it.[118]

In Brabant, guilds were not the only association that successfully deployed the poverty argument. Other recognized associations spoke about their economic situation to legitimize informal trade activities. In Antwerp, the mistress of the Third Order of the Franciscans, a female lay religious group similar to beguines, clashed with the linen weavers' guild in 1461. The guild accused the women of doing guild work illicitly. The Third Order could rely on an old privilege that supported their defense. The privilege gave members of the order the right to work to earn a living "because they had limited resources, and they thought that they could do this to lessen their need, without anyone hindering them."[119] While the preexisting privilege may have been the decisive factor in the conflict between the linen weavers and the Third Order (as discussed in the next section), the privilege was originally given to this recognized community to address its economic needs.

Since the Bilbao town council intervened in women's irregular activities when—according to the councilors—these activities damaged the town economy, it is not surprising that this was also a frequent argument in the court cases about council ordinances. In the case against Mayora de Iturribalzaga, the council argued that they made the ordinance "because of the great disorder and many fraudulent practices from the contrary party and the great damage and harm to the citizens of the foresaid town and to the foreigners that came to it," an argument the council repeated against the *cojedoras* and the hosts of the *plumeras*.[120] The council had designed the ordinances with these motives in mind, so repeating the same argument might have emphasized its sincerity to the judges in the Chancellery. The council was deploying a counterargument based on similar economic motives to the claims of poverty used by Bilbao's female traders.

In both Brabant and Biscay, individuals, associations, and authorities put forward economic arguments in defense of and against irregular trade. Individuals were probably motivated by the desire to win favor or advantage for themselves, while associations or authorities claimed

---

[118] SAM, Visverkopers 670, 1545.

[119] Génard, 'Register van den dachvaerden', 145–6, 21 October 1461.

[120] "[...] e lo otro porque visto la mucha deshorden e muchos fraudes que la dicha parte contraria hazia e el gran dagno e perjuyzio a los vecinos de la dicha villa e otros estrajeros que alla venían rescebian [...]." AFB, Municipal, 0304/001/0011.

concern for the common good. The effectiveness of the argument varied from case to case. On a group level, it only seems to have had an effect if a recognized group offered it. For example, in Bilbao, the hosts of the linen buyers argued that they needed extra income from brokerage to finance the buyers' lodging, which was costly.[121] This argument proved ineffective because the *plumeras* had already compensated their hosts for lodging, and the necessity of their brokering was fundamentally questioned. The judges ruled that the hosts had no legitimate need for additional income through brokerage.[122] Had the judges recognized the hosts of the *plumeras* as a formal occupational group, the outcome of the case might have been different.

Group Recognition

One final factor that had an impact on the Brabantine and Biscayan court cases about irregular trade was membership in a recognized community. Throughout this study, I have shown how guilds limited women's labor opportunities in the Brabantine towns. These predominantly male institutions significantly restricted women's labor opportunities, often attempting to exclude those not integrated into a guild household's production. Guilds, along with other established communities, generated social capital—the collective advantage derived from operating within a defined group—for their members, who all benefited from the institution's well-being.[123] Women who secured guild membership could leverage the privileges and rights associated with such recognition.[124] In Brabant, therefore, a privileged subset of women could utilize their guild or community affiliation as a legal advantage when contesting challenges to their work. Conversely, in Biscay, where such communities were notably absent, women relied more heavily on individual arguments and personal connections. Nonetheless, the Biscayan court records reveal a distinct group consciousness among female traders, a phenomenon rarely observed in Brabantine sources.

The relatively few surviving Brabantine court cases involving guild women highlight the strong position of those who had secured membership

---

[121] AFB, Municipal 0031/002/010, fol. 19r–19v.
[122] AFB, Municipal 0031/002/010, fol. 20v–21r.
[123] Ogilvie, 'How Does Social Capital Affect Women?', 327.
[124] Hafter, *Women at Work in Preindustrial France*, 294.

in a closed, patriarchal community. In 1435, for instance, the Antwerp old clothes sellers sought to expel Liesbet Maes from their guild after she married the tanner Jan Godens. The guild members argued that her marriage to a man from another guild disqualified her from guild membership. In her defense, Liesbet claimed that "she had purchased and received the guild membership herself," asserting that she was a free member. The aldermen of Antwerp ruled in her favor.[125] A similar outcome occurred in the conflict between the Mechelen mercers' guild and Liesbet Coolputs and her husband, as discussed in chapter 3. The aldermen of Mechelen chose not to expel Liesbet because of her marriage, instead upholding her privileges as a guild member.[126] As Peter Stabel has argued, guild membership "was no guarantee of equal social and economic perspectives."[127] While guilds attempted to exclude women from their ranks due to gender, town councils recognized these women as privileged individuals, benefiting from the status that came with guild membership.

Women's affiliation with a recognized institution provided them with the opportunity to use their membership as an argument in court. Despite the guilds' opposition, this affiliation gave women a stronger position than those without guild membership, as demonstrated by Susan Broomhall and Anna Fridrich in their studies of premodern Rouen in France and Laufen in the Holy Roman Empire.[128] While the female defendants may have advanced this argument as a legal strategy, and the councils may have judged their cases individually without considering the guilds' bylaws, the women's guild memberships provided them with an argument that councils took seriously.

To benefit from the protections afforded to privileged groups, women first had to belong to such a group—and the work they performed had to be recognized as falling within that group's accepted domain. Membership in a craft guild was not a requirement. For instance, the women of the Antwerp Third Order of the Franciscans successfully invoked their community's privileges in a dispute with the linen weavers' guild. Not only

---

[125] "[...] de voirscreven oudecleercoepers meynden dat zy haere ambacht niet meer hanteren en soude mids dat zy eenen man van eenen anderen ambachte genomen hadde; daerop dat deselve Lysbet ver- antwoerde, dat zy dambacht van den oudencleercoepers selve gecocht ende gecregen hadde ende vry daerin waere [...]." L. Bisschops, 'Oudt register, mette berderen, 1336–1439 (Vervolg)', 220r, 27 January 1435.

[126] SAM, Kramersambacht 90, 19 August 1489.

[127] Stabel, 'From the Market to the Shop', 81.

[128] Broomhall, 'Women, Work, and Power', 206; Fridrich, 'Women Working in Guild Crafts', 145–6.

were they part of a recognized religious community, but their mistress also presented a formal privilege that authorized them to work informally.[129] As a result, it was more difficult for urban authorities to dismiss their claim. In addition to citing poverty, the women gave the Antwerp council a concrete legal basis to rule in their favor.

A similar dynamic can be observed in a 1452 conflict between the Leuven tailors' guild and the beguines. As in Antwerp, a female lay religious community was accused of informally performing guild work. While the tailors complained to the town council, the council ultimately allowed the beguines to continue their activities, albeit with restrictions: they were not permitted to take apprentices from among the children of Leuven's citizens.[130] These cases show not only that town councils acknowledged the legitimacy of female religious communities but also that the women within them understood how to strategically assert their rights.[131]

The absence of guilds in Bilbao resulted in a distinct organization of labor, particularly for women. Groups of saleswomen came to dominate certain sectors of the market, especially in food and small-scale trade. However, these women faced difficulties establishing themselves as members of privileged communities that could legitimize their commercial activities. While they were undeniably part of the urban fabric, the very institution that represented the urban community—the town government—was also tasked with regulating the trades in which their informal work took place. In this context, women tended to rely on individual defensive strategies, such as invoking poverty when defending their businesses in court. Lacking the support of a formally recognized group, these saleswomen were left without collective protection—a dynamic also noted by other scholars.[132]

Although saleswomen in Biscay often struggled to obtain and prove formal recognition, such recognition appears to have been a crucial factor in defending their access to work. One mechanism for legitimizing their labor was the acquisition of a trade license, which had to be requested from the town council. Possession of a license provided women with both leverage and legal standing. When challenged by the authorities, several

---

[129] Génard, 'Register van den dachvaerden' 20, 145–6, 21 October 1461.
[130] SAL, 4648, fol. 459r–459v, 10 June 1452.
[131] Ormrod, *Women and Parliament*, 64.
[132] Wiesner, 'Gender and the Worlds of Work', 223; Ormrod, *Women and Parliament*, 70; Hafter, *Women at Work in Preindustrial France*, 294.

retailers referred to their licenses to justify their activities. In 1509, for example, the town council of Bilbao questioned María Ochoa de Guinea about her right to sell fresh fish, salted fish, and fruit from a shop. She responded that her father had held the license before his death, and the council granted her permission to continue the business.[133] That same day, María Saes de Arrarte likewise inherited a license from a deceased fruit seller.[134] These examples illustrate how the council sought to regulate the number of peddlers through licensing, while women, in turn, used licenses to assert the legitimacy of their work.

Licenses thus became a crucial point of negotiation: they enabled women to respond to the council's doubts about the legality of their trade, but failing to produce a license when requested could result in fines or bans on further activity.[135] While Biscayan women used licenses to argue for their legitimate place in the urban economy, the Bilbao council often sought to undermine that legitimacy, particularly when it came to organized groups like the *cojedoras*. In court, the council repeatedly asserted that these women should not have been in the grain trade at all. In 1525, for instance, it argued that "there were no similar brokers nor hagglers [female, ed.] like the contrary party wanted to be" anywhere in the kingdom.[136] Had comparable occupations existed in other towns, the *cojedoras* might have used them as precedents to strengthen their claims. However, without privileges or membership in a recognized group, they lacked the institutional backing to mount an effective collective defense.

The Biscayan dynamic stands in contrast to the situation in Brabantine towns, where guild membership—even when limited to a small number of women—provided a stronger foundation for legal recognition. The collective court case of the *cojedoras* suggests they had a type of collective or occupational identity and/or network. Nevertheless, the lack of recognition by the town council of Bilbao prevented them from using this argument in court. In Bilbao, women had to rely on individual claims rather than organized communal defense.[137]

---

[133] Enríquez Fernández et al., *Libro de acuerdos y decretos municipales*, fol. 18r, 9 February 1509.

[134] *Ibidem*, fol. 18v, 9 February 1509.

[135] This punishment happened, for example, to the linen cloth broker, María Ibañez de la Cuadra, in 1515. See: *Ibidem*, fol. 24r, 1 June 1515.

[136] "[...] que en todos los nuestros reynos ni en las comarcas no abia semejantes cogedoras ni barateras como las dichas partes contrarias quería ser [...]." ARChV, Sala de Vizcaya, Caja 3467, 5, fol. 4r.

[137] See also: Montenach & Simonton, 'Afterword', 247; Ormrod, *Women and Parliament*.

Despite the council's refusal to recognize the saleswomen as a formal group, evidence suggests that a sense of community nonetheless developed among them. Following a 1510 petition by the fishmongers, the council implemented a rotation system to allocate the town's limited number of fish stalls—possibly indicating that group membership remained relatively stable. Possession of licenses and council-issued permissions likely contributed to this cohesion, but daily collaboration and shared occupational identity were probably the most significant factors in fostering a collective spirit. These dynamics may have motivated the fishmongers' coordinated efforts to push back against restrictive regulations. Indeed, their solidarity resembles that of other closely-knit female occupational groups, such as the *Keuflinnen*—female secondhand dealers in early modern Nuremberg—whom Merry Wiesner has described as "a close-knit body, tightly bound together by a certain set of rights and privileges."[138]

In the court cases, groups of women sought to safeguard their labor opportunities, although some disputes appear to have been primarily led by individual women. For instance, among the *sardineras*, Mayora de Iturribalzaga took a prominent role, likely supported by other women involved in the informal sale of fresh fish. Likewise, Marina de Bedia led the second legal challenge concerning the *cojedoras*, while Toda de Larrea played a pivotal role in the initial conflict. The visibility of these individuals raises questions about their specific roles: Were they at greater risk of losing their livelihoods if their occupations were banned? This seems unlikely, as testimonies from various *cojedoras* emphasize that all engaged in the work due to economic necessity or long-established practice.

A more plausible explanation is that women like Mayora and Marina were the most well-connected. In Mayora's case, testimonies from the councils of Bermeo and Plentzia lead me to believe that she was a woman of notable connections. Given that access to higher judicial authorities required both networks and resources, it is conceivable that such women were positioned to act as figureheads or representatives in these legal struggles. However, the limited nature of the sources on Bilbao's saleswomen makes it difficult to reconstruct their networks in detail or to determine precisely how social ties translated into legal action.

Even though we cannot fully trace the individual networks of these women, it is evident that connections and influence played a role in

---

[138] Wiesner, 'Paltry Peddlers or Essential Merchants?', 8–9.

shaping their labor conditions. In some cases, saleswomen explicitly invoked the connections of Bilbao's councilors to undermine their authority. The hosts of the *plumeras*, for example, alleged that the councilors only issued the ordinance against brokerage because "their wives were the owners of the linen shops," and would benefit from controlling the price of linen cloth.[139] Similarly, the *cojedoras* accused the council of using them as scapegoats in order to extort the *mulateros* and manipulate grain prices to benefit the wealthy elite. The women argued that: "being rich and powerful, [the councilors] could buy everything and the poor people would die of hunger"—a surprisingly similar argument to that of the Antwerp gardeners in 1492.[140] While the council relied on its formal authority to justify regulation, women used courtroom discourse to expose perceived favoritism and self-interest among the urban elite. Thus, although the concrete impact of personal networks on women's daily trade remains difficult to quantify, it is clear that the politics of connection and accusation played a crucial role in their legal strategies.

3. Conclusion

This chapter began with a depiction of a group of Bilbao saleswomen influencing town regulations and directly impacting Bilbao's councilors. These women appeared politically savvy, strong, and independent, akin to the modern narrative that would earn them a plaque in northern Spain's many homages to the region's fisherwomen. In contrast, the Brabantine sources do not present a similar image of a collective group of women; their voices are harder to discern in the archival documents. In shaping political influence, scholars have indicated the importance of community, whether formal or informal, and the recognition of those communities

---

[139] "[...] e porque a los mismos regidores e otras personas del dicho regimiento las yba yntereses en ello porque sus mugeres tenian tiendas de lienços e otras mercaderías [...]. [...] los mismos regidores que fieron en hazer la dicha hordenança heran los mismos que tenian tiendas de lienços y los vendian al por rebender sus mercaderias [...]." AFB, Municipal, 0031/002/010, 9v–11r, 27 May 1549.

[140] "[...] la dicha hordenanza no tocaba ni fablaba en los mantenimientos ni hera sobre buena gobernacion del pueblo. [...] lo que los dichos regidores querían para que todo el pan que fuese a la dicha villa syendo sus criados e criadas los que entendiesen en la benta dello se lo diesen a los precios que ellos lo quisiesen. E como heran ricos e poderosos lo pudiesen conprar todo e las probes gentes muriesen de abre." ARChV, Sala de Vizcaya, Caja 3467, 5, fol. 9r–9v.

by local governments.¹⁴¹ In Bilbao, women traders had no male institutionalized competitors and, in some labor sectors, were therefore the main economic actors in the town. In Brabant, craft guilds claimed this formal, recognized trade. Furthermore, they positioned themselves as representatives of the common good while excluding large segments of urban society.¹⁴² Therefore, men and women not included in the guilds' networks were excluded from formal participation in guild life, both economic and political.¹⁴³

However, the second part of this chapter paints a different picture. Regardless of gender or location, men and women in the fifteenth- and sixteenth-century towns used the same type of arguments when colliding with the institutions organizing their economic activities. The result for the Brabantine informal and illicit sellers was different than that of Bilbao's women fishmongers and other tradeswomen. Bilbao's tradeswomen seem to have been generally less successful when defending their economic activities in court. This discrepancy illustrates the influence of institutions at the individual level. While the guilds in Mechelen and Antwerp did constrain women's activities, the organization of work within guilds and the household economy might have provided a more stable context to fall back on compared to the absence of these institutions in Bilbao.

Possibly, the close link between the organization of work in guilds and the prevalence of the household economy was exactly what safeguarded some women's economic activities. The absence of these institutions in Bilbao's small-scale trades could explain the saleswomen's lack of effective defense strategies. However, it is important to acknowledge that records of conflict resolution at lower judicial levels are missing for Bilbao. These sources may have offered alternative insights into how tradeswomen navigated disputes and negotiated outcomes outside the formal court system. As a result, the apparent lack of success among Bilbao's tradeswomen in higher courts may not fully reflect the effectiveness of women's conflict resolution strategies in the Biscayan hub.

Ogilvie's concept of 'institutional enforcement,' introduced in the previous chapter, focuses on the negative effects of guilds on women's work but overlooks the support patriarchal institutions could offer

---

[141] Dumolyn, 'Guild Politics and Political Guilds', 30–1; Ormrod, *Women and Parliament*, 64.
[142] Prak, 'Corporate Politics in the Low Countries'.
[143] Van den Heuvel, 'Guilds, Gender Policies and Economic Opportunities', 130.

certain groups of women.[144] Bilbao tradeswomen, lacking this network, faced greater challenges in defending their economic roles, even if it gave them a certain occupational group identity and, with this, political agency. The lack of institutions organizing their work also gave them fewer protective mechanisms to fall back on once the council started scrutinizing their economic activities. This comparison shows how socioeconomic institutions organizing urban work could simultaneously restrict and protect women's economic activities, underscoring the complex interplay between gender, economic control, and institutional frameworks in shaping women's opportunities.

---

[144] Ogilvie, *The European Guilds*, 575.

Understanding Women's Work

I would like to begin by clarifying that this book does not aim to determine whether women's labor opportunities in northern or southern Europe were 'worse' or 'better.' Too often, the historiographical debate has been hindered by appraisals of 'good' or 'bad.' As researchers, our role is not to judge past societies by contemporary standards but to bridge gaps in our understanding of them. The similarities and differences between women's labor opportunities in Brabant and Biscay, as examined in this book, offer a chance to reflect on what shaped gender roles and how these could result in different economic positions for women.

We have seen how various institutions organizing labor influenced women's activities. Deeper insight emerges from understanding how these institutions interwove with each other and with other influential factors. This provides a nuanced framework for explaining variations in women's economic positions. The comparative analysis drawing on normative urban regulations from Bilbao, Antwerp, and Mechelen, as well as judicial sources, guild records (including accounts and membership lists), and tax levies, allowed this study to delve into crucial aspects determining women's economic roles. The findings underscore the complex interplay of institutions and other influences, revealing how women navigated and sometimes overcame structural barriers to shape their work opportunities. Let us explore this assertion point by point, beginning with a brief recap of the fundamental elements of this study: the specific labor sectors and institutions formally organizing urban work in Brabant and Biscay.

Labor sectors form the cornerstone of this comparative analysis, with a focus on fields where women's roles are most prominently documented: small-scale trade in Biscay and Brabant, and, to a lesser extent, small-scale production and wage labor in Brabant. Sources highlight women's pivotal role in sales-related tasks. In Bilbao, women dominated the small-scale trade of commodities, forming a crucial, though sometimes contested, link in the provision chain. They also held intermediary positions in interregional trade networks, providing accommodation or brokering deals. In Antwerp and Mechelen, evidence shows women's involvement in a wider variety of work sectors, encompassing both production and trade.

However, there is little evidence of women dominating a specific market activity. References to women's involvement are scarcer per trade sector compared to Bilbao, and they rarely place women in the foreground.

Two institutions had the legal capacity to formally organize the urban labor markets of Antwerp, Mechelen, and Bilbao: the town councils and craft guilds. The composition and influence of town councils in Brabant and Biscay varied significantly. In Brabant, town governments, heavily influenced by craft guilds, aligned with these corporations' interests. Conversely, Bilbao's council, comprised predominantly of oligarchic landholders and mercantile elites, prioritized safeguarding interregional economic activities. Though typically not directly involved in day-to-day work practices, all three town councils enacted regulations driven by socioeconomic concerns in response to local practices. Regulating women's work could be a part of these concerns, but gender did not take the main role in their regulations.

Craft guilds played a significant role in the Brabantine towns, influencing women's work in complex ways. These guilds did not only possess governmental and economic organizational capacities; they also operated under the belief that they embodied the entirety of urban society—politically, economically, culturally, socially, and religiously. The craft guilds created a structure in the urban Brabantine societies that could not easily be avoided. Consequently, they were deeply interwoven with all other mechanisms shaping Brabantine urban labor markets. This complexity means that for Brabant, they are a crucial factor in understanding women's work opportunities. Especially since guilds were, or aspired to be, explicitly exclusive and predominantly masculine institutions.

The town councils in Brabant and Biscay, alongside the guilds in Brabant, functioned within two distinct regions with diverse economic outputs and organizational priorities. These differences necessitated tailored organizational structures and priorities. However, both regions shared a common feature regarding women's work: formal limitations imposed by institutions. Within patriarchal frameworks, such limitations were entrenched and seldom contested. Restricting women's roles in urban economies required no explicit justification in written documents; changes to existing structures were typically legitimized to maintain (patriarchal) norms, underpinned by social and economic motivations.

Despite these shared limitations, women's work positions in Brabant and Biscay were by no means identical. The differences stemmed from several factors, including the distinct interplay of institutions and local economic conditions, which form the next component of this study's findings.

*

Besides institutions with formal organizational capacity, two additional institutions significantly shaped women's economic positions: the informal market and the household. The informal market is particularly noteworthy due to its lack of legal status. It encompassed all activities outside self-regulatory institutions, often filling gaps in the urban economy and circumventing existing structures—reflected in the roles women occupied within it.

In Bilbao, the informal market was the primary arena for small-scale trade by female retailers and other women selling goods. Their predominance stemmed from the absence of more prestigious formal institutions, though it did not mean their work was unregulated. These women operated under a normative framework set up by the town council, resulting in a dynamic interplay between informal saleswomen and municipal authorities. Informal work could also be irregular and, therefore, deemed illicit, prompting the council to impose fines or engage in lengthy court cases.

In Brabant, evidence of regular yet informal markets in Antwerp and Mechelen is more limited. Examples such as Antwerp's licensing of a married couple to sell fish oil and regulations on the oaths of *uitdraagsters* point to the presence of regulated informal market activity. However, our clearest view emerges through cases of infringement or when such practices were addressed in urban ordinances. These sources pertain to all market participants, not only those fully dependent on informal work. Because of its unofficial nature, women's labor often appears negatively in the sources. A notable—and arguably typical—exception is women's informal work within the household economic unit.

The household economic unit was most advantageous for women who had a household member affiliated with a formal institution. In Brabant, the household was closely tied to the craft guilds and formed a foundational element of the urban economic structure. Women's access to various labor activities often hinged on their household position. As a result, their economic activities within the guilds and the household were not continuous throughout their lives, as their position changed with age and transformative events.

In Biscay, the deeply embedded household unit appears to have been absent in small-scale trade occupations. While women worked in these trades to sustain themselves and their households, similar to the situation in Brabant, the household did not function as a structuring economic unit. Biscayan customary law promoted the nuclear couple and their economic endeavors, but customary law was not written for all social groups. In higher-status trades, such as the linen trade, spousal cooperation followed a similar pattern to the Brabantine model.

Guilds were fundamentally structured around the household economic unit; the household was deeply embedded in the informal market; and the informal market, in turn, operated only in conjunction with urban governments. These four institutions were interwoven, making their impact on women's work opportunities complex and mutually reinforcing. From Biscayan and Brabantine women's perspective, this interaction meant navigating multiple structures simultaneously. This interdependence could increase opportunities, as seen with the Brabantine forum shoppers in chapter 4, who skillfully utilized all available institutions to achieve the best possible outcomes in economic conflicts. The interplay between institutions also meant facing limitations from various sides, as demonstrated by the Bilbao fishmonger Catalina Nafarra, who had to contend with both council regulations and competition from fellow informal traders. The cooperation, interaction, and conflict among these four institutions shaped the very structure of the premodern urban market.

*

Despite their different impacts on different social groups, the town governments and socioeconomic institutions operated broadly consistently within their respective domains. Studying them provides very much a collective perspective on women's work opportunities. However, this institutional perspective overlooks other crucial elements that shaped these opportunities. While institutions can be seen as a fixed genetic code, other factors function as environmental determinants, resulting in each woman's unique experiences and life cycles. These factors are essential for understanding the outcomes explored in this book. For Brabant and Biscay in the fifteenth and sixteenth centuries, we can distinguish three main ones.

(1) The type of work women engaged in significantly influenced their labor opportunities. In Brabant, this impact was particularly pronounced due to the organization of work within craft guilds. Traditional labor sectors, such as fishmongering and butchery, which evolved from domestic production to market-oriented production and eventually into guild structures, were less open to women participating formally in their own right. Moreover, during economic decline, these guilds often imposed increasing restrictions on women's work, even for those involved through the household unit. While guilds encompassed many work fields, their attitudes towards women's work varied considerably across different trades.

In Biscay, there appears to have been a different attitude toward women selling locally produced commodities or those involved in trading imported products. Almost all the women we encountered in this book trading in Biscay operated informally due to the absence of formal institutions. However, the informal market of Bilbao can be viewed as a spectrum with varying 'degrees' of informality. The *panaderas*, *regateras*, *pescaderas*, and *sardineras* of Bilbao faced few barriers other than economically motivated regulations, provided they avoided bulk trade. Only when they engaged in more lucrative trades, such as the sale of fresh fish for the *pescaderas* and *sardineras* or the involvement of the *cojedoras* in the grain trade, did they encounter significant obstacles designed to exclude outsiders. Bilbao's council's priority to safeguard excises from and control interregional trade is reflected in this attitude toward the different groups of saleswomen. The wealthier linen traders, while trading informally, likely did not face any persecution for their work activities.

(2) The different attitudes toward work sectors were closely linked to the next factor: social status. For instance, the positioning of women within Bilbao's informal spectrum was not arbitrary. Wealthier linen traders engaged in lucrative trade did not opt for small-scale sales like the *regateras*; their occupational choices were shaped by their financial status and connections, collectively forming their social status. The findings in this book thus shed light not only on what women were permitted to do but also on what they were compelled to do. Confrontations with urban governments and craft guilds and the risk of fines likely stemmed primarily from the necessity to earn or augment their income. Household unit or not, women had to engage in economic activities to sustain themselves.

The tax levies from Brabant and Biscay reveal that many women household heads operated within the lower financial strata of urban societies. This pattern is particularly evident in Bilbao, where we can directly correlate these lower tax contributions with the tradeswomen under study. Antwerp and Mechelen tax levies leave less evidence about this correlation. In addition to the tax records, our assessment of the economic status of the women discussed in this book relies on their frequent use of the 'poverty argument.' While this argument does not provide a definitive view of their wealth and cannot serve as exclusive proof thereof, it is consistently invoked in court cases where women petition for changes to normative ordinances or seek individual exemptions from them. For some, the argument and actual financial status might well have coincided.

Social status was also shaped by the connections one possessed. The absence of detailed personal information prevents a clear insight into women's networks. Nonetheless, some evidence highlights the importance of their connections. For instance, Machteld van Wynge, the Leuven mercer who secured permission for her husband's training, likely benefited from her family's standing in the mercers' guild. The Bilbao fishmonger Mayora de Iturribalzaga, despite not prevailing in her court case, presented witness statements from town councils in Bermeo and Plentzia suggesting she had influential connections. Complaints from the *plumeras* and *cojedoras* in Bilbao accused councilors of favoring their own overseers, underscoring the role of connections.

Evidence hinting at women's financial status and personal connections does not establish causality. Did wealthier and better-connected women secure better positions due to their advantages, or did their connections and wealth arise from their ability to access better labor positions through other influential factors? Likely, both scenarios hold some truth, a question that warrants more exploration.

(3) A variety of elements related to the distinct socioeconomic contexts of the three towns influenced women's economic positions. When Toda de Larrea and her husband fell into debt due to war in the kingdom, she took up the occupation of *cojedora* (see chapter 2). Wars, crises, and economic booms were unpredictable factors not typically considered in the organization of work, yet they profoundly impacted individual experiences.

More stable contextual factors, such as the size of the towns and their main economic focuses, were equally influential. The smaller size of Bilbao likely facilitated direct interactions between its citizens, including women retailers, and the town council. In contrast, the larger size of the two Brabantine towns and the formal organization of work by guilds obscured many private interactions and informal trades within these communities.

While the socioeconomic contexts of these towns certainly influenced women's labor opportunities, their precise impact often remains obscure.

*

The complex dynamics of women's work become apparent when we consider the myriad factors that shaped the labor market both collectively and individually in the two regions. Broadening our perspective is not merely a matter of nuance; it is essential to fully understanding these past societies. A comparative analysis of women's work opportunities in Brabant and Biscay leads to an overarching conclusion: the 'enhanced guild effect.' This concept captures the deeper and more intricate influence of craft guilds on women's labor opportunities, as demonstrated throughout this study.

Guilds exerted a significant influence across all strata of premodern urban societies. For women, this dominance translated into contending with an institution inherently excluding them from many sectors of the urban labor market. Even with variations among guilds, their obstructive impact remained evident. The scant representation of women as guild members and the imposition of regulations limiting their—informal and formal—participation attest to this power. In this respect, the findings of this study align with previous research, emphasizing guilds as a pivotal factor in restricting women's labor opportunities. Outsiders, by definition, were constrained by this 'guild effect,' with women often finding themselves being defined as outsiders. Craft guilds' roots in the patriarchal context and domestic production had seen to this ramification. This organizational framework likely explains why occupations that in Biscay were largely the province of women faced explicit challenges in the same occupations in Brabant, where guilds wielded significant control.

By no means did this situation imply that women in Biscay worked without limitations. The town council restricted their work, influenced by patriarchal values, albeit primarily driven by socioeconomic motivations rather than gendered ones. While other factors in Bilbao posed limitations for women, as discussed earlier, Bilbao's saleswomen avoided an additional layer of restrictions by not having to compete with craft guilds. Moreover, due to the absence of formal competitors, they even had opportunities to influence the council and its regulations, a phenomenon rarely observed in the Brabantine source material.

The nuances accompanying these findings provide an enriched perspective, hence the concept of the 'enhanced guild effect.' Guilds not only imposed increased limitations on women's work but also established a clearer framework within a predominantly informal economy. Some women operated within the guild structure, particularly within the household economic unit. Although guild regulations constrained their opportunities to work independently, they likely maintained relatively stable—one could even say almost predictable—economic positions. Additionally, they benefited from the guilds' influential political and cultural standing. These were the women who could access the guilds' charitable funds and, upon the death of a husband, could assume the role of a guild member.

For guild outsiders, the structured framework drawn by guilds may have provided more clarity and aligned expectations. The *uitdraagsters* of Antwerp, the *pensvrouwen* of Leuven, and *harincvrouwen* of Mechelen were not guild members, but their close affiliation with recognized corporations afforded them some form of recognition. Mirroring guild strategies, as seen with the Third Order women in fifteenth-century Antwerp, proved successful for informal work. The guild structure in Brabant resulted in limitations while also providing a clearer understanding of what was permissible. Its influence extended beyond group dynamics to significantly shape individual opportunities.

In Biscay, the absence of formal organization in socioeconomic institutions allowed more space for female-dominated labor sectors but also resulted in a lack of structured urban markets. Women working in these traditionally female sectors did so under the direct oversight of the town council, which sanctioned their work insofar as it aligned with their own interests. However, the lack of structural organizations in Bilbao meant they had few defenses when their activities conflicted with the council's policies. The litigations between Bilbao's saleswomen and the town council did not lead to the structural protection of their work. Instead, the saleswomen had to fend for themselves against both fellow informal competitors and the council when facing imposed limitations. Despite a sense of group identity among Bilbao's saleswomen, particularly evident among fishmongers sharing the same market square, this solidarity was not formally recognized and thus did not necessarily offer them protection.

The dual impact of craft guilds underscores the need to stay clear of assumptions that premodern urban women necessarily desired more autonomy. Guilds were neither the oppressors depicted by scholars like Sheilagh Ogilvie, nor solely the protectors as portrayed in the research of Steven Epstein and Maarten Prak. Their complex relationship with 'outsiders' both constrained the opportunities for many urban residents and provided a clearer framework for the urban market, along with a stable framework for women affiliated with the guilds.

*

Instead of a direct one-to-one comparison of each element influencing women's labor in Brabant and Biscay, my focus on similar occupations organized in distinct frameworks has clarified the interactions between institutions and influencing factors, thus illuminating the mechanisms behind the organization of women's work. However, considering alternative scopes raises intriguing questions. What if I had not compared women's work in small-scale trade across the two regions? What if I had focused on a different aspect?

Two groups remain largely invisible in this study due to limitations in scope and the availability of sources. In Bilbao, adding a middling class involved in craft production—those trades traditionally structured in guilds and domestic workshops elsewhere—might complement my findings. The town council regulated artisans involved in craft production. For instance, regulations for the shoemakers focused on the procurement of raw materials. They stay conspicuously silent about women's work in artisan occupations. While groups of artisans operated in Bilbao alongside the retailers and peddlers discussed in this book, there is scarce evidence documenting women's participation in these crafts.

In Antwerp and Mechelen, alongside the influential guilds, there existed a group of itinerant traders who likely conducted their operations similarly to the tradeswomen in Bilbao. Unlike their guild-affiliated female competitors in Antwerp and Mechelen, their work was not defined by marital status or formal guild membership. Evidence regarding the *uitdraagsters* and *harincvrouwen* provides some understanding of these groups. However, it is highly probable that these were not the only labor sectors where many informal traders competed with the guilds. Further exploration could reveal whether these 'missing' groups operated under mechanisms similar to those studied in this book.

Moving beyond a static comparison to a dynamic one appears to be the logical next step in advancing this research. We must delve deeper into women's economic positions to comprehend premodern urban life more fully. Adding the individual level will enable our examination of

Figure 10. Fifteenth-century fresco depicting women traders in a market scene. Located at the Issogne Castle, Valle d'Aosta, Italy.
Source: Giorgio Olivero. By concession of Regione Autonoma Valle d'Aosta.

women's personal networks and how their economic activities evolved over their lifetimes. By incorporating an individual approach, provided there is a viable source base, we can shed light on the precise impact of other influential factors discussed in this study.

This book aimed to give more color to our understanding of women's roles in premodern urban societies. Like the women depicted in the market scene on this book's cover—engaged in trade and negotiation—women in Brabant and Biscay were not peripheral figures but central agents on the urban labor markets. We can now better imagine Gheertruyde van den Broeke disputing with guild officials on Mechelen's IJzerenleen, or Willem De Bruyne and Kateline Dierix establishing their informal fish oil trade in Antwerp. We can also see how Bilbao's dockside saleswomen navigated and contested regulations imposed by the town council. These local examples reveal how economic, institutional, and social dynamics interacted with women's work across regions. While our perspective has deepened, many gray areas remain to be explored. Only through continued research can we fully grasp women's work opportunities, their roles in urban societies, and, by extension, society as a whole. The economic activities of women in Brabant and Biscay provide a starting point for this comprehensive understanding.

Bibliography

1. Archival sources

Biscay

Statutory Archives of Biscay (Archivo Foral de Bizkaia)
    Municipal: 0017/001/051; 0031/002/010; 0034/001/008; 0304/001/011
    Judicial: 0087/291; 1004/067; 1062/029; 1191/119; 1544/050; 2232/084; 2643/014; 2653/058; 2659/493
    Notarial: 0483/0188; 0484/0256; 0486/0005; 0486/0019; 0486/0020

Archives of the Royal Court and Chancellery of Valladolid (Archivo de la Real Audiencia y Chancillería de Valladolid)
    Pleitos Civiles, Pérez Alonso (F): Caja 991, 3
    Registro de Ejecutorias: Caja 273, 12; Caja 308, 31; Caja 359,65; Caja 645, 42; Caja 810,31
    Sala de Vizcaya: Caja 2939, 11; Caja 3467, 5; Caja 4368, 4; Caja 561, 2; Caja, 79,1

Brabant

City Archives of Antwerp (Stadsarchief Antwerpen, FelixArchief)
    Godshuizen: 860#7761; FA#22
    Archieven van de gepriviligieerde ambachten: 4001, Ambachten boeck 1430-1561; 4017, Het Gulden Boek, Lakengilde; 4211; 4212; 4253; 4273; 4274; 4276; 4277; 4363; 4369; 4650
    Afschriften van archiefdocumenten: HN#103
    Privilegiekamer: 1394; 3391; 913, Gebodboek Abis 1439-1496; 915, Gebodboek 1539-1564 B
    Schepenregisters: 12; 5

City Archives of Leuven (Stadsarchief Leuven)
    Oud Archief: 1523, 't Groot Gemeynboeck B; 1524, 't Groot Gemeynboeck B; 1527; 4648; 4652; 4659; 4748

City Archives of Mechelen (Stadsarchief Mechelen)
    Magistraat (Ordonnantiën): Serie I, nr. 3; Serie I, nr. 4, *Ordonnantiën*; Serie III, nr.2, *Novum Chaos* 2; Serie V, nr. 1
    Geldwezen: IV. Belastingen op de huizen, Serie I, nr. 1

Handschoenmakers-, tesmakers-, riem(be)slagers-, witledermakers- en schedemakersambacht: 554bis; 557
Hoedenmakersambacht: 1
Hoveniers-, fruiteniers- en mandenmakersambacht: 7; 16; 17
Kramersambacht: 1; 47; 90
Oudkleerkopersambacht: 1; 21
Visverkopers: 11; 14; 23; 26; 30; 321; 322; 462a; 462b; 670

2. Printed sources

Brabant

Behets, P., *Rollen en aanvullende reglementen van de Mechelse ambachten. Deel I*. Unpublished Transcription Collection, 2024.
Behets, P., *Rollen en aanvullende reglementen van de Mechelse ambachten. Deel II*. Unpublished Transcription Collection, 2024.
Bisschops, L., 'Oudt register, mette berderen, 1336-1439', *Antwerpsch Archievenblad*, 27 (1890), 1-470.
Bisschops, L., 'Oudt register, mette berderen, 1336-1439 (Vervolg)', *Antwerpsch Archievenblad*, 28 (1891), 1-472.
Bisschops, L., 'Oudt register, mette berderen, 1336-1439 (Vervolg)', *Antwerpsch Archievenblad*, 29 (1892), 1-262.
Bisschops, L., 'Het 2e oudt register, in 't perkament gebonden 1438-1459 (Vervolg)', *Antwerpsch Archievenblad*, 29 (1892), 262-471.
Bisschops, L., 'Het 2e oudt register, in 't perkament gebonden 1438-1459 (Vervolg)', *Antwerpsch Archievenblad*, 30 (1893), 1-471.
Génard, P., 'Register van den dachvaerden', *Antwerpsch Archievenblad*, 19a (1882), 1-313.
Génard, P., 'Register van den dachvaerden', *Antwerpsch Archievenblad*, 20 (1883), 1-472.
Geudens, E., *Dit raect het oude cleercoopers ambacht binnen der stede van Antwerpen ende is eene verleeninge vanden jaere M vierhondert ende sessendertich* (Brecht, 1905).
Melis-Taeymans, F., *Correctieboeck 1414-1512* (Antwerp, 1979).
Van den Branden, J., 'Clementijnboek 1288-1414 (Vervolg)', *Antwerpsch Archievenblad*, 26 (1889), 1-136.
Van den Branden, J., 'Oudt register, mette berderen, 1336-1439 (Vervolg)', *Antwerpsch Archievenblad*, 27 (1890), 1-470.

Biscay

de Mañaricua, A.E. *Las Ordenanzas de Bilbao de 1593* (Bilbao, 1954).
Enríquez Fernández, J., Hidalgo de Cisneros Amestoy, C., Lorente Ruigómez, A. & Martínez Lahidalga, A., *Libro de acuerdos y decretos municipales de la villa de Bilbao: 1509-1515* (Donostia, 1995).
Enríquez Fernández, J., Hidalgo de Cisneros Amestoy, C., Lorente Ruigómez, A. & Martínez Lahidalga, A., *Ordenanzas municipales de Bilbao (1477-1520)* (Donostia, 1995).
Enríquez Fernández, J., Hidalgo de Cisneros Amestoy, C., Lorente Ruigómez, A. & Martínez Lahidalga, A., *Repartimientos y foguera-vecindario de Bilbao (1464-1492)* (Donostia, 1996).
Enríquez Fernández, J., Hidalgo de Cisneros Amestoy, C. & Martínez Lahidalga, A., *Colección documental del archivo histórico de Bilbao (1473-1500)* (Donostia, 1999).

Enríquez Fernández, J., Hidalgo de Cisneros Amestoy, C. & Martínez Lahidalga, A., *Colección documental del archivo histórico de Bilbao (1501-1514)* (Donostia, 2000).

Enríquez Fernández, J., Hidalgo de Cisneros Amestoy, C. & Martínez Lahidalga, A., *Colección documental del archivo histórico de Bilbao (1514-1520)* (Donostia, 2001).

Largacha Rubio, E., Hidalgo de Cisneros Amestoy, C., Lorente Ruigómez, A. & Martínez Lahidalga, A., *Colección documental del archivo de la cofradía de pescadores de la villa de Lequeitio (1325-1520)* (Donostia, 1991).

Monreal Zia, G., *The Old Law of Bizkaia (1452). Introductory Study and Critical Edition* (Reno, 2005).

Rodriguez Herrero, Á., *Ordenanzas de Bilbao, siglos XV y XVI* (Bilbao, 1948).

Zugaza, L., *El Fuero Nuevo de Vizcaya* (Bilbao, 1976).

Fueros, privilegios, franquezas y libertades del M.N.Y.M.L. Señorío de Vizcaya (Bilbao, n.d.).

3. Secondary sources

Abreu-Ferreira, D., 'Fishmongers and Shipowners: Women in Maritime Communities of Early Modern Portugal', *Sixteenth Century Journal*, 31 (2000), 7–23.

Abreu-Ferreira, D., 'Neighbors and Traders in a Seventeenth-Century Port Town', *Signs: Journal of Women in Culture and Society*, 37 (2012), 581–87.

Abreu-Ferreira, D., 'Women, Law and Legal Intervention in Early Modern Portugal', *Continuity and Change*, 33 (2018), 293-313.

Armstrong-Partida, M. & McDonough, S., 'Singlewomen in the Late Medieval Mediterranean', *Past & Present*, 259 (2023), 3-42.

Ayuso Sánchez, C., 'El mundo laboral femenino en el País Vasco medieval', *Sancho El Sabio: Revista de Cultura e Investigación Vasca*, 30 (2009), 115–36.

Bailey, M., 'The Black Death, Girl Power, and the Emergence of the European Marriage Pattern in England', *Journal of Medieval and Early Modern Studies*, 54 (2024), 493-528.

Bailey, M.L., Colwell, T.M. & Hotchin, J., 'Approaching Women and Work in Premodern Europe', in M.L. Bailey, T.M. Colwell & J. Hotchin (eds.), *Women and Work in Premodern Europe: Experiences, Relationships and Cultural Representation, c. 1100-1800* (Oxford and London, 2018), 1-29.

Bardyn, A., 'Vermogende vrouwen. Het vastgoedbezit van vrouwen in laatmiddeleeuws Brussel op basis van cijnsregisters (1356-1460)', *Stadsgeschiedenis*, 9 (2014), 1-24.

Bardyn, A., 'Crediting Women? A Comparative Perspective on Credit Markets and Gender Inequality in Late Medieval Brabant' (Conference paper, Leuven, 2016).

Bardyn, A., 'Women's Fortunes. Gender Differences, Asset Management, and Investment in Late Medieval Brabant' (PhD Dissertation, KU Leuven, 2018).

Bellavitis, A. & Zucca Micheletto, B., 'Introduction. North versus South: Gender, Law and Economic Well-Being in Europe in the Fifteenth to Nineteenth Centuries', in A. Bellavitis & B. Zucca Micheletto (eds.), *Gender, Law and Economic Well-Being in Europe from the Fifteenth to the Nineteenth Century: North versus South?* (Oxford and New York, 2018), 1-27.

Bellavitis, A., *Women's Work and Rights in Early Modern Urban Europe* (Cham, 2018).

Bellavitis, A., 'Urban Markets', in C. Macleod, A. Shepard & M. Ågren (eds.), *The Whole Economy. Work and Gender in Early Modern Europe* (New York, 2023), 136–63.

Bennett, J.M., "'History That Stands Still'. Women's Work in the European Past', *Feminist Studies*, 14 (1988), 269–83.

Bennett, J.M., 'Public Power and Authority in the Medieval English Countryside', in M. Erler & M. Kowaleski (eds.), *Women and Power in the Middle Ages* (Athens, 1988), 18-36.

Bennett, J.M., *Ale, Beer, and Brewsters in England: Women's Work in a Changing World, 1300-1600* (New York, 1999).

Bennett, J.M., *History Matters* (Manchester, 2006).

Bolumburu Arizaga, B. & Martínez Martínez, S., *Atlas de villas medievales de Vasconia* (San Sebastian, 2006).

Bolumburu Arizaga, B., Ríos Rodríguez, M.L. & Del Val Valdivieso, M.I., 'La villa de Guernica en la baja edad media a través de Ssus ordenanzas', *Vasconia: Cuadernos de Historia – Geografía*, 8 (1986), 167-234.

Bolumburu Arizaga, B., 'El abastecimiento de las villas vizcaínas medievales: política comercial de las villas respecto al entorno y a su interior', *En la España Medieval*, 6 (1985), 293-316.

Broomhall, S., 'Women, Work, and Power in the Female Guilds of Rouen', in M. Cassidy-Welch and P. Sherlock (eds.), *Practices of Gender in Late Medieval and Early Modern Europe* (Turnhout, 2008), 199-213.

Buchner, T. & Hoffmann-Rehnitz, P.R., 'Introduction: Irregular Economic Practices as a Topic of Modern (Urban) History – Problems and Possibilities', in T. Buchner & P.R. Hoffmann-Rehnitz (eds.), *Shadow Economies and Irregular Work in Urban Europe. 16th to Early 20th Centuries* (Münster, 2011), 3-36.

Burm, E. & De Munck, B., 'Het broodje gebakken? Huwelijksstrategieën en partnerkeuze van de bakkers(kinderen) te Brussel in de overgang van het Ancien Régime naar de negentiende eeuw', *Stadsgeschiedenis*, 2 (2010), 148–68.

Capp, B., *When Gossips Meet: Women, Family, and Neighbourhood in Early Modern England* (Oxford, 2003).

Cappelle, K., "In de macht, plicht en momboorije van Heuren man': de rechtspositie van de getrouwde vrouw in Antwerpen en Leuven (16de eeuw)', *Pro Memorie*, 18 (2016), 48-68.

Cappelle, K., 'Law, Wives and the Marital Economy in Sixteenth-Century Antwerp: Bridging the Gap between Theory and Practice', in B. Zucca Micheletto & A. Bellavitis (eds.), *Gender, Law and Economic Well-Being in Europe from the Fifteenth to the Nineteenth Century* (Oxford and New York, 2018), 228–41.

Cappelle, K., "Out of Extraordinary Love and Affection': Gender, Spousal Wills and the Conjugal Strategy of Commercial Households in Sixteenth-Century Antwerp', *Rechtskultur – Zeitschrift Für Europäische Rechtsgeschichte*, 10 (2022), 1-28.

Carlier, M., 'The Household: An Introduction', in M. Carlier & T. Soens (eds.), *The Household in Late Medieval Cities, Italy and Northwestern Europe Compared* (Leuven and Apeldoorn, 2001), 1-11.

Castrillo Casado, J., 'Mujeres y matrimonio en las tres provincias vascas durante la baja edad media', *Vasconia*, 28 (2012), 9-39.

Castrillo Casado, J., 'Participación de las mujeres en la economía urbana del País Vasco durante la baja edad media', in M.I. Del Val Valdivieso & J.F. Jiménez Alcázar (eds.) *Las mujeres en la edad media* (Murcia-Lorca, 2013), 213–22.

Castrillo Casado, J., 'Las mujeres del común y la sociedad política en al País Vasco bajomedieval', in J.Á. Solórzano Telechea, B. Arízaga Bolumburu & J. Haemers (eds.), *Los grupos populares en la ciudad medieval europea* (Logroño, 2014), 499-522.

Castrillo Casado, J., *Las mujeres vascas durante la baja edad media: vida familiar, capacidades jurídicas, roles sociales y trabajo* (Madrid, 2020).

Castrillo Casado, J., 'Mujeres, negocio y mercaduría a finales de la edad media: algunos apuntes sobre el País Vasco', *Edad Media. Revista de Historia*, 22 (2021), 285-315.

Catalán Martínez, E. & Lanza García, R., 'Crecimiento demográfico en tiempos de crisis: Bilbao en los Siglos XVI y XVII', *Revista de Demografía Histórica*, 35 (2017), 17-54.
Cavallo, S., *Artisans of the Body in Early Modern Italy. Identities, Families and Masculinities* (Manchester and New York, 2007).
Clark, A., *Working Life of Women in the Seventeenth Century* (London, 1968).
Cohn, S.K. Jr., *Women in the Streets: Essays on Sex and Power in Renaissance Italy* (Baltimore, 1996).
Collinge, P., 'Guilds, Authority and the Individual: The Company of Mercers Prosecution of Dorothy Gretton in Early Eighteenth-Century Derby', *Business History*, 61 (2019), 281–98.
Comas-Via, M., 'Widowhood and Economic Difficulties in Medieval Barcelona', *Historical Reflections/ Réflexions Historiques*, 43 (2017), 93-103.
Coomans, J., 'Policing Female Food Vendors in the Late Medieval Netherlands', *Yearbook of Women's History*, 36 (2017), 97-113.
Crowston, C., 'Women, Gender, and Guilds in Early Modern Europe: An Overview of Recent Research', *International Review of Social History*, 53 (2008), 19-44.
Cruchaga Calvin, M.J., 'La mujer en las villas portuarias del Cantábrico: el ejemplo de Santander en la baja edad media' (Unpublished M.A. thesis, Universidad de Cantabria, 2012).
Cuenca, E.L., 'Bad Customs, Civic Ordinances, and 'Customary Time' in Medieval and Early Modern English Urban Law', *Historical Reflections*, 47 (2021), 39-58.
Daems, G., 'De lakenindustrie in de stad Mechelen en in haar omgeving tussen ca. 1480 en ca. 1580' (Unpublished Master Dissertation, KU Leuven, 1974).
Davis, D., *A History of Shopping* (London and Toronto, 1966).
De Longé, G., *Coutumes de la ville de Malines* (Brussels, 1879).
De Moor, T. & Van Zanden, J.L., 'Girl Power: The European Marriage Pattern and Labour Markets in the North Sea Region in the Late Medieval and Early Modern Period', *Economic History Review*, 63 (2010), 1-33.
De Munck, B. & Soly, H., '"Learning on the Shop Floor" in Historical Perspective', in B. De Munck, S.L. Kaplan & H. Soly (eds.), *Learning on the Shop Floor. Historical Perspectives on Apprenticeship* (New York and Oxford, 2007), 3-32.
De Munck, B. & Dumolyn, J., 'The Political Culture of Work', in B. De Munck & T.M. Safley (eds.), *A Cultural History of Work in the Early Modern Age*, 3 (London, 2019), 145–58.
De Munck, B., De Kerf, R. & De Bie, A., 'Apprenticeship in the Southern Netherlands, c. 1400–c. 1800', in M. Prak & P. Wallis (eds.), *Apprenticeship in Early Modern Europe* (Cambridge, 2019), 217–46.
De Munck, B., 'From Brotherhood Community to Civil Society? Apprentices between Guild, Household and the Freedom of Contract in Early Modern Antwerp', *Social History*, 35 (2010), 1-20.
De Munck, B., 'La qualité du corporatisme: Stratégies économiques et symboliques des corporations anversoises, XVIe – XVIIIe siècles', *Revue d'histoire moderne et contemporaine*, 54 (2007), 116–44.
De Munck, B., *Guilds, Labour and the Urban Body Politic: Fabricating Community in the Southern Netherlands, 1300–1800* (New York, 2018).
De Smet, G., 'Bijdrage tot de sociale geschiedenis van het Mechelse ambachtelijke milieu. Het ambacht van de kramers (1712–1749)' (Unpublished M.A. thesis, KU Leuven, 1982).
Deceulaer, H. & Panhuysen, B., 'Dressed to Work: A Gendered Comparison of the Tailoring Trades in the Northern and Southern Netherlands, 16th to 18th Centuries', in M. Prak, C. Lis, J. Lucassen & H. Soly (eds.), *Craft Guilds in the Early Modern Low Countries* (Aldershot, 2006), 133–56.
Deceulaer, H., 'Second-Hand Dealers in the Early Modern Low Countries: Institutions, Markets and Practices', in L. Fontaine (ed.), *Alternative Exchanges: Second Hand Circulations from the Sixteenth Century to the Present* (New York, 2008), 13-42.

Del Val Valdivieso, M.I., 'La solidaridad familiar en Vizcaya en el Siglo XV', in *Vizcaya en la edad media: congreso de estudios histórico* (Donostia, 1986), 333-37.

Del Val Valdivieso, M.I., 'El trabajo de las mujeres en el Bilbao tardomedieval', in *Las Mujeres Vascas en la Historia* (Bilbao, 1997), 65-92

Del Val Valdivieso, M.I., 'Los espacios del trabajo femenino en la Castilla del Siglo XV', *Studia Historica. Historia Medieval*, 26 (2008), 63-90.

Dewilde, B. & Poukens, J., 'Bread Provisioning and Retail Dynamics in the Southern Low Countries: The Bakers of Leuven, 1600–1800', *Continuity and Change*, 26 (2011), 405-38.

Dijkman, J., *Shaping Medieval Markets. The Organisation of Commodity Markets in Holland, c. 1200–c. 1450* (Leiden and Boston, 2011).

Dillard, H., *Daughters of the Reconquest: Women in Castilian Town Society, 1100–1300* (Cambridge, 1984).

Dumolyn, J., 'Guild Politics and Political Guilds in Fourteenth-Century Flanders', in J. Dumolyn, J. Haemers, H.R. Oliva Herrer & V. Challet (eds.), *The Voices of the People in Late Medieval Europe. Communication and Popular Politics* (Turnhout, 2014), 15-48.

Dumont, D., 'Women and Guilds in Bologna: The Ambiguities of "Marginality"', *Radical History Review*, 70 (1998), 4-25.

Edwards, J. & Ogilvie, S., 'What Can We Learn from a Race with One Runner? A Comment on Foreman-Peck and Zhou, "Late Marriage as a Contributor to the Industrial Revolution in England"', *Economic History Review*, 72 (2019), 1439-46.

Eersels, B., 'The Craft Guilds Are the City. Political Participation in Late Medieval Towns. Brabant and Liège (c. 1360–1500)' (Unpublished Ph.D. Dissertation, KU Leuven, 2018).

Eersels, B., 'Requested and Consented by the Good Crafts. A New Approach to the Political Power of Craft Guilds in Late Medieval Maastricht (1380–1428)', in B. Eersels & J. Haemers (eds.), *Words and Deeds. Shaping Urban Politics from Below in Late Medieval Europe* (Turnhout, 2020), 91-112.

Eisenbichler, K., 'Introduction: A World of Confraternities', in K. Eisenbichler (ed.), *A Companion to Medieval and Early Modern Confraternities* (Leiden and Boston, 2019).

Emperador Ortega, C., 'El archivo de la Real Chancillería de Valladolid y la Sala de Vizcaya: fondos documentales producidos por una sala de justicia en el Antiguo Régimen', *Clío & Crímen: Revista del Centro de Historia del Crimen de Durango*, 10 (2013), 13-34.

Erler, M.C. & Kowaleski, M., *Gendering the Master Narrative: Women and Power in the Middle Ages* (Ithaca, 2018).

Erler, M. & Kowaleski, M. (eds.), *Women and Power in the Middle Ages* (Athens, 1988).

Everaert, J., 'Macht in de Metropool. Politieke elitevorming tijdens de demografische en economische bloeifase van Antwerpen (ca. 1400–1550)' (Unpublished Ph.D. Dissertation, Vrije Universiteit Brussel and Universiteit Antwerpen, 2021).

Fontaine, L., 'Makeshift, Women and Capability in Preindustrial European Towns', in A. Montenach & D. Simonton (eds.), *Female Agency in the Urban Economy: Gender in European Towns, 1640–1830* (New York, 2013), 56-72.

Fontaine, L., 'The Role of Peddling in Consumption in Modern Europe', *Field Actions Science Reports. The Journal of Field Actions*, Special Issue 12 (2014), 1-3.

Fridrich, A.C., 'Women Working in Guild Crafts. Female Strategies in Early Modern Urban Economies', in A. Montenach & D. Simonton (eds.), *Female Agency in the Urban Economy: Gender in European Towns, 1640–1830* (New York, 2013), 134-50.

García de Cortázar, J.Á., Arízaga Bolumburu, B., Ríos Rodríguez, M.L. & Del Val Valdivieso, M.I., *Vizcaya en la edad media: evolución demográfica, económica, social y política de la comunidad vizcaína medieval*, vol. 1 (San Sebastian, 1985).

García de Cortázar, J.Á., Arízaga Bolumburu, B., Ríos Rodríguez, M.L. & Del Val Valdivieso, M.I., *Vizcaya en la edad media: evolución demográfica, económica, social y política de la comunidad vizcaína medieval*, vol. 2 (San Sebastian, 1985).

García de Cortázar, J.Á., Arízaga Bolumburu, B., Ríos Rodríguez, M.L. & Del Val Valdivieso, M.I., *Vizcaya en la edad media: evolución demográfica, económica, social y política de la comunidad vizcaína medieval*, vol. 3 (San Sebastian, 1985).

García de Cortázar, J.Á., Arízaga Bolumburu, B., Ríos Rodríguez, M.L. & Del Val Valdivieso, M.I., *Vizcaya en la edad media: evolución demográfica, económica, social y política de la comunidad vizcaína medieval*, vol. 4 (San Sebastian, 1985).

García Fernández, E., 'Las cofradías de mercaderes. Mareantes y pescadores vascas en la edad media', in B. Arízaga Bolumburu & J.Á. Solórzano Telechea (eds.), *Ciudades y Villas Portuarias del Atlántico en la Edad Media* (Logroño, 2005), 257–94.

García Fernández, E., 'Las cofradías de oficios en el País Vasco durante la edad media (1350–1550)', *Studia Historica. Historia Medieval*, 15 (1997), 11-40.

Gelderblom, O., *Cities of Commerce. The Institutional Foundations of International Trade in the Low Countries, 1250-1650* (Princeton, 2013).

Gil, M., 'Les femmes dans les métiers d'art des Pays-Bas Bourguignons au xve siècle', *Clio*, 34 (2011), 231–54.

Gilissen, J., 'Le statut de la femme dans l'ancien droit Belge', in *Extrait des recueils de la Société Jean Bodin* (Bruxelles, 1962), 255-321.

Godding, P. *Le droit privé dans les Pays-Bas méridionaux du 12e au 18e siècle* (Bruxelles, 1987).

Gold, C., 'On the streets and in the markets: Independent Copenhagen saleswomen', in A. Montenach & D. Simonton (eds.), *Female Agency in the Urban Economy: Gender in European Towns, 1640–1830* (New York, 2013), 35-55.

Goldberg, J.P., *Women, Work, and Life Cycle in a Medieval Economy: Women in York and Yorkshire c.1300–1520* (Oxford, 1992).

Goldberg, J.P., 'Household economics: Money, work, and property', in C. Beattie, A. Maslakovic & S. Rees Jones (eds.), *The Medieval Household in Christian Europe c.850–c.1550: Managing Power, Wealth, and the Body* (Turnhout, 2003), 223–29.

González Athenas, M., 'Legal regulation in eighteenth-century Cologne: The agency of female artisans', in A. Montenach & D. Simonton (eds.), *Female Agency in the Urban Economy: Gender in European Towns, 1640–1830* (New York, 2013), 151–68.

Guiard y Larrauri, T., *Historia de la noble villa de Bilbao*, vol. 1 (Bilbao, 1905).

Guiard y Larrauri, T., *Historia del Consulado y Casa de Contratación de Bilbao y del comercio de la villa*, vol. 1 (Bilbao, 1913).

Haemers, J., 'Bloed en inkt. Een nieuwe blik op opstand en geweld te Leuven, 1360–1383', *Stadsgeschiedenis*, 7:2 (2012), 141–64.

Haemers, J., 'Governing and gathering about the common welfare of the town: The petitions of the craft guilds of Leuven, 1378', in H.R. Oliva Herrer, V. Challet, J. Dumolyn & M.A. Carmona Ruiz (eds.), *La comunidad medieval como esfera pública* (Sevilla, 2014), 153–72.

Haemers, J., 'Ad petitionem burgensium. Petitions and peaceful resistance of craftsmen in Flanders and Mechelen (13th–16th centuries)', in J.Á. Solórzano Telechea, B. Arízaga Bolumburu & J. Haemers (eds.), *Los grupos populares en la ciudad medieval europea* (Logroño, 2014), 371–94.

Haemers, J., 'Verraders, muitmakers en boeven! Vrouwen en opruiende woorden in de laatmiddeleeuwse Zuidelijke Nederlanden', *Stadsgeschiedenis*, 19 (2024), 77-92.

Haemers, J. & Delameillieure, C., 'Women and contentious speech in fifteenth-century Brabant', *Continuity and Change*, 32:3 (2017), 323–47.

Haemers, J. & Eersels, B., *Words and Deeds: Shaping Urban Politics from below in Late Medieval Europe* (Turnhout, 2020).

Hafter, D.M., *Women at Work in Preindustrial France* (University Park, 2007).

Hamilton, E.J., *American Treasure and the Price Revolution in Spain, 1501–1650* (New York, 1970).

Hanus, J., *Affluence and Inequality in the Low Countries: The City of 's-Hertogenbosch in the Long Sixteenth Century, 1500–1650* (Leuven, 2014).

Hardwick, J., *The Practice of Patriarchy: Gender and the Politics of Household Authority in Early Modern France* (Pennsylvania, 1998).

Harmsen, K. & Hubers, H., "En zij verkocht de vis ...'. Visverkoopsters in Utrecht en Antwerpen van de veertiende tot en met de zeventiende eeuw', *Dinamiek, 8:2 (1991), 29-40*.

Herlihy, D., *Opera Muliebria: Women and Work in Medieval Europe* (New York, 1990).

Herlihy, D. & Klapisch-Zuber, C., *Les Toscans et leurs familles: une étude du Catasto Florentin de 1427* (Paris, 1978).

Herlihy, D. & Klapisch-Zuber, C., *Tuscans and Their Families: A Study of the Florentine Catasto of 1427* (New Haven, 1985).

Hoffman, P.T., Jacks, D.S., Levin, P.A. & Lindert, P.H., 'Real Inequality in Europe since 1500', *The Journal of Economic History*, 62:2 (2002), 322–55.

Honeyman, K. & Goodman, J., 'Women's Work, Gender Conflict, and Labour Markets in Europe, 1500–1900', *The Economic History Review*, 44:4 (1991), 608–28.

Howell, M.C., *Women, Production, and Patriarchy in Late Medieval Cities* (London, 1986).

Howell, M.C., 'Women, the Family Economy, and the Structures of Market Production in Cities of Northern Europe during the Late Middle Ages', in B.A. Hanawalt (ed.), *Women and Work in Preindustrial Europe* (Bloomington, 1986), 198-222.

Howell, M.C., 'Citizenship and Gender: Women's Political Status in Northern Medieval Cities', in M. Erler & M. Kowaleski (eds.), *Women and Power in the Middle Ages* (Athens, 1988), 37-60.

Howell, M.C., 'Achieving the Guild Effect without Guilds: Crafts and Craftsmen in Late Medieval Douai', in P. Lambrechts & J.-P. Sosson (eds.), *Les métiers au Moyen Âge* (Louvain-la-Neuve, 1994), 109-28.

Howell, M.C., *Commerce before Capitalism in Europe, 1300–1600* (Cambridge, 2010).

Howell, M.C., 'The Gender of Europe's Commercial Economy, 1200–1700', *Gender & History*, 20:3 (2008), 519–38.

Howell, M.C., 'Whose "Common Good"? Parisian Market Regulation, c. 1300–1800', in S. Middleton & J.E. Shaw (eds.), *Market Ethics and Practices, c. 1300–1850* (London, 2018), 46-62.

Howell, M.C., 'The Problem of Women's Agency in Late Medieval and Early Modern Europe', in A. Pipkin & S.J. Moran (eds.), *Women and Gender in the Early Modern Low Countries* (Leiden, 2019), 21-31.

Hufton, O., *The Prospect Before Her. A History of Women in Western Europe. Volume one, 1500 – 1800* (London, 1995).

Humphries, J. & Sarasúa, C., 'Off the Record: Reconstructing Women's Labor Force Participation in the European Past', *Feminist Economics*, 18:4 (2012), 39-67.

Humphries, J. & Sarasúa, C., 'The Feminization of the Labor Force and Five Associated Myths', in G. Berik & E. Kongar (eds.), *The Routledge Handbook of Feminist Economics* (London, 2021), 169–78.

Hunt, M.R. & Shepard, A., 'Introduction. Producing Change', in C. Macleod, A. Shepard & M. Ågren (eds.), *The Whole Economy: Work and Gender in Early Modern Europe* (New York, 2023), 1-25.

Hutton, S., 'Women, Men, and Markets: The Gendering of Market Space in Late Medieval Ghent', in A. Classen (ed.), *Urban Space in the Middle Ages and Early Modern Age* (Berlin, 2009), 409–32.

Hutton, S., *Women and Economic Activities in Late Medieval Ghent* (New York, 2011).

Hutton, S., 'Property, Family and Partnership: Married Women and Legal Capability in Late Medieval Ghent', in C. Beattie & M.F. Stevens (eds.), *Married Women and the Law in Premodern Northwest Europe* (Boydell & Brewer, 2013), 155–72.

Ignacio Salazar, J., 'Gobierno local en el Bilbao bajomedieval', *Bidebarrieta: Revista de Humanidades y Ciencias Sociales de Bilbao*, 12 (2003), 183–97.

Installé, H., 'Bestuursinstellingen van de Heerlijkheid Mechelen (11de Eeuw–1795)', in R. Van Uytven, C. Bruneel & H. Coppens (eds.), *De gewestelijke en lokale overheidsinstellingen in Brabant en Mechelen tot 1795* (Brussels, 2000), 835–64.

Irigoyen López, A., 'Characteristics of Castilian Cities in the 16th and 17th Centuries', in S. Panzram (ed.), *The Power of Cities: The Iberian Peninsula from Late Antiquity to the Early Modern Period*, The Medieval and Early Modern Iberian World, 70 (Leiden, 2019), 289-320.

Iziz, R. & Iziz, A., *Historia de las mujeres en Euskal Herria. 1. Prehistoria, romanización y reino de Navarra* (Tafalla, 2016).

Jacobs, M., 'De ambachten in Brabant en Mechelen', in R. Van Uytven, C. Bruneel & H. Coppens (eds.), *De gewestelijke en lokale overheidsinstellingen in Brabant en Mechelen tot 1795* (Brussels, 2000), 558–324.

Jacobs, R., *Een geschiedenis van Brussel* (Tielt, 2004).

Jacobsen, G., 'Women's Work and Women's Role: Ideology and Reality in Danish Urban Society, 1300–1550', *Scandinavian Economic History Review*, 31:1 (1983), 3-20.

Janssens, A., 'The Rise and Decline of the Male Breadwinner Family? Studies in Gendered Patterns of Labour Division and Household Organisation', *International Review of Social History*, 42 (1997), 1-23.

Jeggle, C., 'Blurred Rules: Regulation and the Problem of Non-Regular Practices in the Linen Trades in Seventeenth-Century Münster/Westphalia', in T. Buchner & P.R. Hoffmann-Rehnitz (eds.), *Shadow Economies and Irregular Work in Urban Europe. 16th to Early 20th Centuries* (Münster, 2011), 73-90.

Johnson, T., *Law in Common: Legal Cultures in Late-Medieval England* (Oxford, 2020).

Jørgensen, D., 'Modernity and Medieval Muck', *Nature and Culture*, 9:3 (2014), 225–37.

Kamp, J., *Crime, Gender and Social Control in Early Modern Frankfurt Am Main* (Leiden, 2019).

Kamp, J. & Schmidt, A., 'Getting Justice: A Comparative Perspective on Illegitimacy and the Use of Justice in Holland and Germany, 1600–1800', *Journal of Social History*, 51:4 (2018), 672–94.

Keuhn, T., 'Household and Family in the *Ius Commune* and *Ius Proprium*', in M. Carlier & T. Soens (eds.), *The Household in Late Medieval Cities, Italy and Northwestern Europe Compared* (Leuven-Apeldoorn, 2001), 37-50.

Kittell, E.E., 'Testaments of Two Cities: A Comparative Analysis of the Wills of Medieval Genoa and Douai', *European Review of History*, 5:1 (1998), 47-82.

Kittell, E.E. & Queller, K., '"Whether Man or Woman": Gender Inclusivity in the Town Ordinances of Medieval Douai', *The Journal of Medieval and Early Modern Studies*, 30:1 (2000), 63-100.

Kittell, E.E. & Queller, K., 'Wives and Widows in Medieval Flanders', *Social History*, 41:4 (2016), 436–54.

Kowaleski, M., 'Women's Work in a Market Town: Exeter in the Late Fourteenth Century', in B.A. Hanawalt (ed.), *Women and Work in Preindustrial Europe* (Bloomington, 1986), 145–64.

Kowaleski, M. & Bennett, J.M., 'Crafts, Gilds, and Women in the Middle Ages: Fifty Years after Marian K. Dale', *Signs: Journal of Women in Culture and Society*, 14:2 (1989), 474-501.

Laenen, J., *Geschiedenis van Mechelen tot op het einde der middeleeuwen*, 2nd ed. (Mechelen, 1934).

Lambert, B., 'Merchants on the Margins: Fifteenth-Century Bruges and the Informal Market', *Journal of Medieval History*, 42:2 (2016), 226–53.

Lambert, B., 'Double Disadvantage or Golden Age? Immigration, Gender and Economic Opportunity in Later Medieval England', *Gender & History*, 31:3 (2019), 545–64.

Lanza, J.M., *From Wives to Widows in Early Modern Paris: Gender, Economy, and Law* (Aldershot, 2007).

Lecuppre-Desjardin, E. & Van Bruaene, A.-L., 'Introduction. Du Bien Commun à l'idée de Bien Commun', in E. Lecuppre-Desjardin & A.-L. Van Bruaene (eds.), *De Bono Communi. The Discourse and Practice of the Common Good in the European City (13th–16th c.)* (Turnhout, 2010), 1–9.

Limberger, M., *Sixteenth-Century Antwerp and its Rural Surroundings: Social and Economic Changes in the Hinterland of a Commercial Metropolis (ca. 1450 – ca. 1570)* (Turnhout, 2008).

Limberger, M., 'The Making of the Urban Fiscal System of Antwerp until 1800: Excises, Annuities and Debt Management', in M. Limberger & J.I. Andrés Ucendo (eds.), *Taxation and Debt in the Early Modern City* (London, 2012), 131–47.

Ling, S., Jansson, K.H., Lennersand, M., Pihl, C. & Ågren, M., 'Marriage and Work: Intertwined Sources of Agency and Authority', in M. Ågren (ed.), *Making a Living, Making a Difference: Gender and Work in Early Modern European Society* (New York, 2016), 80–102.

Lis, C. & Soly, H., *Werken volgens de regels: ambachten in Brabant en Vlaanderen 1500 – 1800* (Brussels, 1994).

Marfany, J., 'Family and Welfare in Early Modern Europe: A North-South Comparison', in C. Briggs, P.M. Kitson & S.J. Thompson (eds.), *Population, Welfare and Economic Change in Britain, c.1270–1834: Historical Studies* (Woodbridge, 2014), 103–27.

Marnef, G., *Antwerpen in de tijd van de Reformatie: ondergronds protestantisme in een handelsmetropool 1550 – 1577* (Antwerp, 1996).

Marnef, G., 'Multiconfessionalism in a Commercial Metropolis: The Case of 16th-Century Antwerp', in T.M. Safley (ed.), *A Companion to Multiconfessionalism in the Early Modern World* (Leiden, 2011), 75-97.

Martin Rodriguez, J., 'Figura histórico-jurídica del Juez Mayor de Vizcaya', *Anuario de Historia del Derecho Español*, 38 (1968), 641–69.

Martini, M. & Bellavitis, A., 'Household Economies, Social Norms and Practices of Unpaid Market Work in Europe from the Sixteenth Century to the Present', *The History of the Family*, 19:3 (2014), 273–82.

Mast, M., 'Politiek, prestige en vermogen: de Mechelse magistraat, 1520–1577' (Unpublished M.A. thesis, KU Leuven, 1990).

Masure, T., 'De stadsfinanciën van Antwerpen, 1531–1571. Een poging tot rekonstruktie' (Unpublished M.A. thesis, UGent, 1986).

McIntosh, M.K., *Working Women in English Society, 1300–1620* (Cambridge, 2005).

McNamara, J.A. & Wemple, S., 'The Power of Women through the Family in Medieval Europe, 500–1100', in M. Erler & M. Kowaleski (eds.), *Women and Power in the Middle Ages* (Athens, 1988), 83-101.

Meulemans, A., 'Leuvense ambachten: de beenhouwers', *Eigen Schoon en de Brabander*, 42 (1958), 412–28.

Monasterio Aspiri, I., 'La condición jurídica de la mujer en el derecho civil-foral de Bizkaia', *Iura Vasconiae*, 3 (2006), 249–81.

Montenach, A. & Simonton, D., 'Introduction. Gender, Agency and Economy: Shaping the Eighteenth-Century European Town', in A. Montenach & D. Simonton (eds.), *Female Agency in the Urban Economy: Gender in European Towns, 1640–1830* (New York, 2013), 1–14.

Montenach, A. & Simonton, D., 'Afterword', in A. Montenach & D. Simonton (eds.), *Female Agency in the Urban Economy: Gender in European Towns, 1640–1830* (New York, 2013), 244–50.

Montenach, A., 'Formal and Informal Economy in an Urban Context: The Case of Food Trade in Seventeenth-Century Lyon', in T. Buchner & P.R. Hoffmann-Rehnitz (eds.), *Shadow Economies and Irregular Work in Urban Europe. 16th to Early 20th Centuries* (Münster, 2011), 91-106.

Montenach, A., 'Legal Trade and Black Markets: Food Trades in Lyon in the Late Seventeenth and Early Eighteenth Centuries', in D. Simonton & A. Montenach (eds.), *Female Agency in the Urban Economy: Gender in European Towns, 1640–1830* (New York, 2013), 17-34.

Montenach, A., 'Creating a Space for Themselves on the Urban Market. Survival Strategies and Economic Opportunities for Single Women in French Provincial Towns (Seventeenth–Eighteenth Centuries)', in J. De Groot, A. Schmidt & I. Devos (eds.), *Single Life and the City 1200–1900* (Basingstoke, 2015), 50-68.

Montenach, A., 'Working at the Margins: Women and Illicit Economic Practices in Lyon in the Late Seventeenth and Eighteenth Centuries', in M.L. Bailey, T.M. Colwell & J. Hotchin (eds.), *Women and Work in Premodern Europe: Experiences, Relationships and Cultural Representation, c. 1100-1800* (Oxford and London, 2018), 192–213.

Muurling, S., *Everyday Crime, Criminal Justice and Gender in Early Modern Bologna* (Leiden and Boston, 2020).

Nausia Pimoulier, A., 'El usufructo de viudedad Navarro como recurso de supervivencia para las viudas (Siglos XVI y XVII)', *Iura Vasconiae: Revista de Derecho Histórico y Autonómico de Vasconia*, 10 (2013), 573–96.

Nicholas, D., *The Domestic Life of a Medieval City: Women, Children and the Family in Fourteenth-Century Ghent* (Lincoln, 1988).

O'Flanagan, P., *Port Cities of Atlantic Iberia, c.1500–1900* (Aldershot, 2008).

Ogilvie, S., 'How Does Social Capital Affect Women? Guilds and Communities in Early Modern Germany', *American Historical Review*, 109:2 (2004), 325–59.

Ogilvie, S., *A Bitter Living: Women, Markets, and Social Capital in Early Modern Germany* (Oxford, 2006).

Ogilvie, S., *Institutions and European Trade: Merchant Guilds, 1000–1800* (Cambridge, 2011).

Ogilvie, S., *The European Guilds. An Economic Analysis* (Princeton, 2019).

Ormrod, W.M., *Women and Parliament in Later Medieval England* (Cham, 2020).

Ortner, S.B., 'Specifying Agency. The Comaroffs and Their Critics', Interventions, 3:1 (2001), 76-84.

Oudemans, A.C., *Middel- en Oudnederlandsch woordenboek*, vol. 1 of 8 (Arnhem, 1870).

Peeters, J.-P., 'De produktiestructuur der Mechelse lakennijverheid en de ambachten van wevers en volders van 1270 tot 1430', *Handelingen van de Koninklijke Kring voor Oudheidkunde, Letteren en Kunst van Mechelen*, 88 (1984), 93–158.

Pilorget, J., 'Circulations féminines et encadrement de l'espace urbain à la fin du Moyen Âge: l'exemple d'Amiens', in Y. Carbonnier, S. Curveiller & L. Warlouzet (eds.), *Mobilités et déplacements des femmes dans le nord de la France du Moyen Âge à nos jours* (Arras Cedex, 2019), 15-31.

Polónia, A., 'Women's Participation in Labour and Business in the European Maritime Societies in the Early Modern Period' (Conference Proceding, Prato, 2009).

Power, E. & Postan, M.M., Medieval Women (repr., Cambridge, 1976).

Prak, M., 'Corporate Politics in the Low Countries: Guilds as an Institution, 14th to 18th Centuries', in M.R. Prak, C. Lis, J. Lucassen & H. Soly (eds.), *Craft Guilds in the Early Modern Low Countries: Work, Power and Representation* (Hampshire, 2006), 74-106.

Prak, M., 'Corporatism and Social Models in the Low Countries', *TSEG/The Low Countries Journal of Social and Economic History*, 11:2 (2014), 281-304.

Prims, F., *Geschiedenis van Antwerpen. VI – Onder de hertogen van Bourgondië – hertogen van Brabant (1406–1477). 1ste boek – de politieke orde*, vol. 13 (Brussels, 1936).

Prims, F., *Geschiedenis van Antwerpen. VI – Onder de hertogen van Bourgondië – hertogen van Brabant (1406–1477). 2e boek – de economische orde*, vol. 14 (Brussels, 1937).

Rábade Obradó, M.P., 'La mujer trabajadora en los ordenamientos de Cortes, 1258–1505', in C. Segura Graiño & Á. Muñoz Fernández (eds.), *El trabajo de las mujeres en la edad media hispana* (Madrid, 1988), 113-40.

Ratcliffe, M., '"Matris et Munium...": Marriage and Marriage Law in Medieval Spanish Legislation', *Revista Canadiense de Estudios Hispánicos*, 13 (1988), 93-109.

Rey Castelao, O., 'Inheritance, Marital Strategies, and the Formation of Households in Rural North-Western Spain in the Eighteenth and Nineteenth Centuries: An Overview', in A.-L. Head-König (ed.), *Inheritance Practices, Marriage Strategies and Household Formation in European Rural Societies* (Turnhout, 2012), 75-99.

Rivera Medina, A.M., 'Pescado, tiempo y distancia: las conservas en Bizkaia (s. XIV–XVIII)', in *Arrain Kontserbak Euskal Herrian: Industria eta Ondarea = Las Conservas de Pescado en el País Vasco: Industria y Patrimonio* (Gipuzkoa, 1997), 15-43.

Rivera Medina, A.M., 'Cuerpos de mujer en el mundo laboral bilbaíno bajomedieval y moderno (s. XIV–XVI)', in *Familia y organización social en Europa y América siglos XV–XX* (Murcia-Albacete, 2007).

Rivera Medina, A.M., '"E tobimos por bien echar sisa". Los impuestos al consumo como media de financiación concejil. Bilbao, 1300–1550', in J.Á. Solórzano Telechea & B. Arizaga Bolumburu (eds.), *La gobernanza de la ciudad europea en la edad media* (Logroño, 2011), 427-43.

Rivera Medina, A.M., 'Superando fronteras. Mujer y cultura laboral en los puertos del norte peninsular, siglos XIV–XVI', in M. García Hurtado & O. Rey Castelao (eds.), *Fronteras de agua. Las ciudades portuarias y su universo cultural (siglos XIV–XXI)* (Santiago de Compostela, 2016), 17-32.

Rivera Medina, A.M., 'Economía informal: la baratería en la frontera marítima Atlántica medieval', in M. García Fernández, Á. Galán Sánchez, R.G. Peinado Santaella (eds.), *Las fronteras en la edad media hispánica, siglos XIII–XVI* (Granada and Sevilla, 2019), 583-96.

Romano, D., 'Gender and the Urban Geography of Renaissance Venice', *Journal of Social History*, 23:2 (1989), 339-53.

Ryckbosch, W., 'Economic Inequality and Growth before the Industrial Revolution: The Case of the Low Countries (Fourteenth to Nineteenth Centuries)', *European Review of Economic History*, 20:1 (2016), 1-22.

Salazar, J.I., 'Gobierno local en el Bilbao bajomedieval', *Bidebarrieta*, 12 (2003), 183-97.

Sarasúa, C., 'Women's Work and Structural Change: Occupational Structure in Eighteenth-century Spain', *Economic History Review*, 72:2 (2019), 481-509.

Sarti, R., Bellavitis, A. & Martini, M., 'Introduction. What Is Work? Gender at the Crossroads of Home, Family, and Business from the Early Modern Era to the Present', in R. Sarti, A. Bellavitis & M. Martini (eds.), *What Is Work? Gender at the Crossroads of Home, Family, and Business from the Early Modern Era to the Present* (New York, 2018), 1–84.

Schmidt, A. & van Nederveen Meerkerk, E., 'Reconsidering the "First Male-Breadwinner Economy": Women's Labor Force Participation in the Netherlands, 1600–1900', *Feminist Economics*, 18:4 (2012), 69-96.

Schmidt, A., Devos, I. & Blondé, B., 'Introduction. Single and the City: Men and Women Alone in North-Western European Towns since the Late Middle Ages', in J. De Groot, I. Devos & A. Schmidt (eds.), *Single Life and the City: 1200–1900* (Basingstoke, 2015), 1-24.

Schmidt, A., *Overleven na de dood: weduwen in Leiden in de Gouden Eeuw* (Amsterdam, 2001).

Schmidt, A., 'Vrouwenarbeid in de vroegmoderne tijd in Nederland', *TSEG: Low Countries Journal of Social and Economic History*, 2:3 (2005), 2-21.

Schmidt, A., 'Women and Guilds: Corporations and Female Labour Market Participation in Early Modern Holland', *Gender & History*, 21:1 (2009), 170-89.

Schmidt, A., 'The Profits of Unpaid Work. 'Assisting Labour' of Women in the Early Modern Urban Dutch Economy', *The History of the Family*, 19:3 (2014), 301-22.

Schmidt, A., 'Contested Authority. Working Women in Leading Positions in the Early Modern Dutch Urban Economy', in M.L. Bailey, T.M. Colwell & J. Hotchin (eds.), *Women and Work in Premodern Europe: Experiences, Relationships and Cultural Representation, c.1100–1800* (Oxford and London, 2018), 214-36.

Schmidt, A., *Prosecuting Women: A Comparative Perspective on Crime and Gender before the Dutch Criminal Courts, c.1600–1810* (Leiden, 2020).

Schoeffer, J., *Historische aanteekeningen rakende de kerken, de kloosters, de ambachten en andere stichten der stad Mechelen* (Brussels, 1996).

Schöts, S., 'Female Traders and Practices of Illicit Exchange. Observations on Leipzig's Retail Trade between the Sixteenth and Nineteenth Century', in T. Buchner & P.R. Hoffmann-Rehnitz (eds.), *Shadow Economies and Irregular Work in Urban Europe: 16th to Early 20th Centuries* (Münster, 2011), 127-40.

Simonton, D., '"Birds of Passage' or 'Career' Women? Thoughts on the Life Cycle of the Eighteenth-Century European Servant', *Women's History Review*, 20:2 (2011), 207-25.

Simonton, D., 'Widows and Wenches: Single Women in Eighteenth-Century Urban Economies', in A. Montenach & D. Simonton (eds.), *Female Agency in the Urban Economy: Gender in European Towns, 1640–1830* (New York, 2013), 93-115.

Simonton, D., *Gender in the European Town – Ancien Régime to the Modern* (London, 2023).

Slokker, N., *Ruggengraat van de stad: de betekenis van gilden in Utrecht, 1528–1818*, ed. M. Muntinga (Amsterdam, 2010).

Smail, D., *The Consumption of Justice: Emotions, Publicity, and Legal Culture in Marseille, 1264–1423* (Ithaca, 2013).

Solórzano Telechea, J.Á., 'La villa de las "Buenas Dueñas Honradas": La condición de las mujeres en el Santander medieval', *Edades. Revista de Historia*, 5:1 (1999), 23-46.

Solórzano Telechea, J.Á., 'Las voces del común en el mundo urbano de la España Atlántica en la baja edad media', in J.Á. Solórzano Telechea, B. Arízaga Bolumburu & J. Haemers (eds.), *Los grupos populares en la ciudad medieval europea* (Logroño, 2014), 301-44.

Solórzano Telechea, J.Á., 'The Politics of the Urban Commons in Northern Atlantic Spain in the Later Middle Ages', *Urban History*, 41:2 (2014), 183-203.

Solórzano Telechea, J.Á., '"Por bien y utilidad de los dichos maestres, pescadores y navegantes": trabajo, solidaridad y acción política en las cofradías de las gentes de la mar en la España Atlántica medieval', *Medievalismo*, 26 (2016), 329-56.

Solórzano Telechea, J.Á., 'Ideologies and Political Participation of the Commons in Urban Life of Northern Atlantic Spain during the Late Middle Ages', in B. Eersels & J. Haemers (eds.), *Words and Deeds: Shaping Urban Politics from Below in Late Medieval Europe* (Turnhout, 2020), 181-94.

Solórzano Telechea, J.Á., 'La configuración política de Bizkaia y sus vínculos con Castilla en la plena edad media. Del conde Momo al conde Don Tello de Trastámara' (Unpublished Book Chapter, 2021).

Sousa Melo, A., 'Women and Work in the Household Economy: The Social and Linguistic Evidence from Porto, c.1340–1450', in C. Beattie, A. Maslakovic & S. Rees Jones (eds.), *The Medieval*

Household in Christian Europe c.850–c.1550: Managing Power, Wealth, and the Body (Turnhout, 2004), 249–69.

Stabel, P., 'Women at the Market: Gender and Retail in the Towns of Late Medieval Flanders', in W.P. Blockmans, W. Prevenier & T. de Hemptinne (eds.), *Secretum Scriptorum: Liber Alumnorum Walter Prevenier* (Leuven, 1999), 259–76.

Stabel, P., 'A European Household Economy?', in M. Carlier & T. Soens (eds.), *The Household in Late Medieval Cities: Italy and Northwestern Europe Compared* (Leuven and Apeldoorn, 2001), 121–26.

Stabel, P., 'Guilds in Late Medieval Flanders: Myths and Realities of Guild Life in an Export-Oriented Environment', *Journal of Medieval History*, 30:2 (2004), 187–212.

Stabel, P., 'From the Market to the Shop: Retail and Urban Space in Late Medieval Bruges', in B. Blondé, P. Stabel, J. Stobart & I. Van Damme (eds.), *Buyers and Sellers: Retail Circuits and Practices in Medieval and Early Modern Europe* (Turnhout, 2006), 79-108.

Stabel, P., 'Workplace Cultures', in V.L. Garver (ed.), *A Cultural History of Work in the Medieval Age* (London, 2019), 85–98.

Staples, K.K., 'The Significance of the Secondhand Trade in Europe, 1200–1600', *History Compass*, 13:6 (2015), 297-309.

Taverner, C., 'Licensing the Informal Economy in Early Modern Europe: Food Hawkers in London and Naples', *The London Journal*, 47:2 (2022), 159-80.

Tomkins, A. & King, S., 'Conclusion', in A. Tomkins & S. King (eds.), *The Poor in England 1700–1850: An Economy of Makeshifts* (Manchester, 2003), 258–80.

Van Aert, L., '"Van appelen tot zeemleer": Koopvrouwen in Antwerpen in de 16de eeuw' (Unpublished M.A. thesis, Vrije Universiteit Brussel, 2002).

Van Aert, L., 'Tussen norm en praktijk. Een terreinverkenning over het juridische statuut van vrouwen in het zestiende-eeuwse Antwerpen', *TSEG / Low Countries Journal of Social and Economic History*, 2:3 (2005), 22-42.

Van Aert, L., 'The Legal Possibilities of Antwerp Widows In the Late Sixteenth Century', *The History of the Family*, 12:4 (2007), 282–95.

Van Aert, L., 'Tot "Leven of overleven"? Winkelhouden in crisistijd: de Antwerpse meerseniers, ca. 1648–1748' (Unpublished Ph.D. Dissertation, Universiteit Antwerpen, 2007).

Van Dekken, M., *Brouwen, branden & bedienen: Werkende vrouwen in de Nederlandse dranknijverheid, 1500–1800* (Amsterdam, 2010).

Van den Heuvel, D., 'Partners in Marriage and Business? Guilds and the Family Economy in Urban Food Markets in the Dutch Republic', *Continuity and Change*, 23:2 (2008), 217–36.

Van den Heuvel, D., 'Selling in the Shadows: Peddlers and Hawkers in Early Modern Europe', in M. van der Linden & L. Lucassen (eds.), *Working on Labor: Essays in Honor of Jan Lucassen* (Leiden, 2012), 125–51.

Van den Heuvel, D., 'The Multiple Identities of Early Modern Dutch Fishwives', Signs: Journal of Women in Culture and Society, 37:3 (2012), 587–94.

Van den Heuvel, D., 'Guilds, Gender Policies and Economic Opportunities for Women in Early Modern Dutch Towns', in D. Simonton & A. Montenach (eds.), *Female Agency in the Urban Economy* (New York, 2013), 116–33.

Van den Nieuwenhuizen, J., 'Bestuursinstellingen van de stad Antwerpen', in R. Van Uytven, C. Bruneel & H. Coppens (eds.), *De gewestelijke en lokale overheidsinstellingen in Brabant en Mechelen tot 1795* (Brussels, 2000), 462-510.

Van Dijck, M.F., 'Towards an Economic Interpretation of Justice? Conflict Settlement, Social Control and Civil Society in Urban Brabant and Mechelen During the Late Middle Ages and the Early

Modern Period', in M. Van der Heijden (ed.), *Serving the Urban Community: The Rise of Public Facilities in the Low Countries* (Amsterdam, 2009), 62-88.

Van Gerven, J., 'Vrouwen, arbeid en sociale positie: Een voorlopig onderzoek naar de economische rol en maatschappelijke positie van vrouwen in de Brabantse steden in de late middeleeuwen', *Revue Belge de Philologie et d'Histoire*, 73:4 (1995), 947–66.

Van Gerven, J., 'Antwerpen in de veertiende eeuw: Kleine stad zonder toekomst of opkomend handelscentrum', *Revue Belge de Philologie et d'Histoire*, 76:4 (1998), 907–38.

Van Houtte, J.A., 'Anvers aux XVe et XVIe siècles: Expansion et apogée', *Annales. Histoire, Sciences Sociales*, 16:2 (1961), 248–78.

Van Nederveen Meerkerk, E., 'Segmentation in the Pre-Industrial Labour Market: Women's Work in the Dutch Textile Industry, 1581–1810', *International Review of Social History*, 51:2 (2006), 189–216.

Van Nederveen Meerkerk, E., 'Gender and Economic History: The Story of a Complicated Marriage', *TSEG / Low Countries Journal of Social and Economic History*, 11:2 (2014), 175–97.

Van Uytven, R., *De geschiedenis van Mechelen: van heerlijkheid tot stadsgewest* (Tielt, 1991).

Vandeweerdt, N., '"Van den vleeschouweren oft pensvrouwen": De economische mogelijkheden voor vrouwen in het Leuvense vleeshouwersambacht in de vijftiende en zestiende eeuw', *TSEG/Low Countries Journal of Social and Economic History*, 15:1 (2018), 5-30.

Vandeweerdt, N., 'Women, Town Councils, and the Organisation of Work in Bilbao and Antwerp: A North–South Comparison (1400–1560)', *Continuity and Change*, 36:1 (2021), 61-87.

Vandeweerdt, N. & Haemers, J., 'Working Women: Women's Professional Activities in and outside the Craft Guilds', in J. Haemers, A. Bardyn & C. Delameillieure (eds.), *Urban Women. Life, Love, and Work in the Medieval Low Countries* (Leuven, 2025), 121–46.

Verstrepen, M.-A., 'Het sociaal-economisch beleid van de stad Antwerpen op basis van de stadsgeboden (1439–1489)' (Unpublished M.A. thesis, Universiteit Gent, 1982).

Verwerft, B., 'De beul in het markizaat van Antwerpen tijdens de Bourgondische en Habsburgse periode (1405–1550)' (Unpublished M.A. thesis, Universiteit Gent, 2007).

Viazzo, P.P., 'What's so Special about the Mediterranean? Thirty Years of Research on Household and Family in Italy', *Continuity and Change*, 18:1 (2003), 111–37.

Vicente, M., 'Images and Realities of Work: Women and Guilds in Early Modern Barcelona', in A. Saint-Saëns & M. Sánchez (eds.), *Spanish Women in the Golden Age: Images and Realities* (Westport, 1996), 127–39.

Von Heusinger, S., 'Vater, Mutter, Kind: Die Zunftfamilie als Wirtschaftseinheit', in E. Jullien & M. Pauly (eds.), *Craftsmen and Guilds in the Medieval and Early Modern Periods* (Stuttgart, 2016), 156–73.

Vos, L., 'Het huwelijksvermogensrecht in het huidige Vlaanderen van de 16de en 17de eeuw: Een vergelijkende studie van de Costumen van Antwerpen, Brussel, Leuven, Gent en Mechelen' (Unpublished M.A. thesis, KU Leuven, 2016).

Walker, G., *Crime, Gender and Social Order in Early Modern England* (Cambridge, 2003).

Wessell Lightfoot, D., *Women, Dowries and Agency: Marriage in Fifteenth-Century Valencia* (Manchester, 2013).

Whittle, J. & Hailwood, M., 'The Gender Division of Labour in Early Modern England', *Economic History Review*, 73:1 (2018).

Whittle, J., 'A Critique of Approaches to 'Domestic Work': Women, Work and the Pre-Industrial Economy', *Past & Present*, 243:1 (2019), 35-70.

Wiesner, M.E., 'Paltry Peddlers or Essential Merchants? Women in the Distributive Trades in Early Modern Nuremberg', *Sixteenth Century Journal*, 12:2 (1981), 3-13.

Wiesner, M.E., 'Guilds, Male Bonding and Women's Work in Early Modern Germany', *Gender & History*, 1:2 (1989), 125–37.

Wiesner, M.E., 'Gender and the Worlds of Work', in B. Scribner (ed.), Germany: A New Social and Economic History, Vol. 1: 1450–1630 (London, 1995), 209–32.

Wiesner, M.E., 'Having Her Own Smoke: Employment and Independence for Singlewomen in Germany, 1400–1750', in J.M. Bennett & A.M. Froide (eds.), *Singlewomen in the European Past, 1250–1800* (Philadelphia, 1999), 192-216.

Wiesner, M.E., *Women and Gender in Early Modern Europe*, 2nd ed. (Cambridge, 2000).

Williams, C.C., *The Informal Economy* (Newcastle, 2019).

Wyffels, C., *De oorsprong der ambachten in Vlaanderen en Brabant* (Brussels, 1951).

Wyffels, H., 'Women and Work in Early Modern Printing Houses: Family Firms in Antwerp, Douai, and Leuven, 1500–1700' (Unpublished Ph.D. Dissertation, KU Leuven, 2021).

Wyffels, H., 'De drukkersvrouwen van Sint Lucas: Gildenlidmaatschap en arbeidspatronen in het vroegmoderne Antwerpse boekwezen', *Nieuwe Tijdingen. Over vroegmoderne geschiedenis*, 5 (2021), 67-87.

Wyssenbach, S., 'Riches of the Sea: Collecting and Consuming Frans Snijders's Marine Market Paintings in the Southern Netherlands', in S. Burghartz, L. Burkart & C. Göttler (eds.), *Sites of Mediation: Connected Histories of Places, Processes, and Objects in Europe and Beyond, 1450–1650* (Leiden, 2016), 328–52.

Zabala Iriarte, A., 'The Consolidation of Bilbao as a Trade Centre in the Second Half of the Seventeenth Century', in O.U. Janzen (ed.), *Merchant Organization and Maritime Trade in the North Atlantic, 1660–1815* (Liverpool, 2017), 155–74.

Zemon Davis, N., 'Women in the Crafts in Sixteenth-Century Lyon', in B.A. Hanawalt (ed.), *Women and Work in Preindustrial Europe* (Bloomington, 1986), 198-221.

Zucca Micheletto, B., 'Reconsidering the Southern Europe Model: Dowry, Women's Work and Marriage Patterns in Pre-Industrial Urban Italy (Turin, Second Half of the 18th Century)', *The History of the Family*, 16:4 (2011), 354–70.

Zucca Micheletto, B., *Travail et propriété des femmes en temps de crise (Turin, XVIIIe siècle)* (Mont-Saint-Aignan, 2014).

Ågren, M., 'Introduction', in M. Ågren (ed.), *Making a Living, Making a Difference: Gender and Work in Early Modern European Society* (New York, 2016), 1-23.

4. Digital sources

David Jacks and Leticia Arroya-Abad, 'Belgium 1366-1603', *Global Prices and Income database*. https://gpih.ucdavis.edu/Datafilelist.htm.

Leticia Arroya-Abad, 'Spain 1351-1800', *Global Prices and Income database*. https://gpih.ucdavis.edu/Datafilelist.htm.

Stapel, Rombert, 2020, 'Duchy of Brabant GIS Collection'. https://hdl.handle.net/10622/UOKBYL.

Index

Abreu-Ferreira, Darlene, 40, 52, 103
agency, 18, 26, 28, 37, 178, 198, 212
Ågren, Maria, 27, 45
aldermen, 95, 146, 148-150, 153, 175, 185, 198-200, 206
Antwerp
    Correctieboeken, 81, 139, 185, 200
    population of, 34, 73
apprentice, 47-48, 86-89, 98-99, 109, 148-149, 176, 207. *See also* mercers
Armstrong-Partida, Michelle, 29
authority, 137, 144
    female occupations and, 176
    gendered limitations and, 174
    marital status and, 176
    See also council, town; widow

Bailey, Mark, 28-29
Bailey, Merridee, 169
bakers
    daughters of guild masters, 111
    guild membership, 49
    guild organization, 47-48
    production and, 48
    taxation and, 48
    See also bread trade; guild, craft; grain trade
Bardyn, Andrea, 27
barriers to women's work, 23
    economic arguments and, 131, 133, 140, 142, 150, 168
    gendered arguments and, 131, 135, 137-138, 150, 169
    public weights and, 145
Basque Country, 14, 69, 102, 105, 132
beguines, 204, 207
Bellavitis, Anna, 29, 40, 78
Bennett, Judith, 18-19
Bergen-op-Zoom, 34
Bermeo, 13, 56, 88, 104, 124, 137, 179, 209, 218
Bilbao
    maritime economy of, 31, 106

market space and, 33
population of, 33, 73
bread trade
    horneras, 50, 182
    illicit trade and, 134, 139
    informal organization of, 49
    organization of, 50
    panaderas, 50-51, 101, 133, 182, 217
    public ovens and, 101
    public weights and, 177
    See also bakers; guild, craft; women's work
brokerage, 213
    centralization of, 190
    cojedoras, 52, 92, 102, 105-106, 120, 164-165, 176-177, 186, 189-196, 203-204, 208-210, 217-218
    corredoras, 65-66
    illicit trade and, 164, 189
    labor structures and, 177
    limitations by town council and, 66, 158, 164-166, 187-189
    monopoly on, 193
    necessity of work as argument and, 192
    precedent in litigation and, 190, 193, 208
    public weights and, 169
    See also grain trade; linen trade; litigation
Broomhall, Susan, 206
Brussels, 53, 199
bulk trade. *See* wholesale
Burm, Ellen, 111
butchers
    absence of female guild membership and, 107
    informal trade and, 118
    inherited membership and, 111
    masculinity and, 117
    pensvrouwen, 55, 118, 220
    petition by, 179
    spousal cooperation and, 96, 104, 154
    widow's right and, 162, 201
    See also guild, craft

candlemakers, 104, 120
candle sellers (*candeleras*), 59
capital investment, 49, 113, 115
Capp, Bernard, 181
Cappelle, Kaat, 27
Carlier, Myriam, 87
Castile, kingdom of, 31, 178, 186, 195, 203
Castrillo Casado, Janire, 69
Catalina Nafarra, 13, 124, 129, 179, 216
Collinge, Peter, 140
Colwell, Tania, 169
common good, 132, 180, 192, 203, 205, 210, 211
comparative methodology, 14, 16, 18, 20, 29, 37-38
competition, economic, 59, 184
    formal, 96
    guilds and, 17, 19, 116, 120, 149, 155
    informal, 55, 61, 119-120, 124-125
    interregional difference, 117
    labor structures and, 116, 125, 211
    litigation and, 124
    single women and, 150
    spousal cooperation and, 48, 156, 162
    violence and, 124-125
    See also guild, craft; informal market; verbal violence
connections. *See* network
consent, 27, 171, 182-183
Corregidor, 90-91, 135, 164, 179, 186, 189-190, 195
council, town
    authority and, 46, 193, 210
    composition of, 33, 35-37
    control of women's work by, 57, 59, 133, 138, 165
    control of work by, 59
    criteria for regulating work and, 122
    economic centralization by, 158, 163-166
    leniency towards informal trade, 117, 193, 202
    limits on women's work by, 120, 163, 189
    oligarchy, 33, 37, 174
    organization of women's work by, 64
    organization of work by, 46, 122, 132
    taxation revenue and, 51, 71, 131, 138, 165
    See also informal market; institutions; ordinances, town
Crowston, Claire, 18

decline thesis, 158, 163
Delameillieure, Chanelle, 184
Del Val Valdivieso, María Isabel, 182
De Moor, Tine, 87
De Munck, Bert, 17, 111, 151
drapery, 34-36, 70

economic decline
    women's work opportunities and, 162
economic strategy, women, 185
Enríquez Fernández, Javier, 71, 73, 76
Epstein, Steven, 19, 220
Erler, Mary, 173

female occupations, 45, 49-51, 56-57, 163, 207
    political strategy and, 183
    privileges and, 183
femme sole, 26, 97, 110, 112
financial status, 14, 21, 25, 40, 46, 71, 74, 77, 81, 83, 101, 105, 217, 218
    gender and, 79
    guilds and, 82
    marital status and, 75
    occupational identifiers and, 77
    women's work and, 75
    See also litigation; poverty
fishmongers
    absence of female guild membership, 107
    daughters of guild masters and, 53
    debt and, 154
    guild control, 120
    guild entrance, 53
    guild exclusivity, 105, 154
    guild limits on household cooperation, 154-155, 162
    guild masculinity, 53, 146
    guild membership list, 54
    guild monopoly, 120
    guild monopoly by, 146
    guild sentence book, 41, 55, 99, 125, 141, 147, 152, 170, 185
    harincvrouwen, 55, 94, 97, 120, 122
    inherited guild membership, 111
    pescaderas, 56-58, 100, 102, 136, 164, 184, 217
    sardineras, 56-58, 100, 102, 167, 191-192, 194, 209, 217

spousal cooperation and, 54, 99, 105, 153, 155-156
See also informal market; guild, craft; women's work
fish trade
  changes in, 154-155, 161, 165-166
  illicit trade and, 99, 122-123, 135-136, 140-141, 146, 153, 157, 184
  informal trade and, 118, 156
  limitations by town council and, 164-165
  litigation and, 136
  market space and, 55, 57, 94, 118, 120, 146, 179-180
  organization of, 56-57, 137, 155
  public weights and, 137
  skill and, 137
  taxation and, 53
  town officials and, 137
  town ordinances and, 166
  women's work and, 54, 136
Flanders, 34, 58, 139
forum shopping, 198
  ambivalence of judicial authorities and, 198, 200
  appeal and, 198-199
  individual advantage and, 200
  leverage and, 198
free market days, 48, 96
Fridrich, Anna, 95, 101, 206
fruit sellers (*fruteras*), 59, 208
furriers, 67

García de Cortázar, José Ángel, 132
gardeners
  female guild membership, 60, 150, 160
  guild account book, 108
  guild exclusivity, 151
  parentage and, 115
  single women and, 203
  verbal violence and, 144
Gheertruyde van den Broeke, 13, 22, 153, 156-157, 185, 224
glove makers
  female membership and, 109-110
  guild account book, 89, 175
  guild entrance list, 109
  guild poor box, 88

Goldberg, Jeremy, 176
Gold, Carol, 77
grain trade
  gendered restrictions in, 50
  mulateros, 52, 164, 177, 192, 210
  public weights and, 92, 100, 163, 177
  rents and, 103, 190
  roderas, 51, 163
  See also brokerage, *cojedoras*
Guernica, 133
Guiard y Larrauri, Teófilo, 33
guild, craft, 16
  access through household, 19, 48, 63, 66, 69, 86, 93
  ambivalence and, 54, 97, 121, 156
  barriers for membership and, 112
  complaints by women and, 185
  control of women's work by, 61
  control of work by, 153
  cultural organization by, 141, 147
  differentiation between labor sectors and, 98, 150, 157, 161
  dissolution of, 21
  double membership and, 122
  economic pragmatism and, 97, 147
  exclusivity of, 53, 109, 145, 156, 163
  exemptions for household members by, 94, 150-151
  female members, 63, 107, 109-110, 205
  female members and marital status, 109
  female members and parentage, 113
  female wage workers and, 67
  forum shopping and, 201
  gendered limitations, 147, 150
  household economy and, 19
  impact on women's opportunities, 115
  impact on women's work, 30
  implicit gendering of work by, 144
  informal trade and, 121-122
  leniency towards informal trade, 121, 147
  limits on female members, 150
  limits on female wage workers, 94
  limits on household cooperation, 87, 151, 153-156, 161
  limits on women's influence, 180, 184
  limits on women's work, 18-19, 54, 62, 115, 143, 162, 169, 181, 206

masculinity and, 17, 54, 148, 150, 161, 163
masters' daughters, 113, 115
membership list, 39, 108
monopolies and, 17, 54, 146, 170
organizational capacity of, 19-20, 146
organization of work by, 49, 122
patriarchy and, 17-18, 95, 97, 149-150
political power of, 17, 35-36, 172, 180
political representation by, 17, 37, 172
poor box and, 88, 151
privileges of, 35
temporary ban from, 156-157
women's opportunities in, 20, 64
guild debate, 18, 158
guild effect, 19-20, 30, 130, 145-146, 150-151, 157, 169-170, 219

Haemers, Jelle, 184
Hafter, Daryl, 21, 39, 104, 111, 150
Hanus, Jord, 79
hatters, 67, 147
hidden workforce, 70, 221
Hotchin, Julie, 169
household economy, 87
    absence in records, 87, 103, 106
    guilds and, 211
    household production unit, 25, 48, 64, 70, 85-86, 90, 96
    life cycle changes and, 87
    See also guild, craft; marital status; spousal cooperation; widow
household head, 40, 71, 74-76, 82, 89, 93, 101, 184, 217
    male breadwinner model, 151
    widows and, 89
house rent levy, 71-75, 77-78
Howell, Martha, 19, 23, 30, 39, 63, 86
Hufton, Olwen, 162
Humphries, Jane, 67
Hutton, Shennan, 27

identity and group status
    belonging, 178, 193, 209
    masculinity and, 151
    occupational affiliation, 52, 63, 76-78, 102, 181, 205, 208-209, 220
    pescaderas, 220

privileges, 193, 204, 206-207
recognition/absence of, 64, 183, 205-206
illicit trade, 117, 152
    leniency towards, 191, 197, 200, 203
imprisonment, 190
informal market, 23-24, 61
    control over, 24, 50
    institutions and, 116-117, 123
    market space and, 146
    monopoly and, 133
    organization of, 21
    persecution of, 60
    spousal cooperation and, 96
    women's access to, 48
innkeepers (*huespedas*), 65-66, 70, 82, 194, 196, 213
    complaints about, 187
    illicit trade and, 93, 187
    spousal cooperation, 92
innkeepers (*mesoneros*), 51
institutional enforcement, 18, 130, 169, 211
institutions, 16
    differentiation between type of, 127
    impact on women's opportunities, 193, 197
    impact on women's work, 18, 25, 122, 170, 186
    interconnectedness, 85, 118
    limits on women's work by, 121, 205
    organizational capacity of, 16, 25
    organization of women's work by, 38
    organization of work by, 104
    protection by, 60, 177
interregional trade, 34. *See also* wholesale
Iziz, Ana, 69, 105
Iziz, Rosa, 69, 105

Jacobsen, Grethe, 170
journeyman, 86-87, 110, 150
Juan de Larrea, 90-91

Kittell, Ellen, 28, 48, 88
Kowaleski, Maryanne, 18, 49, 173

Lambert, Bart, 116, 139
legal system
    customary law, 26, 93, 110, 136
    fueros, 26

INDEX 245

inheritance law, 26
property rights, 26, 90, 101
Roman law, 26
versus daily practices, 26-27
women's legal capacity and, 26, 90
See also litigation
Leuven, 37, 55, 62, 96, 98, 117, 141, 146-147, 154, 162, 174, 176, 181, 201, 207, 218, 220
leverage, 180, 182, 184
license
    informal trade and, 24, 59, 133, 135
    legitimization and, 207-208
linen trade, 65, 125, 217
    brokerage and, 187-188, 196
    lenceras, 27, 65
    plumeras, 65-66, 82, 187-189, 193-196, 204-205, 210, 218
    spousal cooperation in, 216
litigation, 22
    appeal and, 93, 103, 135, 186, 188, 195, 198, 202
    change regulation through, 193-194
    collective advantage through, 196
    costs of, 81, 194
    court reports and, 39, 70
    customary law and, 189
    economic arguments and, 136, 191, 204
    group recognition and, 206-208
    individual advantage through, 196-197, 207-208
    initiation of, 194-195, 197
    innkeepers and, 186-188, 205
    judicial records and, 41, 92-93
    legal strategy and, 171, 181, 206, 216
    mercers' guild and, 199
    necessity of work as argument in, 192
    outcome versus daily practice, 188-190, 194, 197
    personality and, 136
    prohibition of brokerage through, 190
    reduced fines after, 196, 203
    Royal Chancellery of Valladolid, 41, 81, 88, 93, 124, 135, 186-190, 195-196
Luiten van Zanden, Jan, 87

María Ibáñez de Jáuregui, 90, 91
María Pérez de Bermeo, 13, 124
Marina de Bedia, 190, 209

marital status
    impact on women's work of, 24
market space, 13, 56, 62
    gendering of, 58, 117
    informal trade and, 117-118
Mast, Marleen, 72
Mayora de Iturribalzaga, 13, 103, 122, 135-138, 164-165, 179, 185-186, 191, 194-195, 204, 209, 218
McDonough, Susan, 29
McIntosh, Marjorie, 49
Mechelen
    population of, 72
mercers
    differentiation between labor sectors and, 109, 113
    economic trends and, 163
    female guild membership, 97, 109, 151, 159-160
    guild apprentices, 176
    guildapprenticeship list, 109
    guild entrance fee, 112
    guild entrance list, 42, 108, 112, 159
    guild limits on women's work, 160
    guild organization, 63, 108
    guild sentence book, 41, 125, 141-142
    illicit trade and, 140-141, 198
    marital status and, 110
    parentage and, 112, 115, 176
    single women and, 115
    verbal violence and, 141
    widow's right and, 89
Montenach, Anne, 120
Muurling, Sanne, 197

network, 81, 124-125, 154, 205, 209
    litigation and, 209-210
northern Low Countries, 111, 113, 136, 144, 194
north-south divide, 14, 28-29, 31. *See also* comparative methodology

Ogilvie, Sheilagh, 18-20, 25, 162, 169, 211, 220
oil sellers (aceiteras), 59, 100, 102, 123, 133, 183
oil workers, 63-64, 109, 113
ordinances, town
    after complaints, 46, 178
    gendered language in, 47-48, 51, 54, 64, 151, 161

narratios, 38, 131, 134, 179
  old clothes sellers and, 161
  repetition of, 38, 59, 66, 134, 165, 188, 191
  requested by guilds, 46
  versus daily practice, 39, 69, 164, 191
  See also council, town
Ormrod, Mark, 178

patriarchy, 17, 25
  gendered arguments and, 151
  gender norms and, 25, 131, 143
  implicit gendering of work, 134
  limits on women's work, 169
personality, saleswomen, 124-125, 136, 196
petition, 178-179, 195
  guilds and, 178, 180, 185
  pescaderas and, 179
plenary meeting, 174
Plentzia, 104, 137, 209, 218
Portugalete, 37, 56, 100
poverty, 34, 79, 103, 105, 160, 201
  argument, 65, 76, 79, 200-204, 218
  women's work and, 105
power, 173
  indirect influence, 180, 185
  women and, 183
Prak, Maarten, 19, 220
protection of the consumer, 51, 132-133, 136
purse and glove makers
  limits on women's work by, 148, 169
  power of, 180
  spousal cooperation and, 82, 94, 149
  See also glove makers

Queller, Kurt, 48, 88

reputation, 136, 140, 144
retailers (*regateras*), 58-59, 166, 179, 184, 217

Sarasúa, Carmen, 67
Schmidt, Ariadne, 20, 74, 115, 136, 194
Schöts, Susanne, 117
secondhand trade
  estimators, 61, 143, 145, 175
  female old clothes sellers, 95, 110, 143
  guild organization, 61

guild privilege, 62
illicit trade and, 200
old clothes sellers, 61
uitdraagsters, 61-63, 81, 121, 181, 215, 220, 221
servants, 19, 40, 47, 50-51, 74, 76-77, 87, 92, 98, 99-101, 131, 142, 147, 198
shopkeepers, 64, 109
  female guild membership, 110-111, 147, 160
  guild organization, 63
  parentage and, 113
  See also mercers
single women
  work limitations and, 150
skill, 20, 137, 143, 176-177
Smail, Daniel, 196
social capital, 18, 76, 205
social status, 197. *See also* financial status
Sousa Melo, Arnold, 103
spousal cooperation, 91, 104
  absence of husband and, 106, 156, 203
  debts and, 91
  financial status and, 91
  guilds and, 95
  type of, 93, 96, 154
Stabel, Peter, 206
staple rights, 53
suspicion, 131-132, 143

tanners, 36, 88, 94, 206
Taverner, Charlie, 24, 30
taxation
  female taxpayers and, 74, 81
  gender inequality and, 74-75, 79
  hearth count, 74, 87
  interregional gender differences and, 79
  register, 40, 42, 71, 77, 83, 105
  See also financial status
Third Order of the Franciscans, Antwerp, 204, 206
Toda de Larrea, 102-103, 105, 203, 209, 218
type of work, 22-23
  artisan occupations, 31, 66, 104, 109
  differentiation between labor sectors, 170

Van Aert, Laura, 108, 112, 142, 160
Van Dekken, Marjolein, 111

Van den Heuvel, Danielle, 52, 93, 96, 112, 144, 154-155
Van Nederveen Meerkerk, Elise, 74, 115
verbal violence, 125, 141-142, 144, 154, 199
    gender and, 144
Vierschaar, tribunal, 139

wage workers, women, 50, 60, 67, 94, 146, 149
wholesale, 52, 56, 163, 165
widow
    as substitute, 175
    authority and, 174
    debt and, 88
    financial status and, 75-76, 90
    guild administration and, 89
    power and, 89

widow's right, 69, 105, 110, 148, 174-176, 202
    restriction of, 162
Wiesner, Merry, 86, 162, 196, 209
women's work
    as substitute, 54, 99, 110
    customary activities, 55, 162, 181, 187, 191, 193
    declining opportunities and, 154, 161, 165
    distinction based on marital status, 92
    independent, 53, 59, 64, 97, 101, 103, 157
    marital status and, 102-103
    recognition of, 53, 61
    short-term changes in opportunities, 160, 162
work, 22

Zunftzwang, 17

www.ingramcontent.com/pod-product-compliance
Lightning Source LLC
Chambersburg PA
CBHW051610230426
43668CB00013B/2057